STATE AND RESERVATION

STATE AND RESERVATION

New Perspectives on Federal Indian Policy

EDITED BY

GEORGE PIERRE CASTILE AND ROBERT L. BEE

The University of Arizona Press   Tucson & London

The University of Arizona Press
Copyright © 1992
Arizona Board of Regents
All Rights Reserved

⊛ This book is printed on acid-free, archival-quality paper.
Manufactured in the United States of America.

97   96   95   94   93   92   6   5   4   3   2   1

LIBRARY OF CONGRESS CATALOGING-IN-PUBLICATION DATA

State and reservation : new perspectives on federal Indian policy /
   edited by George Pierre Castile and Robert L. Bee.
      p.   cm.
   Includes bibliographical references and index.
   ISBN 0-8165-1319-8 (alk. paper). —
   ISBN 0-8165-1325-2 (pbk. : alk. paper)
      1. Indians of North America—Reservations.   2. Indians of
North America—Government relations.   3. Indians of North
America—Politics and government.   4. United States—Politics
and government.   I. Castile, George Pierre.   II. Bee, Robert L.
   E93.S75   1992   92-8229
   323.1′197073—dc20   CIP

British Library Cataloguing-in-Publication Data
A catalogue record for this book is available from the British Library.

Contents

Contributors

ROBERT L. BEE (co-editor) is Professor of Anthropology at the University of Connecticut. He has conducted extensive research on the impact of federal policy on the Quechan Indian community of the Fort Yuma reservation and other ethnographic studies of the Prairie Potawatomi of Kansas and a rural region of highland Mexico. In 1978 he went to Washington, D.C., to study the implementation of Indian policy. His books on policy issues include *Cross-Currents Along the Colorado* and *The Politics of American Indian Policy.*

GEORGE PIERRE CASTILE (co-editor) is Professor of Anthropology at Whitman College. His ethnographic and ethnohistorical research with Native American peoples has focused on problems of national indigenous policies in state-enclave relations in Latin America and the United States. His publications include the books *Persistent Peoples* and *The Indians of Puget Sound* as well as numerous articles on the federal-Indian relation.

GEORGE S. ESBER, JR., is Ethnographer with the Office of Native American Programs, National Park Service. His field research has emphasized applied work with Native American communities and is best represented by his work in the Tonto Apache community in Payson, Arizona, where his study of space needs for housing design won him a Praxis Award. He has published numerous articles related to the design of the built environment.

JOHN M. FINDLAY is Assistant Professor in the Department of History at the University of Washington. A historian of the American West, he focuses particularly on California and Nevada. He has published the book *People of Chance: Gambling in American Society from Jamestown to Las Vegas* and co-authored the chapter "Euro-American Impact Before 1870" for the *Great Basin* volume of the *Handbook of North American Indians*.

FREDERICK E. HOXIE is Director of the D'Arcy McNickle Center for the History of the American Indian at the Newberry Library. He is the author of *A Final Promise: The Campaign to Assimilate the Indians, 1880– 1920* (1984) and editor of *Indians in American History* (1988) and other works. Dr. Hoxie is a historian interested in the interplay between native communities and American society and is currently at work on a community history of the Crow reservation in the late nineteenth and early twentieth centuries. In addition to his other duties, he is also director of the American Indian Family History Project and chairman of the editorial committee for the forthcoming book *America in 1492*.

MARTHA C. KNACK is Professor of Anthropology in the Department of Anthropology and Ethnic Studies at the University of Las Vegas, Nevada. Her research has concerned Northern and Southern Paiute peoples with a particular emphasis on Indian–non-Indian resource competition. Her publications include numerous articles and research reports on Native Americans and the recent book, with Omer Stewart, *As Long as the River Shall Run: An Ethnohistory of Pyramid Lake Reservation, Nevada*.

DAVID C. MAAS is Associate Professor of Political Science at the University of Alaska, Anchorage. His research focuses on questions of development and democracy in the context of relations between indigenous peoples and contemporary states. He has written numerous articles on Alaska natives, self-determination, tribal governments, and federalism.

THOMAS R. MCGUIRE is a research associate with the Bureau of Applied Research in Anthropology, University of Arizona. His publications include *Politics and Ethnicity on the Rio Yaqui: Potam Revisited*, articles in *Human Organization, Urban Anthropology*, and *Journal of the Southwest*, as well as a monograph on the historical development of the Fort Apache cattle industry. He is currently initiating a long-term study of the Guyamas shrimp industry.

JOHN H. MOORE is Chair and Associate Professor of Anthropology at the University of Oklahoma. He is the author of *The Cheyenne Nation: A Social and Demographic History* (1987) and articles in *American Ethnologist, Science, Ethnology, Ethnohistory,* and other journals. He is primarily interested in the relationship between kinship and demography, and in other aspects of culture that illuminate this relationship. Dr. Moore has done fieldwork among Native Americans in Montana, Michigan, Tennessee, Florida, and Washington. He is presently working with Creek Indian elders in Oklahoma to prepare a history of their tribal towns since 1540.

FRANK W. PORTER III is Director of the Chelsea House Foundation for American Indian Studies. He holds a B.A., M.A., and Ph.D. from the University of Maryland. He is general editor of *Indians of North America* and is the author of numerous articles on the history, archaeology, and ethnography of the Indians of the Eastern United States. His books include *The Bureau of Indian Affairs, Native American Basketry: An Annotated Bibliography, The Nanticoke,* and *Strategies for Survival: American Indians in the Eastern United States.*

LAWRENCE DAVID WEISS is Assistant Professor of Sociology at the University of Alaska, Anchorage. His work focuses on historical and contemporary political economic analyses of Native Americans and also on Native American health issues. His publications include the book *Development of Capitalism in Navajo Nation* and several articles about native health care issues and political economy.

STATE AND RESERVATION

Introduction

GEORGE PIERRE CASTILE AND
ROBERT L. BEE

The political and legal system of Native American reservations in the United States is an unusual structural arrangement between enclaved peoples and the larger political state that encapsulates them. The forms of "native administration" that developed here and in other English colonies such as Australia, Canada, and New Zealand have in common the almost total displacement of an aboriginal population by massive European migration, followed by the development of a system of permanent political reserves and administered communities. This pattern is by no means a common, inevitable, or self-explanatory outcome of culture contact; nor was it even in the era of colonialism. Most models of the relationship of ethnic groups to the state seem inappropriate here because they describe the structural interrelations of constituent groups in "plural societies" that are more nearly balanced in their political and economic power.

The original essays collected in this volume examine a number of perspectives on the rise, change, and persistence of the relationship between the federal government and Indians in the United States. What began as a simple colonial policy of land acquisition and "peace making" gradually evolved into the unique "special" federal-Indian relationship. Although Congress periodically moves to abrogate the system entirely, the structural arrangements currently described as a "government-to-government" relationship have survived. No other ethnic group's political status has such considerable claims to self-determination and sovereignty; yet, ironically, the reservation peoples remain among the poorest and most powerless of the ethnic elements in the United States.

There is a need for more inquiry into this relationship. The bulk of the work concerned with Indian peoples has not explicitly focused on the reservation system and federal policy per se, and studies that have focused on the system have been primarily descriptive, atheoretical, and generally lacking in historical context. Except for a few landmark efforts such as Edward Spicer's *Perspectives in American Indian Culture Change* (1961), explicitly theoretical attempts by anthropologists to come to grips with the changing reservation relationship have been few.

Historians such as Francis Paul Prucha have had much to say about the development of federal Indian policy and administration on the reservations, but generally less than anthropologists and with less concern about the Indians' end of the relationship (Prucha 1984). Some scholars of jurisprudence have recently begun to produce valuable analyses of the legal roots of the relationship, although these tend to concentrate on the law itself (Wilkinson 1987). In the rest of the Americas, self-conscious theory regarding the relation of the state to indigenous peoples is far more actively debated under such labels as the "national question" and "indigenismo," but this ongoing debate has found little reflection in U.S. scholarship (Bollinger and Lund 1982).

The contributors to this volume were asked to consider the obvious basic questions: Why did the reservation system come into existence and take the form it did? And, most important, why does it persist? If there are problems with this system—the ever-recurring "Indian problem"—are they somehow inherent in the system itself or the result of deliberate policies? The individual essays focus on a variety of revealing and meaningful aspects of the larger issues. There is in this diversity a common analytical theme: the concept of *reservation* conveys quite different meanings to the different parties involved—the Indians, other local inhabitants, and the federal government.

The federal-Indian relationship has obviously evolved as a reflection of shifting policy emphases at the congressional level. Two of the contributors are historians who offer insights into the formative stages of the system. John Findlay examines the reservation system during the tumultuous gold rush period between 1850 and 1865 in California. Although California itself was late in the contact sequence of Indian and white, the chapter opens a window into the nature of the whole reservation program before the mid-nineteenth century. Not only here but everywhere along the advancing edge of the "frontier" the initial policy concern that led to the establishment of reservations was simple land clearance coupled with the need for military control of the displaced Native Americans.

California is an extreme instance of this period of relatively naked resource looting. Indians there were shifted from place to place in "movable asylums," ostensibly for their own benefit. But in addition to chronicling the devastating impact of this period on the native peoples, Findlay illustrates the conflicts of interest that resulted in a variety of "meanings" attached to the reservations. From the beginning to the present, the federal-Indian relation has not been simply two-handed. It also includes local and state players, whose interests in native affairs are often at variance with the federal government and almost always counter to those of the Indian peoples themselves. As a result, Findlay says, "National policy tended to function only so far as it suited the needs and wishes of state and local interests." The outcome for the Native Americans has often been a capricious and unpredictable quality of life on the reservations; one of his sources said that many "looked upon the reservations, rather as a hell than a home."

In the late 1800s the relatively raw phase of shunting aside native peoples for land clearance was largely completed and most Native Americans were successfully confined to much-diminished parcels of land. There then emerged a new policy emphasis on "assimilation," designed to eliminate these last enclaves by absorbing their people through enforced "civilization" and freeing their "surplus" land from communal ownership. This assimilationist policy is perhaps the most durable and historically recurring view of reservations as temporary instruments to instill conformity to Anglo ways rather than permanent homelands. Indeed, such a perspective is often seen as the "natural" policy for all states confronted with ethnic heterogeneity—the classic melting-pot philosophy.

Frederick E. Hoxie examines the Crow in the context of this era. The policy dilemma that emerged at that time was that the "vanishing Americans" refused to vanish; and although much of their surplus land was eliminated under the 1887 Dawes Act, the peoples endured. Hoxie illustrates the process of endurance and persistence of the Native American peoples in the face of the "oppression" of concerted policy efforts to dismantle their lifeways. Specifically, he examines Crow political life and internal leadership and reminds us that regardless of federal intentions, the Native Americans have molded the reservation system to serve their own purposes. They may have become "reservation peoples," but they are still peoples, with a surviving structure of leadership, pursuing their own goals.

Not all Indian peoples were confined to the federally administered community status of reservations. Two contributors focus on historical analyses of the experience of those "without reservation." The lives of these peoples are still very much influenced by federal Indian policy, but they are very different from those of the "recognized" tribes. The issue of who is or is not a "legal"—that is, federally recognized—tribe entitled to the "special" relation has become of very great interest in recent years as policy has shifted toward granting such tribes permanent sovereign status.

Martha Knack examines the situations of two small groups in Utah: Kanosh and Washakie. The history she offers is to some extent an interesting instance of parallel social evolution of the reservation relationship in that she illustrates the Mormons' "national" efforts to deal with Native Americans. Very much like the larger-scale federal efforts, Mormon policies were directed toward both land clearance and assimilation through civilization. However, lacking federal authority, the Mormons worked largely through smaller-scale land colonization schemes using Indian "homestead" laws.

The experience of these peoples in nonreservation enclaves is not entirely unique. Many other smaller Western tribal groups found themselves similarly situated on small parcels of land without the status of reservations— land they themselves acquired through purchase or through a variety of federal land schemes. The 1887 Dawes Act's emphasis on allotment of land in severalty aimed at breaking up the reservations into individual freehold, but it left behind many such pockets of enduring enclaves. Provisions of the act for the assignment of public domain lands and the two variants of "homestead" law examined by Knack could be, and in some cases were, used to create more such "reserves." The status of these nonreservation peoples has been much debated, but their very presence demonstrates that the preservation of Native American "peoples" is not solely an artifact of the federal relation manifest in the reservation system.

Frank W. Porter is similarly concerned with the small tribes of Puget Sound, many of whom were left landless and without federal recognition as tribes by the "Stevens" treaties of 1855. Porter describes how many of these landless tribes have survived as coherent peoples even though some are widely scattered "diaspora" groups with only memories of aboriginal homelands. Ironically, while reservations have been "hells" for many Native Americans, the possession of such a reserved territorial base with treaty rights and the sovereignty granted to tribes by federal decree have in modern times been important keys to tribal survival. As Porter suggests, while the existence of these Indian peoples is by no means purely a function of being granted official status by the federal government, the denial of the "special" federal-Indian relation creates special problems. Since 1978 the Federal Acknowledgment Project has attempted to solve these conundrums for a variety of tribes, including those of Washington, but to the satisfaction of almost no one. Porter considers the travails of the process, and in particular the symbolic importance of a land base—a homeland—suggesting a recognition paradox for the landless tribes: "no land, no recognition."

John H. Moore raises larger-scale problems about Native American peoples who have endured without reservation status: those of the supposedly defunct Oklahoma reservations, often officially referred to as the "historic areas of Oklahoma." The status of the various refugee "civilized" tribes of the former Indian Territory is one of the most tangled and long-standing problems in Indian policy history. Like Porter, Moore argues against "the idea that Indianness is something bestowed by the federal government, in some mysterious way, when a reservation is created, and thus something withdrawn when a reservation is dissolved."

Also like Porter, Moore tends to see the denial of reservation status as a product of continuing resource competition—denial of access to land. He emphasizes local-level conflicts between Indian and non-Indian politics after Oklahoma became a state and the reservations were "dissolved." Moore very clearly illustrates the basic problem (also touched on by Findlay) of the tension between non-Indian local and state governments and sovereign Indians placed outside state jurisdiction by the federal relationship. Both suggest that federal policy has most often in the past tended toward the support of these non-Indian "citizen" interests to the detriment of its trust obligation to the Native Americans. In Oklahoma, Moore suggests, "the continuing refusal of the dominant society and its agencies to use the word *reservation* to describe Oklahoma Indian lands is only part of the continuing propaganda aspect of this war."

More often than not, simple resource competition, especially for land, has been offered as the key to understanding Indian–non-Indian relations and federal Indian policy, and there is no doubt that it explains much. However, Moore introduces as well the importance of the "symbol" of reservation status in these economic matters. Carrying this further, the essays by Robert Bee and George Castile both examine the sources of policy since the turnaround from land expropriation—usually dated from John Collier's administration of the Indian Reorganization Act in the 1930s and 1940s. Since land loss was largely halted at that time, they argue that Indian policy afterward cannot be understood solely in terms of neocolonial models of economic exploitation. Both look entirely away from the reservation and the relatively small-scale local resource conflicts to a more general analysis of federal decision-making strategies.

After Collier and the 1934 Indian Reorganization Act, the federal policy position regarding reservations has fitfully but generally shifted away from seeing them as temporary impounding points for ultimate assimilation and toward a recognition of their status as permanent homelands. Barring the brief resurgence of abolitionist sentiment epitomized by the "termination" resolution of 1953,[1] the tendency of federal policy since the 1930s has been toward economic development and strengthening of the reservations as communities. The ultimate legislative expression of this policy is the Indian Self-Determination Act of 1975, which seeks to make the Native American peoples entirely self-administering and to eliminate their dependent status as administered communities. Both Bee and Castile attempt to account for these dramatic shifts away from the "natural" policies of expropriation and assimilation.

Bee argues that federal policy since 1960 has lost its focus and has steadily become the accumulated precipitate of specific solutions to largely local problems. An important factor in explaining this trend is the relationships of power that link Congress with the executive, the Indians, and the courts in the policy dynamic. Using Weberian concepts to trace the interplay of politics and bureaucracy, and of tribal sovereignty and federal trusteeship, he shows how the present condition came to prevail and suggests that radical and innovative policy reform is unlikely in the face of these relationships. As the present dynamic is played out, it places increasing policymaking power in the hands of the federal courts.

Castile critically examines a number of models of economic exploitation that have been offered to explain Indian policy, but concludes that these by themselves are inadequate. Like the War on Poverty of the 1960s, he argues, many of the modern programs and policies that strongly affect the reservations are simple reflections of policy made for larger constituencies, and not Indian policy at all. He offers an alternative model of Indian policy per se, suggesting that the continued existence of the reservations is itself a form of "exploitation," but one that benefits the larger surrounding state principally in the realm of the symbolic and the political rather than the economic. Building on the theories of "cultural hegemony" of Antonio Gramsci, he suggests that Indian policy finds its significance in the larger arena of national ethnic policy and in its contribution to maintaining the cohesion of all ethnic elements.

By no means do Bee and Castile argue for a total absence of economic and resource competition factors in explaining Indian policy, but rather simply for the inclusion of other factors. Clearly much that happens in modern times—if no longer the naked exploitation of the pre-1900 era—is still influenced to some degree by local and national economic concerns. The essays by Lawrence Weiss and David C. Maas, and by Thomas R. McGuire, address important areas of the modern policy process which are very much resource centered.

Weiss and Maas focus on Alaska, which has always been somewhat outside the mainstream of developments in Indian policy. The structural relations of the Alaska natives to the federal government rather belatedly underwent considerable rearrangement after Alaskan statehood and the sorting out of local versus national land interests. Many have felt that the "clearing" of title to Indian lands embodied in the Alaska Native Claims Settlement Act of 1971 is simply a latter-day replay of the resource confiscation era of the Dawes Act. Weiss and Maas strongly endorse such a resource-oriented view of this policy.

They explore the source and implications of the Alaska Native Claims Settlement Act using the Marxist concept of "primitive accumulation" as their key to policy formation in a capitalist society. They suggest that "the history of primitive accumulation in the United States is largely the history of the repeated expropriation of Native Americans from their lands." They explore this general history and then focus on the situation of the Alaska natives as an extension of the general process, arguing that it differs from earlier, more naked expropriation because "politically acceptable ways were found to expropriate the lands in politically more sophisticated ways."

George Esber extends this theme of new sophisticated ways of doing business at the same old stand even to modern policies of self-determination. He examines recent policy moves in an effort to explore the "latent dangers" of seemingly benign policy. He suggests that self-determination is in fact a policy of "participation," and as such the "new" policy is little more than a born-again termination program to rid the government of the responsibilities of the special relationship. Since final decision-making power still rests with the federal government, empowerment is incomplete, and the policy is in Esber's view "an invitation to participate" that might be better called "the Indian Participation Act." In fact, he suggests, "self-determination as a policy of a dominant group toward a minority people is a contradiction in terms and can never be a reality."

Generally, in discussions of Indian policy there has been a tendency to see the Indians as possessing certain "rights" alleged to be "inalienable." But despite the present apparent policy commitment to the permanency of the special government-to-government relationship, the relationship has changed a great deal over the years—and is still changing. Congressional power is plenary, and today's inalienable right may be tomorrow's bargaining chip.

Thomas McGuire focuses on the process of "negotiation" by which abstract rights take real forms through accommodation and compromise. McGuire's analysis is specifically based on the question of the allocation of water rights, an important area of ongoing resource conflict. He concentrates on the give-and-take of such "negotiation" and asks how the federal government's policy of negotiation affects the negotiation of policy. He examines the complex history of settlements arrived at over *Winters* doctrine rights at Salt River, San Luis Rey, and Colorado Utes, with an eye toward the implications for national-level federal Indian policy. In the process he illustrates that federal policy, now as in the past, is often guided more by practicality than by principle. In the negotiation process, "fundamental concepts of trust, equity, and entitlement are thrown open to interpretation," and "the one consistent line" is " 'to execute a waiver or release' of all past and future Indian claims to water."

A final word. In this collection we aim more to open a debate that has been neglected than to finally resolve the issue of federal-Indian relations. The contributors have come to their own conclusions, and we will leave our certainties at that level. The record of the past that we touch upon is clearly a monument to the ability of the Native American peoples to endure in the face of overwhelming and often deliberate pressure for their cultural dissolution. Much of the pressure in the early era is obviously understandable, if not excusable, in simple terms of population pressures and resource competition.

New explanations are needed for why the reservation system and federal-Indian relations have seemingly become permanent. Many feel that times have changed since the 1930s and that federal policy is no longer guided mostly by the interests of local rapacious land seekers. Policy itself has become meandering, unfocused, and preoccupied with local issues and negotiated settlements. Some of the contributors are obviously pessimistic about these recent trends, seeing them simply as more of the same under new names. The powerlessness of the Indian peoples before political pressures to usurp their resources is a consistent and depressing theme that emerges in any examination of federal-Indian relations. Yet if that were all there was to it, the "Indian problem" would long ago since have ceased to exist.

NOTES

1. The "termination" policy took its cue from U.S. House Concurrent Resolution 108 (83d Congr., 1st sess., August 1, 1953), wherein it became the declared

policy of Congress to terminate its special trust relationship with Native American tribes as soon as possible. Indians in specified states and tribes "should be freed from Federal supervision and control and from all disabilities and limitations specially applicable to Indians."

REFERENCES

BOLLINGER, WILLIAM, and DANIEL LUND. 1982. "Minority Oppression: Toward Analyses That Clarify and Strategies That Liberate." *Latin American Perspectives* 9(2):2–28.

PRUCHA, FRANCIS PAUL. 1984. *The Great Father: The United States Government and the American Indians.* Lincoln: University of Nebraska Press.

SPICER, EDWARD H. 1961. *Perspectives in American Indian Culture Change.* Chicago: University of Chicago Press.

WILKINSON, CHARLES F. 1987. *American Indians, Time and the Law.* New Haven: Yale University Press.

PART I

HISTORICAL FOUNDATIONS OF THE RESERVATION SYSTEM

An Elusive Institution

The Birth of Indian Reservations in
Gold Rush California

JOHN M. FINDLAY

In recent years historians of the American West have
stressed anew the need to comprehend how different groups experienced
and understood the same event in different ways (Limerick 1987). This
concern has enriched the study of Indian-white relations. Historians are
now less likely than before to see any one group or side as monolithic in its
thought and practice, and more inclined to appreciate the agency of natives
as they confronted the changes resulting from the arrival of whites. Greater
allowance for multiple points of view will surely enhance historical understanding of Indian reservations.

One way to account for differing perspectives is to recognize reservations
as physical components of the cultural landscape capable of eliciting diverse
meanings from the people associated with them. Seeing reserves as places to
be defined and planned, experienced and modified, resisted and abandoned,
permits us to invoke insights into the significance of the built environment. Amos Rapoport explains that "designers and users, and different user
groups, perceive and evaluate environments differently so that meanings
intended by designers may not be perceived; if perceived, not understood;
and, if both perceived and understood, may be rejected." Furthermore,
designers are inclined to conceive the built environment in "perceptual"
terms that measure it against an ideal. They often see it rather abstractly as a
setting highly susceptible to rational manipulation. Different groups of
users, on the other hand, assign meanings more in "associational" terms.
They come to identify certain attitudes or feelings or circumstances with a
setting as they are "taking possession [of it], completing it, changing it," or

(Rapoport might have added) rejecting it. Users and designers, in other words, develop a variety of understandings of "the nature of the rules embodied or encoded" in the built environment (Rapoport 1982:76, 15–22; 1977:14–15, 24–25, 52). And when these understandings clash with one another, so, often, do the people holding them.

Rapoport's terms can help to illuminate the fact that non-Indians and Indians, as well as non-Indian and Indian subgroups, experienced reservations in diverse, often contradictory, ways. This essay analyzes the wide-ranging perceptions of the institution and assesses how these perceptions affected the implementation of reservation policy in one historical setting—the state of California between 1850 and 1865.

Gold rush California provides an exceptionally rich example of the diversity of meanings elicited by reservations because it acquired some of the very first reserves established by the U.S. government as it turned away from removal policy. Because reserves were relatively undefined in their formative years, they were susceptible to a broad range of interpretations by those who designed, or would design, them. The commissioner of Indian affairs, his appointed agents in California, military officers ordered to uphold Indian policy, and assorted advocates and critics of reserves throughout the state treated the reservation as a kind of blank slate upon which they could write a variety of definitions. Meanings attached to the reserve reflected the diverse experiences and expectations of those who planned, supported, or criticized the institution. Reserves were variously likened to farms, fortresses, asylums, schools, final refuges, and Spanish missions as those involved sought to identify the novel institution with more familiar models.

The turbulent world of the gold rush, combined with rapid modifications of federal policy, ensured that non-Indians' understanding of reservations changed constantly. In this process of continual redefinition, meanings did not endure; older interpretations first coexisted with, then gave way to, newer ones. Those in charge of implementing reservation policy found that experience altered their expectations and forced them to modify the institution. The reserve of 1863 was in vital respects radically different from that of 1853, in the minds of both designers and users. Moreover, in the course of continual redefinition, roles changed. Some designers became users; many whites responsible for implementing federal policy behaved less like subordinates charged to establish and uphold the designs of their superiors than as free agents intent upon exploiting reservations for personal gain.

Designers were compelled to redefine reserves not only because of the

turmoil and corruption in California but also because of concerted resistance
to federal policy by state and local interests. Perhaps even more boldly than
in other times and places in the United States, white settlers in gold rush
California defied federal Indian policy, with the open support of the state
government. These opponents of the reservation were special kinds of users
whose understanding of the institution derived in large part from the
alternative *uses* to which they hoped to put its land and inmates. Farmers,
ranchers, and miners in California desired greater access to both the grounds
occupied by reserves and the labor of reservation Indians.

   The majority of California Indians—the group of users for whom federal
policy was mainly intended—also resisted the reservation, although their
reasons for doing so were based on their own distinctive understandings of
it.[1] Some natives, particularly those upon whose lands reserves were situated, accepted the institution as a form of protection for themselves, but
most did not. Again, reasons for rejecting reserves varied according to
different groups of natives. Many, for example, hoped to remain in their
traditional homelands so that they could retain their culture and self-
sufficiency as long as possible. Others preferred making their own arrangements within the white world, but without the reservation. The resistance
of California Indians to reserves, like that of white settlers and other users,
helped to alter the designers' understanding and thus contributed to
changes in federal policy.

   Given the wide range and shifting nature of the meanings attached to
early reservations in California by designers and users, it is not surprising
that the institution failed to achieve the goals of federal Indian policy. Few
groups concurred on what the reservation meant or ought to mean. In fact,
there tended to be only one point of agreement—that the institution would
not endure. For a wide variety of reasons, both designers and users believed,
or came to believe, that reserves would be temporary. As a result, California's first reservations were marked by an extreme transiency that added to
their inability to serve the purposes of federal agents or California Indians.
Fixed neither in place nor in people's minds, they were an elusive institution.

THE RESERVATION IDEA AND GOLD RUSH CALIFORNIA

As the centerpiece of federal policy, the reservation emerged during the
1850s as a replacement for Indian removal. General guidelines issued by the
commissioner of Indian affairs in 1850 sketched out the new direction.
Rather than being assigned to a remote, somewhat vaguely defined region

and left largely to their own devices, Indians were now to be "colonized" systematically on smaller parcels of land in the midst of territory occupied by non-Indians. Some colonial and early national precedents existed for mid-nineteenth-century reserves, but never had such a policy been so carefully formulated or so broadly implemented. By concentrating natives on well-defined plots, usually of 25,000 acres or less, federal officials hoped to convert Indians from their supposedly habitual hunting and foraging to the fixed lifestyle of agriculture. Under the new regimen the government would assign to each "tribe" some farmland "of limited extent and well-defined boundaries," on which virtually all Indians "should be compelled constantly to remain until such time as their general improvement and good conduct may supersede the necessity of such restrictions." Reserves necessitated not only a more active role for whites in socializing the Indians to Anglo-American ways through education, example, and coercion, but also a more concerted program of government subsidy until Indians were capable of supporting themselves in the new mode and entering into full relations with the larger society (CIA 1851:35–36; Trennert 1975).

Between 1846 and 1851 the perceptions of officials in the nation's capital and of Indian agents on the Great Plains and in the Southwest were instrumental to the evolution of the reserve as "an alternative to what seemed to be the inevitable extinction of the Indian." But initial implementation of the new policy occurred not east of the Rockies but west of the Sierra Nevada, where Indian extinction was a much more likely prospect during the early 1850s (Caughey 1952:35–36; Trennert 1975:viii). The tens of thousands of people streaming into California after 1848 entered a region where relations between natives and non-natives had already begun to change drastically. While Mexico's protection of Indians diminished following the secularization of the missions in the mid-1830s, California's economy, based on ranchos and the stirrings of commerce, absorbed more natives as laborers at the same time that it displaced others from their traditional territories (Hurtado 1988).

The role of natives in California society was thus already in flux when the conquest of the region by the United States and the subsequent discovery of gold attracted immigrants from around the world and heightened a demographic catastrophe for Indians. The approximate native population of the state dropped from 150,000 in 1845 to 100,000 in 1850, 50,000 in 1855, and 35,000 in 1860 (Cook 1976b:44, 59). Increases in the non-native population so taxed resources, so multiplied the incidence of disease, and so intensified violent conflict that the survival of the remaining native population was jeopardized.

Few of the single-minded adventurers who inundated the mining frontier concerned themselves with the welfare of California's Indians. Some
viewed them as a "useful class" (Rawls 1984:67) to be employed in a labor-
scarce economy, but many saw Indians as a hindrance to their exploitation of
the opportunity of a lifetime and sought the most convenient way to
eliminate them. Frontier attitudes thus combined with a rapidly changing
ecology to produce tremendous dislocation and destruction among already
weakened Indian groups. The need to save Indians "from extermination, or
if not to smothe their path to the grave," became steadily more urgent.[2]

In response to the dangers faced by California Indians, federal officials
turned to the untested policy of reservations. They first proposed reserves
for the Golden State in a series of eighteen treaties negotiated in 1851 and
1852 with numerous bands and villages of natives. These agreements assigned Indians to specific territories in the state, promised a subsidy of food
and livestock, and offered instruction and supervision for at least five years.
They fell through, however, when the U.S. Senate voted against their
ratification on July 8, 1852 (Heizer and Almquist 1971:61−79; Kelsey
1973; Rawls 1984:141−47). Even as the senators rejected the treaties,
however, the Office of Indian Affairs prepared to found reservations in
California in a manner that would not require Senate ratification. It appointed Edward F. Beale, a prominent frontier adventurer and officeholder,
as superintendent of Indian affairs in the state and instructed him to establish a "system of colonization" for the purpose of "making useful, our
present worthless, and troublesome Indian population."[3]

In establishing California's first reservations during the 1850s and early
1860s, Beale and his successors focused attention not so much on the coastal
strip between Sonoma and San Diego, where Hispanic settlement had
either eliminated or absorbed most natives, but rather on the great interior
valley and the northern coast, where contact with Indians had been limited
before the 1840s. A pattern typifying the implementation of policy during
the gold rush emerged from the state's first three reservations, each of which
was located in or adjacent to the Central Valley: an experimental reserve
started in the San Joaquin Valley in 1852, often called the Fresno farm; the
state's first full-fledged reserve, founded in 1853 in the Tehachapi Mountains and known as El Tejon or San Sebastian; and the Nome Lackee
Reservation, established in 1854 amid the western foothills of the Sacramento Valley. Approved and funded by the U.S. Congress, each of these
reserves opened to enthusiastic reviews, and together they appeared to
constitute a humane and practical solution to the problem of the California
Indians (Thompson 1983:56−57, 66). On paper, the system reached its

peak in 1857 when Thomas J. Henley, Beale's successor as superintendent of Indian affairs in California, reported that the reservations served 12,000 natives, perhaps one third of the Indian population of the state.[4]

By the following year, the reality of failure overwhelmingly belied the "flattering accounts" of the first hopeful years.[5] At El Tejon, Nome Lackee, and the Fresno farm, starvation, encroachment by white settlers, and incompetence or corruption on the part of Indian agents served to undermine reservation policy. Finding security and subsistence inadequate, most reservation Indians left the institutions; other natives avoided them altogether. Fleeing Indians were not the only party responsible for the demise of the first generation of reservations, however, because white officials proved just as likely to abandon the establishments. Between 1852 and 1855 six reservations or farms were founded in California by agents of the Office of Indian Affairs. All were closed within ten years, including Nome Lackee, El Tejon, and Fresno, and their inhabitants were forced to move to other sites. Between 1856 and 1870 another six reserves were founded in the state, but only three of them remained in 1871 (Browne 1861:310; Rawls 1984:151–53).

Transiency and instability characterized reservations in early American California, in part because there was no lasting consensus on what reservations were. Indian agents and their allies continually redefined the institution, often in response to local problems in implementing federal designs, and various groups of users compelled additional reinterpretation through their resistance to the institution.

PLANNING THE RESERVATION: MODELS, MOBILITY, AND COERCION

Today, the reservation survives as a bastion of Indian nationalism and a monument to the antagonism between native and non-native cultures. During the 1850s, however, the architects of the institution hoped to prepare Indians for eventual assimilation into the greater society. Unwilling to accept coexistence with Indian cultures, they designed reservations so that they resembled variations of the mid-nineteenth-century American asylum.

During the antebellum era, many Americans embraced reformers' new versions of the penitentiary, the insane asylum, and the almshouse, both as solutions to the apparent ills caused by social instability and as models of how people might begin to restore order. Believing increasingly that background, and not an intrinsically flawed character, caused such problems as crime, insanity, and poverty, reformers touted asylums as special environments in which those regarded as deviant might be isolated, concentrated, and resocialized through discipline and routine, and then integrated anew into the larger world. Despite the highest expectations, however, these visionaries encountered difficulties with their models. By the 1850s, asylums that once had been devoted to rehabilitation of deviants and regeneration of stability "were losing their reformist mission and becoming storage bins for society's outcasts" (Rothman 1971:xix, 107–8, 129; Walters 1978:194–206).

Reservations suffered much the same fate, albeit slightly later. In California, by the end of the Civil War, they had become places to segregate Indian "misfits" from the rest of society, but they had been designed as a means to incorporate Native Americans into the mainstream. Indeed, in a burst of optimism that typified the period's evangelical mentality (Prucha 1984, 1:226–37), reformers believed that reserves would exert their influence so quickly and thoroughly that salvation for the natives, in the sense of their conversion from "primitive" to "civilized" ways, would occur almost immediately. The *Daily Alta California* (San Francisco) echoed official views when it predicted in 1853 that reserves would transform Indians within five years "from a state of semi-barbarism, indolence, mental imbecility, and moral debasement, to the condition of civilization, Christianity, industry, virtue, frugality, social and domestic happiness and public usefulness" (cited in Ellison 1922:62; cf. CIA 1855:223–24).[6] There seemed to be no problem that reservations could not solve in just a few years.

Indian agents heightened anticipation of the natives' conversion in the early 1850s by portraying California natives as cooperative and susceptible to reform influences.[7] In the eyes of reformers, Indians must have seemed ideal subjects for asylums. Their supposedly rootless lifestyle stood as the exact antithesis to the restraint and stability that reformers hoped to encourage in their own society; by compelling Indians to settle down, the reserve might illustrate for all Americans the proper path to a more virtuous social order. Furthermore, Indians appeared to be highly vulnerable to the very vices—drinking, gambling, laziness, and promiscuity—that reformers hoped to root out of the larger society.

If Indians were so vulnerable to negative influences, it was perhaps thought, they must surely be equally susceptible to corrective actions. Observers commonly regarded California Indians as a "most abject poor stupid and filthy" people, yet simultaneously believed their degraded character to be malleable. Some held that the Indian had the potential to assimilate fully into American society, while others thought that even the reformed native would remain comparatively childlike. Few agents of the Office of Indian Affairs, however, doubted that there was some capacity for "rapid and permanent improvement," and most saw the reservation as fertile soil in which to cultivate whatever seeds of "civilization" lay dormant in Indian souls.[8]

Local history in California reinforced the official optimism and helped to explain exactly how the new kind of asylum would work on its inmates. Some non-Indians came to terms with the idea of a reservation by likening it to the legendary missions established by Spain and Mexico. They recalled the institution, fondly if not accurately, as the hallmark of a golden age in Indian-white relations (Caughey 1952:xxvi–xxx; Rawls 1984:149–50). Perceptions of the paternalistic mission informed some early proposals to move Indians to reservations in the hope that natives would become self-supporting contributors to the burgeoning economy and learn the habits of white culture, reenacting what was believed to have occurred among mission Indians in Hispanic California. Americans seemed confident that with their Protestant culture and "beneficent" government, they could surpass the purported achievements of Spanish-speaking missionaries (Browne 1861:308). "Surely that which was attempted by a few poor priests," said the first superintendent of Indian affairs in the state, "is not too great a task for the mighty republic of the United States."[9]

Asylums and missions as models for the reservation suggested a primarily hopeful outlook, but some people voiced different views. The optimistic perspective of most Indian agents was complemented by a much more pessimistic current of thought, much in favor among settlers and state officials. In sharp contrast to reformers' expectations of a rapid transformation, some observers anticipated the imminent extinction of the California Indians. In this view, reserves should serve as asylums where natives went to die. In 1855, U.S. Army Captain E. D. Keyes praised the superintendent at Nome Lackee because, instead of holding expectations about the Indians' ultimate survival and acculturation, he reportedly understood that his chief purpose "must be to deprive the red man of his power to do mischief" during the few years he had remaining on earth. "We ought . . . to act," Keyes wrote, "on the determined certainty that the aborigines of this Country will soon become extinct."[10]

The duality of views reiterated the official estimate of the choice confronting California Indians as *extermination or domestication* (Thompson 1983:50; Rawls 1984:141). Regardless of whether one held an optimistic or pessimistic view, however, whites assumed that reservations would be short-lived. The inmates would assimilate into white society within five to twenty-five years, or else disappear from the face of the earth. Either way, the reserve would soon become obsolete. During the 1850s virtually nobody saw a need for a permanent institution where surviving Indians could remain in the event they refused to accept white culture, so little long-term thinking characterized the establishment of gold rush reservations.

In founding the asylums, federal officials signed no treaties (and thus gave no recognition to Indian land rights), offered no long-term federal commitment, and made no provision for a permanent land base or sanctuary for natives. Indian agents had not only become dissatisfied with the treaty system but also felt no compunction to make deals with the California Indians because they believed that the Spanish and Mexican regimes had already stripped them of all rights to the land. As a result, Indians assigned to the first reserves in California simply went as temporary guests on lands set aside nominally for military uses. Upon founding the Fresno farm, Beale carefully explained that the natives possessed no title to the lands but rather stayed at "the will of the Government" and "may at any time be removed at its pleasure."[11] Not surprisingly, then, federal agents frequently responded to such reservation problems as crop failure or increasing pressure from settlers by proposing relocation to a new site—down the valley, across the mountains, outside the state altogether.

Because it had been designed as a movable asylum, both keepers and inmates came to see the reserve as a transient institution. Seldom thinking that reserves would last very long, Indian agents rather carelessly established and safeguarded them. The Fresno farm and El Tejon, which were located on private property, became subject to pressure from white landowners, and settlers clustering around Nome Lackee claimed the public land set aside there for Indians. The presence of non-natives eager to purchase parcels of the reserve loomed large in the abandonment of Nome Lackee in 1863. The government also ultimately abandoned the reserve at El Tejon in 1864 after it was asked to pay a higher rent by its new owner—former superintendent Beale. The Indians from El Tejon were resettled along the Tule River on a farm leased by the government for two years from another private owner.[12]

By marching Indians from one site to another, agents demonstrated that early reservation policy assumed not only a high degree of impermanence but also a substantial amount of coercion. Officials often wrote, particularly in the early years, as if residence at reserves and conversion to white ways were matters of choice for Indians. And in fact, reservations in gold rush California did not exert pressure like that directed against Plains and Southwestern Indians during the later nineteenth century. Nonetheless, besides protecting and assimilating Indians, reservations were also charged with the responsibility of controlling them. Consequently, Indian agents looked to the military both for an example of how to organize life within reservations and for assistance in forcing the Indians to do as they were told.

The military provided another model for those planners of reservations concerned with matters of control. When Edward F. Beale added flesh to the bones of the reservation idea in 1852 and 1853, he made it clear that El Tejon would be half farm and half fortress. A former lieutenant at sea, he meant to impose "a system, and regularity, acquired by eighteen years experience in the strict school of naval discipline." He once wrote that his "system of Discipline and instruction" was sustained "by a moral force," but when moral force failed to persuade Indians to work, "the indolent are punished, and compelled to labor . . . and so it should be with the children when schools are established." Moreover, as reservations tried to instruct Indians in the arts of farming and manual labor, they also supported troops who not only were paid from "the surplus product of Indian labour" but also were responsible for controlling uncooperative natives.[13]

The reservation served a military purpose that often seemed inconsistent with its reform and welfare functions. The importance of managing Indians, as opposed to providing for their welfare, was illustrated in the selection of the site for the first full-scale reserve in the state. Some had argued for locating it in the Sacramento or San Joaquin Valley, near the mining regions, where Indians were most threatened.[14] Beale, however, placed the reserve farther south at El Tejon, near a mountain pass linking southern California with the Central Valley, because Indians in that region were allegedly more troublesome and because he feared that the state's ranching industry might be jeopardized if southern California natives were not pacified. Admitting that the fate of the supposedly less warlike natives in central and northern California was "no idle decimation," Beale wrote, "I cannot help them. Humanity must yield to necessity. They are not dangerous; therefore, they must be neglected."[15]

Another year passed before a reservation was started in the Sacramento Valley, closer to the wholesale destruction caused by gold mining. In the summer of 1854 Thomas J. Henley found the Indians of north-central California "in the most miserable, degraded and destitute condition."[16] In establishing Nome Lackee, government agents consulted with nearby Indians who, because of various threats from whites—including periodic slave raids—expressed an interest in the protection available on federal reserves.[17] If some Indians willingly joined the reservation, however, the pressure on others to relocate to a reserve would apparently be increased.

Henley tried to compel Indians to accept the reserve by withholding virtually all assistance from those who refused to "submit to the policy of removal" to reservations. Taking Henley's proposal to its logical conclusion, one army officer suggested making the Indians "understand that in every other place except the Reserves, they will be considered outlaws, and that every man will have a right to hunt them and to steal their children." Additionally, like Beale, Henley requested that an ample number of soldiers be stationed at reserves in order that the "savages . . . be controlled and kept in subjection."[18] Military coercion was deemed essential to the success of reservation policy.

REDEFINING RESERVES: FAILURE, RESISTANCE, AND CORRUPTION

The increasing advocacy of compulsion during the later 1850s served as an indication of agents' rising frustration with the original ideals of reserves, of heightened tensions between whites and natives, and of the growing awareness that policymakers' initial estimation of the Indians as docile and tractable was wrong. Even more important than the increasing discussion of coercion, however, was the accumulating evidence that the reservation had generally failed to control, protect, or retain its inmates. All talk of compulsion notwithstanding, most Indians who went to California's first three reserves either died there or departed. The institution was too weak to provide them with food and clothing, too weak to protect them from white attacks, and too weak to make them stay. Furthermore, both white settlers and Indians were determined to resist the reservation and its aims. The experiences of the many users of reserves compelled designers to modify, and in some cases abandon, the institution.

Devised to provide Indians with sustenance and sanctuary, reservations in some cases provided no safety at all. Indian agents' inability to check the interference of settlers became apparent at Nome Lackee. The reserve was relatively isolated at its inception in 1854, but settlers quickly crowded around it. Because government agents never realized plans to fence the Indians' fields, settlers regarded the acreage as pasture for their livestock. If Indians tried to drive off or kill the white men's stock, they were threatened, beaten, or shot.[19] By trampling fields at Nome Lackee, the livestock generated in northern California the same phenomenon that plagued early reservations throughout the state—crop failures. Each of the early reserves underwent periods of severe food shortage, and in numerous cases agents had to ration food and restrict diets.[20]

The inadequate food supply modified official policy regarding the confinement of Indians on reserves and weakened further the reservations' ability to retain their charges. Thomas Henley had initially rejected the idea of permitting the "Indians at any time to escape from the Reserves." Less than a year later, however, he essentially reversed his stand by directing all agents to encourage Indians to gather traditional foods from lands surrounding reservations. By 1862 sites for reservations were valued less than before for their farming potential, and more for their proximity to supplies of foods traditionally hunted and gathered by Indians. Converting natives into farmers had not succeeded, and whites tacitly admitted that many Indians could better provide for themselves outside the environment of the reservation. Now, of course, it became "almost impossible to prevent the escape of the Indians . . . disposed to leave."[21]

After internees were allowed to depart reserves to procure food, estimates of how many Indians truly fell within the orbit of the institutions became even more dubious than before. Visitors who remarked on the small numbers of natives at reserves were regularly told by agents that most of the inmates were out foraging for food. This explanation became a kind of standing joke to investigators, who had heard the excuse all too often. J. Ross Browne finally grew tired of the deceit, which in his perception masked pervasive corruption:

> A very large amount of money was annually expended in feeding white men and starving Indians. Much of the latter as were physically able took advantage of the tickets-of-leave granted them so freely, and left. Very few ever remained at these benevolent institutions when there was a possibility of getting any thing to eat in the woods. . . . [It] inevitably happened, when a visitor appeared on the reservations, that the Indians were "out in the mountains gathering nuts and berries." This was the case in spring, summer, autumn, and winter. They certainly possessed a remarkable predeliction for staying out a long time. Very few of them, indeed, have yet come back. (Browne 1861:311–12)

The inability to feed reservation Indians, to get them to raise crops, or to keep them on reserves epitomized the futility of government efforts to protect and control natives in gold rush California. At each of the early reserves, inflated estimates of resident populations collapsed. Indians who had come from other regions of the state usually "scattered to their former Homes and retreats," where they figured to obtain food more easily.[22] Only Indians who had resided nearby before the reserves were established, and who therefore knew best how to exploit the surrounding terrain, remained at the first three reservations until they were closed.[23] And then these natives too either drifted away or were forcibly relocated.

California's first reserves were undermined not only by defects in design but also by opposition from white settlers. Dependent on Indian labor, many settlers resisted the relocation of natives to reservations. One supervising agent at Nome Lackee explained that settlers commonly held that Indians belonged to them "as much as an African slave does to his master. . . . Many of these Indians have left their places and come to the reservation, and have been followed and demanded by the persons claiming them as private property." Another official noted that agents or soldiers removed Indians to reservations when whites gave approval and support but could do little when citizens refused to cooperate.[24]

National policy tended to function only so far as it suited the needs and wishes of state and local interests. While federal agents tried to isolate and concentrate natives in order to assimilate them into American society, some whites attempted to use Indians as labor, and others carried out a war of extermination against them (Rawls 1984). Settlers thus pressured Indian agents to modify federal policies. They consistently disregarded the purposes and practices of reserves and lobbied to get them closed down.[25] Their opposition to federal programs was openly supported by state officials. Once California was admitted to the Union in 1850, it immediately denied civil and political rights to Indians and supported removal efforts by authorizing and financing military campaigns against them (Caughey 1952:xxii–xxiii). Governor John Bigler accepted the destruction of Indians as a matter of course on the frontier and explained that local political realities precluded him from either criticizing the actions of white settlers or adopting programs that favored the natives: "As a private intercessor between American citizens and their savage enemies, consanguinity, and the sentiments which it inspires, would incline me to favor the cause of my countrymen: and as a public magistrate chosen by American citizens, I cannot yield my approbation to any imputations upon their intelligence or patriotism."[26]

The weakness of federal programs in the face of resistance from state and local interests provides perspective on the obstacles faced by reservations during the mid-nineteenth century. The power of the Union over the states had not yet been proven. In addition, the distance between California and Washington, D.C., militated against successful implementation of federal policy. Difficulties on the Pacific Coast also reflected both the confusion in the Indian service resulting from the transition in policy around mid-century and the spoils system of politics before the establishment of a strong civil service ethic. The Office of Indian Affairs generally had inadequate staff. Furthermore, its poorly paid employees, whose appointments frequently represented political favors, were all too often tempted by illicit opportunities (Browne 1861:308–9; Danziger 1974:6–7, 15–16). Frustrated by the low caliber of agents at El Tejon in 1856, one army captain wrote that the government should have "selected honest men, not politicians, to have managed the reserves."[27]

These conditions, combined with gold rush attitudes, produced in early American California a "record of fraud and corruption remarkable even for the Indian Bureau" (Utley 1984:52). Malfeasance and incompetence plagued the implementation of reservation policy from the outset. Upon taking office as superintendent of Indian affairs in 1852, Beale found evidence of "neglect" and "official recklessness" and reported the diversion of supplies purchased for Indians to whites, a common complaint throughout the 1850s.[28] Two years later Beale himself was removed from office amid charges of dishonesty. His problems perhaps derived more from inattention and ill luck than anything else. Yet Beale had located the Tejon reserve not on the public domain but rather on lands already claimed, contrary to his instructions. Moreover, although he reported great progress in teaching Indians how to farm, critics pointed out that the ex–mission Indians situated at El Tejon had been farming those lands for years.[29] Thomas J. Henley replaced Beale as state superintendent in 1854, promising to practice "strict and rigid economy," but by 1858 Henley had also been accused of fraud, and in 1859 he was replaced.[30]

Henley's greatest offense may have been not his own activities but his negligence in overseeing the Nome Lackee reserve. To supervise the property Henley appointed E. A. Stevenson—a man who apparently gambled and drank to excess and kept his own stable of race horses on the reservation.[31] In 1857 Stevenson was succeeded by another political appointee, Vincent E. Geiger, who ran the establishment into the ground through theft and incompetence. The improprieties of Beale, Henley, and Stevenson all paled in comparison with Geiger's. He defrauded the government in reports about conditions on the reserve, employed a "worthless horde" of agents who exploited and abused natives, appropriated government land and equipment for his own use, failed to protect the reserve from white encroachments, and, taking advantage of state law, indentured more than seventy young reservation Indians as his "apprentices" upon being dismissed from the Indian service.[32] Designers could become the worst kind of users.

With men like Geiger in charge, it was no surprise that white employees on the reservations failed to measure up to reform standards. According to George M. Hanson, superintending agent of Indian affairs in northern California during the early 1860s, one special problem was the disruption caused by sexual relations between the white male employees and Indian women, which produced "*half breeds Jealousies* disease and death on every hand." In an 1863 letter to Abraham Lincoln explaining that an "old friend" of the president had been discharged from service for having "Contact" with a native woman, Hanson recalled that when he first "came into office, every employee in the service [was] unmarried, and all but *one,* had each, from one to three squaws to use when they pleased."[33]

The incompetence, corruption, and exploitation of Indians by those managing the reservations added to the frustrations faced by federal policy-makers as they tried to implement an ambitious scheme in a frontier state whose settlers cared less about humanitarian reform than about getting rich quickly—without much regard for the means. Not all the employees in the Indian service in California betrayed their purpose, but it proved very difficult to keep in mind the good intentions that underlay the program. By the late 1850s and early 1860s, support for the reservation had become increasingly qualified, and even those who continued to regard themselves as reformers became cynical about its prospects. These attitudes were conveyed by special agents assigned to examine conditions in the state and report back to the nation's capital. One of the investigators, Godard Bailey, concluded in 1858 that California reservations had become "simply Government Almshouses," thus sharing the fate of other antebellum versions of the asylum. Similar thoughts were expressed by white citizens who had also learned not to trust the Indian service. The *Daily Alta California,* which had held such high hopes for reserves a few years earlier, now termed them "vast elymosinary establishments for the support of pets and paupers."[34]

J. Ross Browne, another special investigator, commented more poignantly on the gold rush reservation experience between the mid-1850s and the mid-1860s. Browne initially expressed enthusiasm for the system's progress. During the late 1850s, however, his tone changed. He contended that the Indians were "no better off" because of the establishment of reserves and argued that Spanish-speaking missionaries had bettered the performance of American reservation agents. But in 1858 Browne was not yet prepared to abandon the institution "because it has not been properly tested."[35] To give the reserve a fair trial, Browne recommended enforcing stricter rules of economy in administering reservations, separating children from the influence of their parents, applying greater pressure on Indians to work and conform to white ways, recruiting better employees, enacting stronger safeguards for the system, and acquiring more money and land for Indian programs.[36]

These proposals illustrated the impulse to modify reservations in response to their failure in California. In many people's minds, however, reform was quickly succeeded by despair. By the early 1860s, after witnessing continued "fraud and mismanagement," "encroachments of white settlers on the reservations," the absence of "either civil or military protection" for natives, and general "neglect, starvation, and disease," J. Ross Browne gave up altogether on the ability of reservations to fulfill the goals originally outlined for them. In both official correspondence and published writings (Browne 1861:311–13) he broadcast his growing disillusionment and criticism. The only option he saw remaining for Indians was to place them under the exclusive protection of the military and remove them altogether from contact with whites, or they would "suffer speedy extinction."[37] Such comments perhaps foreshadowed post–Civil War developments in other parts of the American West where reservations became still less a vehicle for assimilation and more a place to keep defeated Indians apart from white society until they died (CIA 1865:158; Rawls 1984:157–61). Yet in California, the old, discredited reserves endured until they were supplemented by a new generation of smaller reserves and rancherias during the late nineteenth and early twentieth centuries (Rawls 1984:211–13).

INDIAN ALTERNATIVES TO RESERVATIONS

In implementing federal policy during the 1850s, agents rigidly formulated the choice before the Indian as one between certain death without the reserve and survival through assimilation within the reserve. The reservation hardly proved asylum enough, however. Most inmates simply left, not just to secure food to supplement their meager diets but also to find a different environment in which they might survive. Clearly, they sought some option besides "domestication or extermination." These natives tended to believe that outside the reservations they could more successfully develop their own strategies of coexistence, which many had been trying to pursue since initial contact with whites.

Indians' rejection of the white man's alternative to extinction derived from many sources. In the early 1850s, agents reported that natives neither trusted the white authorities with whom they dealt nor had confidence that reserves would protect or subsidize them, and the reservation experience certainly proved these doubts to be well founded. By collecting Indians together, the reserves also facilitated the spread of deadly diseases. But the Indians' primary objection seemed to be that the institution proposed to strip them of what remained of their culture and autonomy. Indians in the vicinity of the Mother Lode generally opposed relocation to the reservation, according to one observer, because they had heard that the reserve could provide no acorns for the traditional diet, no pine pitch for burial cere- monies, and no clothing whatsoever, and because they objected to leaving the land where "they have lived and their forefathers have lived and died & their ashes have been burried." Furthermore, the natives understood that the reservation system would combine and treat all Indians as one, and this threatened their diverse and decentralized social organization.[38] In short, reservations offered the Indians virtually no control over the terms on which they would enter the white man's world.

The alternative path taken by many California natives corresponded to the suggestion of John Bidwell, a distinguished pioneer settler who was as familiar with the state's Indians as any white man. Bidwell argued against reservations in 1851 by pointing out that settlers had already claimed most of the suitable land and that Indians had already begun to adapt to white society without reserves. Instead of a federal institution, Bidwell explained, natives needed stronger legal protection, some land "just where they live" for crops and pasture, opportunities to work nearby as they pleased, and the latitude to "cling around and shelter themselves under the protection of him who treats them best."[39]

The record of mistreatment of California Indians clearly did not justify Bidwell's optimism about the ability of Indians to find safety among set- tlers, and his proposals implied a high degree of Indian dependence on whites. (Bidwell himself made money as an Indian labor contractor [Hur- tado 1988:103, 193–94].) Nevertheless, faced with the failure of federal programs and the hostility of state government, many Indians saw in some variation of Bidwell's strategy a greater chance for both physical and cul- tural survival.

Agents in the Indian service reported during the 1850s that natives in many parts of California had begun to integrate themselves into the larger economy. These Indians tended to dwell in their traditional territories but now worked for white farmers, ranchers, and miners. In depicting one employer's paternalistic attitudes, a correspondent explained that there existed a "reciprocity" in such Indian-white relations that the government could never match. Indeed, as the failure of reservations became increas- ingly apparent, officials in the Indian service gradually accepted private arrangements between whites and natives as an expedient alternative.[40]

In 1860 A. B. Greenwood, commissioner of Indian affairs, instructed his superintending agents in northern and southern California to economize by placing as many Indians as possible under the supervision of private employers: "it is deemed advisable, so far as practicable, to make suitable arrangements with the farmers and tradesmen . . . by which to procure situations for those Indians who do not live upon the reserves, where they will be treated with kindness and humanity, and be comfortably supported, free of all expense to the government. You will also pursue the same course with the Indians living upon the reservations."

Only truly unemployable Indians were to be kept on reserves, and even they were to be made as cost-efficient as possible. Unless expenses were reduced, Greenwood concluded, the federal government must "abandon the system of managing the Indians of California, and leave them to the control of the State, or subject to the mercy or charity of the white citizens."[41] Of course, Greenwood's cost-cutting proposals in effect legitimized the very thing he said he wanted to avoid. California Indians had already been all but abandoned by the U.S. government. Now they were to be, even more expressly than before, the responsibility of private parties rather than the public sector.

Deemphasizing the reservation may have actually worked to the benefit of some native peoples. A few Indians looked upon the reserve as a source of occasional food and temporary protection, and thus incorporated it into their patterns of travel and subsistence.[42] But they preferred to remain free from it unless it occupied their traditional territory. By resisting the reserves, Indians demonstrated a preference for a less institutionalized relationship with white society.

Ironically, although reserves originally were intended to facilitate the integration of Indians into white society, some natives appeared to regard them as an obstacle to entering the settlers' economy. The complaints of one of the most discontented bands at Nome Lackee suggested that the reserve suffered by comparison with opportunities available in the outside world. These were natives from the Mother Lode country who, prior to their removal to Nome Lackee, had toiled at mining and farming for wages and supplemented their incomes with a greater array of traditional subsistence resources. In accounting for why they now kept running away from the reserve, one soldier explained, "On the Reservation . . . they are furnished with flour and clothes—nothing more. If they want anything besides bread to eat they must go out and hunt for it as they did years ago."[43] These Indians from the Mother Lode, like others who fled the reserves, evidently preferred their chances in the midst of white society to the arrangements offered at reservations. Paiutes and other natives removed to El Tejon after military defeat in the Owens Valley during the early 1860s similarly left the reservation and returned to their traditional territory, where they found positions in the white economy (Busby et al. 1980:54–57).

The experience of the Nomlaki, the native group for whom the Sacramento Valley reservation was named, also illustrates the precarious course open to some California Indians. Nome Lackee had been established within Nomlaki territory in 1854. With the abandonment of the reserve in 1863, the Nomlaki were "herded" westward over the mountains to the Round Valley Reservation and there forced to live adjacent to their traditional enemy, the Yuki. Conditions at the new establishment discouraged them from staying, and by the late 1860s many had drifted back to their traditional lands, which were now occupied by whites. In addition to restoring old subsistence patterns, the Nomlaki survived by working for whites— men herded and sheared sheep, harvested hay, and cut wood; women toiled as domestic servants. In some cases the natives adopted the surnames of the white families for whom they worked. Several ranchers and farmers permitted the Indians to dwell on their lands in rancherias and small villages where, by sustaining community life and maintaining such facilities as a burial ground and a dancehouse, they ensured the persistence of aspects of Nomlaki culture, a feat that reservations had attempted to prevent (Goldschmidt 1978:342; Findlay 1983:47–48, 51–52).

The opportunities available to the Nomlaki and some other native groups to persist on the fringes of white society were not available to all Indians in California. Neither were they without peril, for various kinds of dependency, mistreatment, and threats to Indians' survival continued. Most Indians in the frontier state, it should be remembered, simply died or were killed, and those who rejected reservations faced enormous risks.

Nonetheless, the apparent preference for one imperfect alternative over another demonstrates that many Indians regarded the reservation as a highly unpromising prospect during the 1850s. While white authorities retained their commitment to the institution, in part because they could offer nothing else, many Indians deduced that gold rush reservations provided little more than a temporary respite or a final resting place for them.

By the 1860s, surviving natives had to concede white domination of California, but in their struggles to keep themselves and their cultures alive they carved out social spheres that permitted them a degree of autonomy. Persisting in this world required Indians to use any strategies within their power to come to terms with the drastic changes brought by settlers to California. For most, this meant resisting reservations and eking out a day-to-day existence. At the same time, however, some considered a more distant future as well.

In 1861 one group of California Indians explained its understanding of both reserves and the hereafter to George M. Hanson, who in turn translated the natives' sentiments into Christian terms. The Indians, Hanson reported, "have looked upon the reservations, rather as a hell than a home." Their attitudes toward the institution gained clarity as they described a vision of a heaven where, in contrast to the poverty and hunger on reservations, "deer and fish abound." Perhaps anticipating the message of the Ghost Dance religion, the Indians further emphasized that the white man could not get to their "future spirit land."[44] For some, survival entailed looking ahead to an as yet unbuilt environment—the next world—to be designed and used on the Indians' own terms.

NOTES

1. Hurtado 1988 discusses federal policy and reservation realities while focusing mainly on Indian survival strategies. The book is especially valuable for identifying how several specific tribes, bands, or villages underwent distinctive experiences shaped by their respective cultures, size, extent of previous contact with nonnatives, and a host of other factors. My essay, by contrast, generally groups diverse natives together as "California Indians" for the purpose of analyzing the meanings of reservations. The extremely wide variety of Indian experiences, coupled with historical documents that do not always distinguish effectively between different native groups, makes it impossible to discuss more than a few specific Indian groups and their strategies in the given space.

2. W. P. Crenshaw to Thomas J. Henley, December 16, 1854, Letters Received by the Office of Indian Affairs from the California Superintendency, Reel 34 [hereinafter cited as Letters:34]. Conditions faced by Indians during the gold rush are detailed in Heizer 1974; Cook 1976a; Rawls 1984; and Hurtado 1988.

3. Edward F. Beale to Luke Lea, December 14, 1852, Letters:33.

4. Henley to John W. Denver, September 4, 1857, Letters:35.

5. J. Ross Browne to Denver, January 14, 1858, Letters:36.

6. Rawls (1984:153–55, 161–62) explains that in California urban attitudes were more favorable toward Indians than frontier attitudes.

7. George W. Barbour to Lea, July 28, 1851, and Barbour to Lea, n.d., Letters:32; Beale to Lea, December 14, 1852, Letters:33.

8. Quotations from Peter Campbell to Commissioner of Indian Affairs [hereinafter cited as CIA], June 1, 1851, Letters:32; George M. Hanson to William P. Dole, July 15, 1861, Letters:38. For other examples of white officials' estimate of the Indians as obedient, "tractable," and childlike, turn to O. M. Wozencraft, "To the People Living and Trading Among the INDIANS in the State of California"

(1851 broadside), Letters:32; Caughey 1952:35; Beale to George W. Manypenny, February 8, 1854, Letters:33; CIA 1861:249–50.

9. Beale to Lea, November 22, 1852, in USSI 1853:380.

10. Captain E. D. Keyes to Major E. D. Townsend, August 15, 1855, Letters:34; cf. Browne to James Guthrie, March 3, 1857, Letters:35. Additional expressions of belief in the "fixed" fate of extinction for California Indians can be found in Heizer and Almquist 1971:26; Heizer 1974:36, 1979:46–47.

11. Beale to Lea, December 14, 1852, Letters:33; Beale to Lea, October 29, 1852, Letters:32. On impermanence and the absence of treaties, consult Kelsey 1973:234–35; Dippie 1982:76; Rawls 1984:148, 150–51.

12. The problems presented by extensive white ownership of prospective reservation lands were noted early by Wozencraft to CIA, July 18, 1851, Letters:32; John Bidwell to James W. McCorkle, December 20, 1851, Letters:32; Beale to Manypenny, September 30, 1853, in CIA 1854:469–71. On the pressure to sell Nome Lackee to white settlers, see Petition from Tehama County citizens to Secretary of the Interior, 1859, in Heizer 1974:138–39; E. A. Stevenson to Milton S. Latham, August 12, 1861, Letters:38; Henley to Latham, January 10, 1862, Letters:38; Hanson to Dole, September 1, 1862, Letters:38. On the last days of the reserve at El Tejon, see John P. H. Wentworth to Dole, September 1, 1863, in CIA 1864:219–23; Wentworth to Dole, September 14, 1863, Letters:39; Austin Wiley to Charles E. Mix, June 1, 1864, Letters:39.

13. Beale to Manypenny, February 8, June 20, 1854, Letters:33; Beale to Lea, October 29, 1852, Letters:32.

14. Colonel E. A. Hitchcock to the Adjutant General, U.S. Army, November 29, 1852, Letters:33.

15. Beale to Lea, November 22, 1852, in USSI 1853:377–78; Beale to Manypenny, September 30, 1853, in CIA 1854:470–71; Giffen and Woodward 1942:61. Beale's reasoning is defended by Thompson (1983:57–58, 63–64, 66).

16. Henley to Manypenny, August 28, 1854, Letters:33.

17. On the problem of Indian slavery near Nome Lackee and Indians' consequent willingness to join a reservation, see Henry L. Ford to Henley, September 4, 1854, Letters:33; William McDaniel and William McQueen to Henley, October 4, 1854, Letters:33.

18. Henley to Manypenny, October 14, 1854, Letters:34; Keyes to Townsend, August 15, 1855, Letters:34; Henley to Manypenny, October 4, 1856, Letters:35.

19. Browne to A. B. Greenwood, October 18, 1859, Letters:37; John A. Dreibelbis to Greenwood, September 24, 1860, Letters:37; Hanson to Dole, July 15, 1861, Letters:38; Hanson to Dole, July 18, 1863, Letters:39.

20. Reports of crop failures, food shortages, and restricted diets pervaded dispatches from the Fresno farm, El Tejon, and Nome Lackee. See, for example, Browne, "Letter on the Condition of the Indian Reservations in California," in Browne to Guthrie, March 3, 1857, Letters:35; Henley to Manypenny, December 7, 8, 1854, Letters:34; Dreibelbis to Greenwood, November 22, 1860, Letters:37.

21. Henley to Manypenny, November 3, 1855, Letters:34 (quotation); Henley to Manypenny, August 8, 1856, Letters:35; Geiger to James Y. McDuffie, August 31, 1859, in CIA 1860:807 (quotation); Elijah White to Dole, March 8, 1862, Letters:38; Hanson to Dole, September 1, 1862, Letters:38.

22. Hanson to Dole, July 15, 1861, Letters:38.

23. Henley to Manypenny, August 29, 1854, Letters:33; Browne to Greenwood, November 4, 1859, Letters:37; McDuffie to Greenwood, September 4, 1859, Letters:37.

24. E. A. Stevenson to Henley, July 31, 1856, in CIA 1856:802 (quotation); Geiger to Henley, July 1858, in CIA 1859:641–42; Geiger to Henley, April 12, 1858, Letters:36; Crenshaw to Henley, December 16, 1854, Letters:34.

25. Hanson to Dole, July 15, 1861, Letters:38; Browne 1861:312–14; Henley to Latham, January 10, 1862, Letters:38.

26. John Bigler to Redick McKee, April 9, 1852, Letters:32.

27. Captain E. O. C. Ord to Major W. W. Mackall, August 9, 1856, in Heizer 1974:32.

28. Beale to Lea, September 16, 1852, Letters:32.

29. For instructions regarding public lands, see Manypenny to Beale, November 18, 1853, in CIA 1854:480–81. For criticisms of Beale and El Tejon, consult Henley to Manypenny, October 14, 1854, Letters:33; Henley and Browne to Manypenny, December 8, 1854, Letters:34; J. Lancaster Brent to Mix, April 7, 1858, Letters:36; Caughey 1952:140–42.

30. Henley to Manypenny, September 25, 1854, Letters:33; *Daily Morning Call* (San Francisco), February 19, 1858; Browne to CIA, April 19, May 4, 1858, Letters:36; Browne to Greenwood, September 19, 1859, Letters:35.

31. Henley to Manypenny, March 17, 1857, Letters:35; Henley to Denver, June 1, 1857, Letters:35.

32. Petition from Tehama County citizens to Secretary of the Interior, 1859, in Heizer 1974:138–39 (quotation); Browne to Greenwood, October 1, 18, 1859, Letters:37; McDuffie to Greenwood, October 19, 1859, Letters:37; Charles A. Kyle to Dreibelbis, December 29, 1860, Letters:38; clipping from *Sacramento Union,* January 30, 1861, Letters:38; Dreibelbis to CIA, March 30, 1861, Letters:38; Hanson to Dole, July, 15, 18, August 19, 1861, Letters:38.

33. Hanson to Dole, July 15, 1861, Letters:38; Hanson to Mix, July 23, 1861, Letters:38; Hanson to Abraham Lincoln, June 4, 1863, Letters:39.

34. Bailey to Mix, November 4, 1858, Letters:36; *Alta* clipping enclosed in Henley to Denver, December 18, 1858, Letters:37.

35. Browne to Manypenny, December 1, 1854, Letters:33; Browne to Guthrie, March 3, 1857, Letters:35 (quotation); Browne to Mix, September 18, 1858, Letters:36; Browne to Mix, September 29, 1858, in Heizer 1974:115 (quotation).

36. Browne's suggestions, which were echoed by other critics of reserves in California, were made in Browne to Guthrie, March 3, 1857, Letters:35; Browne to Denver, January 14, 1858, Letters:36; Browne to Mix, September 18, 1858,

Letters:36; Browne to Mix, October 8, 1858, reprinted in Heizer 1974:116–17; Browne to Jacob Thompson, October 16, 1858, Letters:36; Browne to Dole, December 27, 1863, Letters:39.

37. Browne to Dole, December 27, 1863, Letters:39.

38. Crenshaw to Henley, December 16, 1854, Letters:34 (quotation); Wozencraft to Lea, July 12, 1851, Letters:32; Dreibelbis to CIA, February 19, 1861, Letters:38.

39. Bidwell to McCorkle, December 20, 1851, Letters:32.

40. Quotation from Bailey to Mix, November 4, 1858, Letters:36. Recognition of Indians' integration into the white economy and white households was frequent. See Henley to Mix, November 19, 1858, Letters:36; John A. Sutter to Henley, December 1, 1856, Letters:35; Henley to Sutter, December 4, 1856, Letters:35; Henley to Manypenny, December 4, 1856, Letters:35; Henley to Manypenny, September 4, 1856, in CIA 1856:790–95; Browne to Greenwood, November 5, 1859, Letters:37; Browne 1861:306. Hurtado (1982) examines how Indians lived among whites.

41. Greenwood to Dreibelbis, July 30, 1860, in CIA 1861:455–56.

42. Browne to Greenwood, November 4, 1859, Letters:37; Hurtado 1988: 152–53.

43. Morgan to Mackall, September 1, 1857, in Heizer 1974:106–7. See also Browne to Mix, September 18, 1858, Letters:36. These natives fleeing from Nome Lackee may have been the same group that recalled its forcible relocation to the reserve as a "death march" (Currie 1957:314–18).

44. Hanson to Mix, July 23, 1861, Letters:38.

REFERENCES

BROWNE, J. ROSS. 1861. "The Coast Rangers. A Chronicle of Events in California. II. The Indian Reservations." *Harper's New Monthly Magazine* 23 (135):306–16.

BUSBY, COLIN I., JOHN M. FINDLAY, and JAMES C. BARD. 1980. *A Culture Resource Overview of the Bureau of Land Management Coleville, Bodie, Benton and Owens Valley Planning Units, California.* Bakersfield, Calif.: U.S. Bureau of Land Management.

CAUGHEY, JOHN WALTON, ed. 1952. *The Indians of Southern California in 1852: The B. D. Wilson Report and a Selection of Contemporary Comment.* San Marino, Calif.: Huntington Library.

CIA [U.S. Commissioner of Indian Affairs]. 1851. *Report of the Commissioner of Indian Affairs* [1850]. In Serial Set 587, 35–175. Washington, D.C.: Union Office.

———. 1854. *Report of the Commissioner of Indian Affairs* [1853]. In Serial Set 690, 243–481. Washington, D.C.: Beverley Tucker.

——. 1855. *Report of the Commissioner of Indian Affairs* [1854]. In Serial Set 746, 211–544. Washington, D.C.: Beverley Tucker.

——. 1856. *Report of the Commissioner of Indian Affairs* [1856]. In Serial Set 875, 554–832. Washington, D.C.: A. O. P. Nicholson.

——. 1859. *Report of the Commissioner of Indian Affairs* [1858]. In Serial Set 974, 353–669. Washington, D.C.: William A. Harris.

——. 1860. *Report of the Commissioner of Indian Affairs* [1859]. In Serial Set 1023, 373–819. Washington, D.C.: George W. Bowman.

——. 1861. *Report of the Commissioner of Indian Affairs* [1860]. In Serial Set 1078, 235–466. Washington, D.C.: George W. Bowman.

——. 1864. *Report of the Commissioner of Indian Affairs* [1863]. In Serial Set 1182, 129–634. Washington, D.C.: Government Printing Office.

——. 1865. *Report of the Commissioner of Indian Affairs* [1864]. In Serial Set 1220, 147–651. Washington, D.C.: Government Printing Office.

COOK, SHERBURNE F. 1976a. *The Conflict Between the California Indian and White Civilization.* Berkeley: University of California Press.

——. 1976b. *The Population of the California Indians 1769–1970.* Berkeley: University of California Press.

CURRIE, ANNE H. 1957. "Bidwell Rancheria." *California Historical Society Quarterly* 36(4):313–25.

DANZIGER, EDMUND JEFFERSON, JR. 1974. *Indians and Bureaucrats: Administering the Reservation Policy During the Civil War.* Urbana: University of Illinois Press.

DIPPIE, BRIAN. 1982. *The Vanishing American: White Attitudes and U.S. Indian Policy.* Middletown, Conn.: Wesleyan University Press.

ELLISON, WILLIAM H. 1922. "Federal Indian Policy in California, 1846–1860." *Mississippi Valley Historical Review* 9(1):37–67.

FINDLAY, JOHN M. 1983. "Historic Settlers and Native Americans." In "A Cultural Resources Overview and Inventory of the Proposed Thomes-Newville Reservoir, Glenn and Tehama Counties, California." Ed. Basin Research Associates, Inc., and Cultural Systems Research, Inc., 37–55. Report prepared for the California Department of Water Resources, Northern District, Red Bluff, California.

GIFFEN, HELEN S., and ARTHUR WOODWARD. 1942. *The Story of El Tejon.* Los Angeles: Dawson's Book Shop.

GOLDSCHMIDT, WALTER. 1978. "Nomlaki." In *California.* Ed. Robert F. Heizer, 341–49. Vol. 8 of *Handbook of North American Indians.* Washington, D.C.: Smithsonian Institution.

HEIZER, ROBERT F., ed. 1974. *The Destruction of California Indians.* Santa Barbara: Peregrine Press.

——. 1979. *Federal Concern About Conditions of California Indians 1853–1913: Eight Documents.* Socorro, N.M.: Ballena Press.

HEIZER, ROBERT F., and ALAN J. ALMQUIST. 1971. *The Other Californians;*

Prejudice and Discrimination Under Spain, Mexico, and the United States to 1920. Berkeley: University of California Press.

HURTADO, ALBERT L. 1982. "'Hardly a Farm House—A Kitchen Without Them': Indian-White Households on the California Borderland Frontier in 1860." *Western Historical Quarterly* 13(3):245–70.

———. 1988. *Indian Survival on the California Frontier.* New Haven: Yale University Press.

KELSEY, HARRY. 1973. "The California Indian Treaty Myth." *Southern California Quarterly* 55(3):225–38.

Letters Received by the Office of Indian Affairs, 1824–1881. California Superintendency, 1849–1880. Reels 32–39. U.S. National Archives, Microcopy 234.

LIMERICK, PATRICIA NELSON. 1987. *The Legacy of Conquest: The Unbroken Past of the American West.* New York: W. W. Norton.

PRUCHA, FRANCIS PAUL. 1984. *The Great Father: The United States Government and the American Indians.* 2 vols. Lincoln: University of Nebraska Press.

RAPOPORT, AMOS. 1977. *Human Aspects of Urban Form: Towards a Man-Environment Approach to Urban Form and Design.* Oxford: Pergamon Press.

———. 1982. *The Meaning of the Built Environment: A Nonverbal Communication Approach.* Beverly Hills, Calif.: Sage Publications.

RAWLS, JAMES J. 1984. *Indians of California: The Changing Image.* Norman: University of Oklahoma Press.

ROTHMAN, DAVID J. 1971. *The Discovery of the Asylum: Social Order and Disorder in the New Republic.* Boston: Little, Brown.

THOMPSON, GERALD. 1983. *Edward F. Beale and the American West.* Albuquerque: University of New Mexico Press.

TRENNERT, ROBERT A., JR. 1975. *Alternative to Extinction: Federal Indian Policy and the Beginnings of the Reservation System.* Philadelphia: Temple University Press.

USSI [U.S. Secretary of the Interior]. 1853. *Report of the Secretary of the Interior, Communicating, in Compliance with a Resolution of the Senate, a Copy of the Correspondence Between the Department of the Interior and the Indian Agents and Commissioners in California.* In Serial Set 688. Washington, D.C.: Robert Armstrong.

UTLEY, ROBERT M. 1984. *The Indian Frontier of the American West 1846–1890.* Albuquerque: University of New Mexico Press.

WALTERS, RONALD G. 1978. *American Reformers, 1815–1860.* New York: Hill and Wang.

Crow Leadership Amidst Reservation Oppression

FREDERICK E. HOXIE

I

Recently scholars have become aware of a truth long apparent, if only dimly acknowledged, within American Indian communities in the United States: a century ago Indian reservations were oppressive and unsuccessful instruments of imperial control. During the years between 1870 and 1930 the United States—which one modern Indian poet has called "this viper nation"—consolidated its control over aboriginal peoples in the West (Louis 1989:1). Initially this control took the form of direct federal governance of relatively small units in which agents, supported by regular army units, implemented policies formulated in Washington, D.C. Officials forced the indigenous populations under their authority to attend school, to stop practicing traditional religious rituals, to marry and divorce like white men, and to participate in a cash economy.[1]

At least for the Plains region, it is not an overstatement to call reservation life in this period oppressive. Nor is it an exaggeration to declare that allotment—which broke most Western reservations into individual land-holdings—did not end this authoritarian rule. Even after Native Americans had received individual titles to real estate previously occupied communally, federal agents continued to incarcerate Indians for infractions of reservation rules and to enforce their "civilization program" with military power. Schoolmasters continued to separate children from their parents. Religious organizations continued to operate with a level of federal support that clearly violated the First Amendment of the U.S. Constitution. Authorities continued to break up unauthorized religious activities and destroy sacred objects. Officials could even "withhold rations" from tribal members who opposed them.

Not even the allotment law's grant of citizenship to Indians taking up individual landholdings ended federal supervision over native communities. In 1910 the Supreme Court spoke for the entire bureaucracy when it declared that "Congress, in pursuance of the long-established policy of the Government, has the right to determine for itself when the guardianship which has been maintained over the Indian shall cease. It is for that body, and not for the courts, to determine when the true interests of the Indian require his release from such condition" (U.S. Supreme Court 1910).

In 1908 Z. Lewis Dalby, an attorney conducting an investigation of the Montana Crow reservation for the Bureau of Indian Affairs, focused the Court's broad proposition on an isolated locale. Speaking to Plenty Coups, one of the Crow tribe's most influential chiefs, Dalby warned, "Your position here as chief is not an official or necessary position. You have such influence as the Department of the Interior is willing that you should exercise. If the Department of the Interior finds that you are exercising that influence to the detriment of the Crow Indians, then your influence will be taken away from you" (Dalby 1908:412–13). The fact that Plenty Coups occupied a two-story frame house, operated a store, and farmed a productive allotment did not affect Dalby's attitude toward him.

In 1930 an outside observer traveling through the American West in a railroad car would have had to conclude that the oppression of the early reservation era had succeeded in destroying the political power of nineteenth-century tribes. Even though the aggregate North American Indian population was on the rise for the first time since 1492, native communities were mired in poverty and confined to the margins of state and national politics. Federal officials and state politicians ignored Indian leaders and ran roughshod over tribal interests because they were convinced that autonomous native communities were extinct.

But if that observer had left the train and settled into a reservation community, the Indian world of 1930 would have looked very different. From the perspective of local native communities, the reservation system had not achieved its objectives. While outsiders had succeeded in altering Indians' dress, economic life, and religious practices, the oppressive reservation regimes had not succeeded in "dissolving the bonds of tribalism" as so many nineteenth-century reformers had hoped they would. Most residents of areas whose majority traced their descent from aboriginal populations continued to think of themselves as members of a distinctive group. As distinct social entities, these ethnic enclaves continued to recognize their own leaders and to pursue a unique, community agenda. They thought of themselves as Indians first and Americans second.

The persistence of a Native American cultural identity, striking in the face of determined efforts to destroy traditional lifeways, raises several questions: How did Indian communities survive the hostile pressures of the early twentieth-century reservation environment with their sense of identity intact? What did that survival cost? And since tribal leaders continued to surface and defend their communities well into the twentieth century, what was the relationship between cultural persistence and community politics? For example, did political competition define cultural values? Or did the defense of the community's ethnic traditions call up particular political issues?

Answering these questions about Indian communities propels scholars into the wider arena of American history and social theory. Since the reservation era coincided with the emergence of race as a factor in American political competition—both in the ethnic politics that emerged in the wake of unprecedented levels of European and Asian immigration and in the racial politics of the post–Civil War South—the persistence of other groups might offer useful models for the Indian experience. Did Native Americans behave like other ethnic and racial groups during this same crucial time period?

Because the early twentieth century was a period when ethnic and cultural politics reached a new level of sophistication, we are also prompted to ask how Indian communities participated in or contributed to a new era of pluralistic ethnic competition. One scholar has declared that "minority races were politically impotent and socially invisible during much of the time when American pluralism was taking shape—and the shape it took was not determined by their presence or by their repression" (Walzer 1980:6). Is he right? Parallel processes of cultural adaptation and survival occurring in several parts of the nation at once seem to suggest otherwise. Perhaps there was an interplay of ethnic and racial experiences in the first third of the twentieth century that affected public life and contributed to a new, plural vision of society. Perhaps the presence of these "impotent" groups *did* make a difference.

Explaining changes in modern American Indian political life and exploring the reasons for native cultural persistence are therefore linked to larger themes of cultural and racial transformation in the United States. Understanding the story of individual Native American communities should help us to trace the emergence of viable contemporary Indian cultures as well as to grasp the complex outlines of the history of American pluralism. If one wishes to trace the story of Indian cultural survival through the reservation era, as well as to link that narrative to broader themes in American social history, it is vital to avoid models and explanations that are either parochial or misleading. Chief among these is the romantic notion that nativistic conservatism was solely responsible for community survival. According to this approach, the determination of a few conservative elders blunted, and then defeated, the efforts of various white "do-gooders" who wanted to alter the group's way of life. Historians frequently paint this portrait in biographical terms. A few good people—usually men—kept the old ways alive despite the efforts of mean-spirited agents, stiff-necked preachers, and community quislings who "sold out" to the white Americans and their cash. Holding off these evil "progressive" forces were nativist community leaders who often appear as Indian versions of the aging Kentucky colonel. Defeated but proud, they posed for photographs in their old uniforms, condemned the carpetbaggers, saved their equivalent of Confederate money, and waited for their West to rise again.

William T. Hagan's history of the Comanches in the reservation era asserts, for example, that Quanah Parker's "frustrations and triumphs" as a defender of his people were those "of the average Comanche writ large" (Hagan 1976:289). Similarly, Donald Berthrong maintained that the survival of the Southern Cheyennes during the same period "is a singular testament to their inner strength and a way of life based upon time-honored customs and spiritualism" (Berthrong 1976:49). Arrell Gibson wove these impressionistic and individualistic assertions into a portrait in his textbook *American Indian: Prehistory to the Present,* which claims that while many Indians were "desolated" by reservation life, they "refused to submit to the new order passively." This resistance took the form of a "near zealous commitment to old customs" (Gibson 1980:464).

Without denying the significance of Quanah's leadership or the power of Cheyenne values, none of these phenomena can explain the survival of Indian communities as social and political entities. There are at least three reasons why this is true.

First, the opposition of conservatives cannot account for the fact that native communities contained a variety of interest groups which took a variety of positions on public issues during the reservation era. Deep divisions existed among people on reservations, and contests among rival groups were a constant feature of native life. Nevertheless, community members continued to believe that they belonged to a single cultural entity. Tribal life encompassed more groups than simply "conservatives" and "progressives." In fact, there were always more than two sides to disputes, and no single group embodied the cause of resistance or tribal survival.

For example, in the Crow community of Pryor, Montana, Plenty Coups, the Crow chief whom Inspector Dalby threatened to fire, wrote to the commissioner of Indian affairs in 1927 urging him to ban the use of peyote on the reservation because it was corrupting the tribe's young people (Plenty Coups 1927). For the previous two decades Plenty Coups had been a frequent opponent of federal policy; now he supported it. In the peyote dispute, neither the Pryor chief nor his opponents had a monopoly on Crow values, and both groups had a history of resisting federal authority. Accounting for community survival by praising one group as the defenders of traditional values and condemning another as tradition's enemies flattens history and distorts the complexity of reservation life.

Second, survival through conservative opposition does not explain how people endured the period of reservation oppression while changing their community's cultural life to secure the tribe's existence. Many of those we might identify in the 1930s as "distinctly Indian" appeared dramatically different from their parents. For example, many "traditional" leaders of the twentieth century participated in Christian churches and sent their children to public schools. They were players in a cash economy; they cut their hair; some were even active in the local Republican party.

Painting a picture with only two colors—one for surrender and the other for unbending opposition—gives a severely constricted vision of social change within the reservation world and no vocabulary with which to describe Crow men like Bear Claw. A tribal elder, Bear Claw presided over the Crow Court of Indian Offenses during the 1920s. Despite the fact that he had been appointed to his post by the reservation superintendent, Bear Claw was a community leader whose authority and prestige were upheld by young people in the tribe. In presiding over the trials of young Crows who had been arrested by the agency police for offenses such as "immoral conduct," he was both an instrument of federal oppression and a descendant of the tribal elders who had disciplined the young in the old buffalo days (see Hoxie 1986:351–57).

Finally, focusing on conservative resistance to the "new order" of the reservation gives federal administrators too much credit. Although agents could call on massive firepower for support in moments of crisis, few such moments occurred—particularly after the carnage at Wounded Knee. While often earnest and hardworking, federal agents were frequently as inefficient, isolated, and broke as the Indians themselves. They could withhold rations and put people in the guardhouse, but they could not monitor daily behavior very effectively, nor could they prevent their charges from complaining to the press, mobilizing their allies back East, or—worse— ignoring them.

The district farmer for the Big Horn valley on the Crow reservation, for example, was charged with supervising Indian agriculture in his area and reporting weekly to Crow Agency regarding the progress of his charges. Disobedience could jeopardize future federal assistance. And yet the Big Horn district farmer reported in August 1925 that "quite a number of the Indians of this district are still up in the mountains. Some of them have been there for nearly a month now. And of those who are in the valley, a large percentage of them have been camping around the dipping vat nearly all week" (Records of Crow Agency 1925).

If the story of tribal survival is to be told accurately, and if scholars wish to discover the relationship between reservations and other racial and ethnic enclaves in early twentieth-century America, we must look beyond a few charismatic elders for an explanatory model. An alternative is a narrative framed in terms of the interaction between an ongoing native political structure and a shifting political and social environment. Through time, the native political structure—which traditionally incorporated ongoing rivalries, loyalties, and inefficiencies—was forcibly incorporated into an alien local and national order. Reservations were characterized by sharp geographic boundaries, limited economic resources, and intrusive, alien institutions such as Christian churches and government schools. Because this reservation setting was artificially constructed by outsiders and im- posed on native people, it directly prohibited some forms of political be- havior (such as selecting leaders on the basis of war honors) while allowing other activities (such as favoring kinsmen) to continue. In the process of incorporation, the new environment also modified many of the traditions that did survive (such as reaching community decisions through the use of councils; see Hall 1987:21–30).

By 1930 the interplay between the inherited political structure and the new reservation environment had altered tribal politics and modified indig- enous cultural traditions throughout the United States. This transforma- tion of prereservation lifeways into a modern Native American ethnic polity is the central fact of recent Indian history. Versions of this transformation can also be detected in the emerging ethnic and racial leadership of the 1930s in other parts of the country. Just as the incorporation of Indians during the reservation era coincided with social changes in the larger Amer-

ican society, so the political adjustments Indians made to their new environment could find parallels among non-Indian cultural and racial minorities
such as African Americans and Eastern European immigrants.

Obviously it is not enough simply to assert that an important process has
occurred. Moving from a generic to a convincing argument requires the
precise examination of a sample case. The Crow Indians of Montana constitute such a case, for their experience largely typifies the fate of tribal
communities assaulted by the oppressive forces of the reservation era.

II

Crow people first encountered Europeans at the close of the eighteenth
century, but they were not forced to make substantial land cessions to them
until 1868. Even after the Crows accepted American dominance they were
able to continue their equestrian existence. Hunting formed the basis of
tribal subsistence until 1884, when the buffalo became extinct and the federal government ordered the tribe to relocate from an agency in the foothills
of the Big Horn Mountains to a new outpost on the flatland of the Yellowstone Valley.

During the 1880s and 1890s the Crows confronted a series of crises.
They could not travel beyond the invisible boundaries of their reserve; they
could not resist the power of federal troops; they could not escape the
government-subsidized missionaries who now lived among them; their
children could not avoid the white man's schools. They seemed faced with
what white administrators proclaimed were the only two roads open to
Indian people in the twentieth century: civilization or death. And yet this
apparently powerless community of Indians avoided both options.

In the 1930s, when the Bureau of Indian Affairs offered the Crows the
chance to write a tribal constitution and organize themselves into a government that conformed to American law, they declined. By better than an
eight-to-one margin, the reservation population declared that it preferred
its own reservation-grown political system to government-approved tribal
status. The Crow story thus provokes in stark terms a question that is
frequently raised in generic form: How and in what way did native communities and indigenous political structures become incorporated into the
United States and still survive?

Four events mark an answer to that question and together trace the outlines of the process on other reservations across the West: the 1887 Sword
Bearer "uprising," the negotiation of the last major land cession agreement

in 1899, the Helen Grey affair of 1906–7, and the rise to prominence of the Crow tribe's general council form of government in the mid-1920s.

III

At five o'clock on the evening of September 30, 1887, as Crow Reservation Superintendent Henry Williamson and his wife sat on the front porch of their quarters near the banks of the Little Bighorn River, a group of sixteen young men, painted and dressed for battle, rode into view. Beginning at one end of the horseshoe-shaped agency compound, they began firing their pistols at the roofs of all the government buildings and into the air. When they reached the agency office, their leader, a twenty-two-year-old youth called Sword Bearer, thrust his gun in the belly of the superintendent's interpreter and then fired wildly into space. In a few minutes they were in front of the agent's home, and they shot at his chimney and roof before riding off into the twilight. Throughout the "attack" Agent Williamson sat frozen and slack-jawed, his unopened mail in his lap (Calloway 1986).

These few minutes of harmless gunfire represent the most direct challenge to federal authority in the history of the Crow reservation. The death of Sword Bearer and seven of his followers in a showdown with the U.S. Army on November 5, five weeks after the September 30 "raid," marked the end of that challenge. In the month that separated Sword Bearer's "raid" and his death, the government issued several pleas to Crow elders to arrest the young warriors and restore order on the reservation. The last of these requests took place on the morning of November 5 itself; the chiefs' failure to comply pushed the military to launch its final offensive.

The Crow leaders' inability to act—either in defense of Sword Bearer or in opposition to him—indicated their unwillingness to choose between a struggle for independence (and sure defeat) and surrender. Their acquiescence in his death at the hands of the soldiers marked the beginning of an era in which leaders were required to recognize publicly the final authority of the U.S. government. Following November 5, there would be no complete freedom from federal authority; the event marked the beginning of the incorporation of Crow political structures into the national order being imposed on them by the United States.

Scholars have generally understood Sword Bearer's flamboyant attack as the action of a frustrated warrior, the thwarted start of a religious revival movement, or the product of generational tensions between remote leaders and unhappy young people (Calloway 1986:50–51). While all of these explanations are plausible, the symbolic quality of the incident—a young man flaunting the authority of the government—suggests a more sophisticated political agenda. This agenda comes more sharply into focus when the political context of the event is considered.

Like other equestrian hunters on the Plains, the Crows were a fluid, band-level society. Their clans and societies inspired unity in times of stress, but typically they hunted and camped in bands that owed their allegiance to one of three major divisions: River Crows, Mountain Crows, and Kicked in the Bellies. Within the bands, authority was in the hands of elders and religious visionaries; their orders were enforced by soldier societies whose membership was drawn from the group's young men. While clan membership and tribal division were fixed at birth, membership in a soldier society and a band was voluntary and of variable length. Because of this fluidity, it is impossible to speak of a single tribal government or principal chief prior to the enforced confinement of the reservation era (Colson 1986:5–19).

The Crows signed their first formal agreement with the United States in 1825 when a Mountain Crow band leader named Long Hair came to the Hidatsa villages on the Missouri River to sign a treaty of friendship offered by an American general, Henry Atkinson. Significantly, however, a man named Red Plume or Long Hair signed the agreement while a River Crow band leader called Sore Belly (Eelapuash) refused to appear; still others were ignorant of the meeting.

Although the Crows signed their first treaty in 1825, it was not until 1851 that Crow leaders agreed to define the boundaries of their homeland and accept payments from the United States. In 1868 Crow leaders again agreed to a treaty. The later agreement set reservation boundaries dramatically smaller than those recognized in 1851 and provided for a resident government agent and the construction of schools.

Despite a record of friendly relations and a series of formal agreements with the United States, there was little intrusion of federal power into Crow life prior to the 1880s. The tribe had no resident agent until 1869, and their agency was largely inaccessible to outsiders until the late 1870s. Most significant, the principal Crow bands avoided even minimal contact with the U.S. government for most of each year. These groups traveled regularly beyond the boundaries set by their treaties, moving between winter camps near the headwaters of the Yellowstone (the location of the first Crow agency), hunting expeditions on the prairies of eastern Montana and central Wyoming, and gatherings for berry picking and hunting in the Big Horn Mountains.

Portions of the River Crow division of the tribe preferred the upper Missouri and rarely came to the agency. Others, primarily Mountain Crows, often spent the winter near the agency, but early government officials reported that they felt they were maintaining an outpost without Indians. Agent Henry Armstrong wrote in 1882, for example, that "these Indians have never been governed but allowed to do pretty much as they pleased" (Armstrong 1882).

During the early 1880s the federal presence became evident in the daily life of the tribe because game grew scarce (buffalo were virtually extinct by 1883), local white ranchers began complaining of Indian trespassing, and the Northern Pacific Railroad began lobbying for a right-of-way along the southern bank of the Yellowstone. At the same time, the Indian Office began to plan for the allotment of the reservation. A group of 107 "chiefs"— leaders of the Crow bands—signed a right-of-way agreement with the Northern Pacific in the summer of 1881. While the right-of-way provoked a great deal of debate, there was little protest once the negotiations had been completed. Differences began to arise immediately afterward, however, as the agent began to funnel federal dollars to leaders who agreed to farm and to pressure the entire group to relocate onto the allotted flatland east of Billings. It was these differences that underlay the Sword Bearer incident.

Between 1882 and 1887 three groups emerged within the Crow community. First was a group of men in their fifties and sixties who stood aloof from the agent's ambitious plans but favored cooperation with the United States. Many of them, such as Iron Bull and Thin Belly, were former army scouts who had cast their lot with the cavalry during the Sioux wars of the 1860s and 1870s. (Iron Bull, often referred to as "principal chief" by resident agents, participated in driving home the last spike in the Northern Pacific Railroad when it was completed in 1883.) Second was a group of younger men who were willing to accept the agent's orders in exchange for favors from the government. Among these eager young entrepreneurs were Plenty Coups, Pretty Eagle, and Medicine Crow, three leaders in their late thirties who spent a substantial amount of time at the agency and who voluntarily began to cut hay on the prairies and to take some preliminary steps toward farming. Third was a group of family and band leaders who resented the agent's plans and urged the younger men to oppose him. Agent Armstrong wrote at the end of 1882 that "there is a disposition shown by some of the young men to pull away from the older chiefs who have made themselves unpopular by working on the [agency] farm. These young men want to form new bands which they call prairie bands composed entirely of Indians who oppose all civilizing influences" (Armstrong 1882).

Several band leaders encouraged this tendency, among them Crazy Head, Deaf Bull, Spotted Horse, and Bear Wolf. For example, in 1883 Crazy Head left the reservation without permission and was pursued by a detachment of soldiers nearly to North Dakota before he agreed to return to the reservation. Early in 1885 Spotted Horse and Bear Wolf were confined to Fort Custer following an incident in which Agent Armstrong was threatened and assaulted.[2] Following their imprisonment, one of their supporters—Deaf Bull (described by the agent as a member of Pretty Eagle's band)—warned that his friends were determined to seek revenge if they were set free. Agent Armstrong urged that Spotted Horse and Bear Wolf be transferred to a prison in the East, predicting that "if these Indians should be released . . . their influence will be stronger than it has been; their party will undoubtedly grow and increase and may cause the government much trouble" (Armstrong 1885:3).

The opposition of men like Spotted Horse appeared to threaten the peace of Crow Agency in 1886 when Hunkpapa leader Sitting Bull and fifty of his disciples suddenly arrived on the Little Bighorn for a visit. While there, Sitting Bull asked for a meeting with Agent Williamson. "During the talk," Williamson later reported, "several of the Crow chiefs—who had never before uttered one word against the allotments, but had . . . acted and spoken in favor thereof—came forward and took the same stand that Sitting Bull said *he* had taken at *his agency.* Among the Crows speaking after this manner was 'Spotted Horse' who stated that this country was his, and he would put the Crows on places where *he* wished them to live."[3] Although overt opposition died down once Sitting Bull left the reservation, the determination of Spotted Horse, Crazy Head, and their shadowy "prairie bands" to operate beyond the agent's control was a regular source of political agitation during the winter of 1886–87.[4]

When Sword Bearer rode into Crow Agency the following year, one of his companions was Crazy Head's son, Knows His Coups, and his fiercest defenders within the tribe were the boy's father and Deaf Bull. Deaf Bull traveled with Sword Bearer to the Northern Cheyenne reservation in an attempt to rally support following the September 30 incident, and Crazy Head urged his son and the other young men to resist the soldiers. Deaf Bull and Crazy Head were imprisoned with the rebels following the army's victory on November 5, effectively removing them—and their "party"— from tribal politics (Ruger 1887a).

Significantly, the thirty-five-day interval between the September 30 shootings at the agency and the November 5 showdown with federal troops was marked by silence from Plenty Coups and others who had previously played the role of reservation middlemen. General Ruger repeatedly asked Crow leaders to turn Sword Bearer over to them, but no one would act. Five of the twenty-one men who participated in the September 30 incident were enrolled as members of Plenty Coups's band; two were with Medicine Crow. Rumors circulated that Pretty Eagle, and perhaps even Plenty Coups, might join the rebellion, but clearly the chiefs chose cautious neutrality instead. The result of this tactic is epitomized by a note General Ruger scribbled three days after Sword Bearer's death, preserved today with Plenty Coups's other personal papers: "This is to certify that Chief Plenty Coups is an intelligent Indian and worthy of trust and confidence" (Ruger 1887b).

IV

Twelve years after the Sword Bearer incident the Crow community was completely contained within the boundaries of the reservation. In 1899 Pretty Eagle, Plenty Coups, and other band leaders were settled into four districts on the reservation. In fact, over the previous decade they had formed a kind of presidium which met with the agent to discuss grazing leases and right-of-way agreements, gathered people together to ratify their decisions, and distributed agency patronage to their supporters. Speaking at a council with the government's agent in 1889, for example, Plenty Coups indicated that he expected to dispense jobs at the agency. He noted that he had urged his followers to send their children to school. "Then," he observed, "when they come back they can work in the issue room, can talk Indian and English." The same was true for the agency police force. "The police are now all discharged and I am going to make some more," the forty-year-old chief declared. "If you [the agent] say twenty, thirty, or forty policemen you want, I make them. I will pick out all brave good men; what I say is true" (U.S. Office of Indian Affairs 1889). Just as the reservation was now equated with the Crow homeland, so these tribal leaders now presented themselves as the community's political leaders.

The sale of 1.1 million acres of reservation land to the U.S. government in the summer of 1899 illustrated how this new political leadership operated. Pretty Eagle and Plenty Coups were the principal spokesmen for the Crows in the negotiations. They agreed to the sale even though it would likely displace the River Crows, who had recently resettled in the contested area, north of the new agency. Prior to their relocation, the River Crow bands had split their time between the Big Horn country and the headwaters of the Missouri, where they lived peacefully with the Assiniboin and other tribes on the Fort Peck reserve.

Significantly, both Plenty Coups and Pretty Eagle indicated in their formal speeches to the commissioners that younger people who had been away at school would also speak at the treaty session. Pretty Eagle concluded his opening address this way: "I have said all that I care to say at this time; my young men will read a paper to you that will tell the things that I have been thinking of." Immediately, Carl Leider, the thirty-year-old son of a Crow woman and a white man, rose and declared, "This is the first time in the history of the Crows we younger men have been allowed a voice in the Crow council." He then went on to list former promises that had not been kept and annuity payments that had not been made. As soon as he ended, Spotted Horse, whom Agent Armstrong had imprisoned in 1885, rose to declare, "We want a settlement of those back accounts; we must have those back monies paid to us before we will talk any more about that land" (U.S. Office of Indian Affairs 1899).

Unlike the divided and indecisive leaders of 1887, the Crow spokesmen of 1899 were a formidable political machine. The group's leaders had decided ahead of time who would speak, and no one other than the designated leaders—Pretty Eagle, Plenty Coups, Leider, and Spotted Horse—appear in the transcript of the session. The internal power of this machine becomes even more apparent when one examines who signed the final land sale agreement.

Even though 518 adult male Crows put their mark of approval on the accord, 162 men listed as heads of households in the 1900 census did not. Of this group of nonsigners, 119 selected allotments on the reservation in the first decade of the twentieth century. Seventy-two of these (about 60 percent) selected allotments in the areas closest to the 1899 land sale. It appears that the people who lived close to—or on—the area being sold either opposed the sale or stayed away from the negotiations. In other words, not only were Plenty Coups, Two Leggings, Medicine Crow, and the others speaking for a group the government now equated with "the tribe," but they seem to have been successful in orchestrating a coalition of followers to back them and override a determined band of local opponents. The 1899 sale also accommodated outside pressures, for the sale allowed land developers to carry out their plans to establish a town site at the confluence of the Little Bighorn and Bighorn rivers. Immediately after the former tribal lands were opened for white settlement, Hardin, Montana, struggled into existence on what had been part of the Crow reservation.

The 1899 negotiations indicate that Plenty Coups and the other recognized leaders had completed a transaction that satisfied the government's demand that they sell some of their lands but did not endanger their own settlements at the south end of the reserve.[5] The efficiency of the sale might also have contributed to the tribal divisions that became apparent a decade later.

V

The third crucial event in the political evolution of the Crow reservation community began when a white woman from the East arrived at Crow Agency in the fall of 1906. Helen Pierce Grey was a muckraker. She spent the winter of 1906–7 among the Crows, collecting complaints against Superintendent Samuel Reynolds and the tribal leadership. These included favoritism in agency hiring and dissatisfaction over a series of grazing leases with local white ranchers. Significantly, Grey's chief informants were disaffected younger men, many of them former students at government boarding schools.

By the spring of 1907, dissatisfied Crows had organized the Crow Indian Lodge, an organization with chapters in the Lodge Grass, Pryor, and Big Horn districts. The group was led primarily by men in their twenties and thirties, and while its complaints were aimed at Agent Reynolds, it didn't take much imagination to realize that they were fed up with the presidium arrangement that had been so evident since 1899. They criticized the agents, but Plenty Coups must have known who their next target would be.

In May 1907 the Indian Office dispatched Z. Lewis Dalby, a Washington attorney, to investigate Helen Grey's charges. Interestingly, when Dalby arrived, Agent Reynolds discovered that Plenty Coups was suddenly very difficult to reach. The cozy relationship between the agent and the chief seemed to have disappeared at the moment of truth. Reports began to circulate that the fifty-eight-year-old leader was meeting with the Crow Indian Lodge and abandoning his former alliance with Reynolds.

Superintendent Reynolds began to breathe more easily, however, after Dalby held a series of rancorous meetings with the Crow Indian Lodge and its sympathizers. The agent's enemies had little hard evidence, and it became plain that the inspector's report would exonerate the reservation administration. Sensing this shift in atmosphere, Plenty Coups—who earlier had met openly with the malcontents in the Crow Indian Lodge—now backed off. But he did not return to the agent's fold. Instead he charted an independent course; to have done otherwise would have severely undermined his credibility with the community.

In early 1908 the Indian Office offered Plenty Coups the perfect issue to rebuild his tribal support when Inspector James McLaughlin appeared at

Crow Agency to negotiate yet another large land sale. This would not be a repeat of 1899. Plenty Coups quickly rallied his followers and produced a solid wall of tribal opposition to the scheme. Even Big Medicine, the agency chief of police and Reynolds's most reliable supporter, declared, "We need our land to share and share alike in the making of allotments" (Hoxie 1984:82).

But Plenty Coups's reassertion of leadership did not return the community's political system to the presidium system of the 1890s. Tribal leaders must have been surprised by the depth of the discontent unleashed by Grey's visit, for in its aftermath they set out to construct a means for encompassing and managing dissent should it arise again. The principal means of accomplishing this was a tribal business committee, which was created in 1910 and on which many former members of the Crow Indian Lodge sat. One of its most energetic leaders was James Carpenter, a mixed-blood former schoolboy who had been born in 1881 and was one of Helen Grey's hosts when she first came to the reservation.

The consequences of this constitutional reform of tribal politics seems clear. Plenty Coups and others such as Bell Rock, Spotted Rabbit, and Medicine Crow had risen to leadership by serving as mediators between the power of the government and the independent desires of an older generation of band leaders and warriors. In this process they risked losing their influence by appearing to be corrupt instruments of the agent's policies, but they also managed to portray themselves as leaders of a community-wide entity, the Crow tribe.

The "scandal" of 1907 exposed the alliance of the middlemen with both the agent and local non-Indian ranchers, so they switched their allegiance back to their critics—who were now young people angry at being excluded from the patronage and economic benefits owed to the entire reservation community. Once Plenty Coups and the leaders had proven their loyalty to their reservation constituents, and after they realized that their protests would not unseat the agent, they were able to reassert themselves as tribal leaders. Opposition to additional land sales was the perfect issue on which to base this political comeback.

Plenty Coups's zig-zag course through the Helen Grey affair traced a reservation equivalent to political maneuvering in mainstream American society, in which leaders often used appeals to racial or ethnic loyalty to mobilize their constituencies. The chief's actions were reminiscent of the Republican party's bloody shirt of the 1870s, or the Southern Democrats' appeal to white supremacy amidst the populist revolt of the 1890s. His was an appeal to broad cultural loyalties which overrode the community's class and ideological divisions. His words echoed the positions of a previous generation's leaders, but his objective of consolidating political power was both pragmatic and immediate.

The differences between incidents in the Indian and non-Indian worlds were enormous, but the dynamic was the same: an embattled political leadership asserted a cultural theme (in this case tribal unity in defense of a common homeland) in the face of a threat to its authority in order to preserve its control for the future. The results too were similar: a hardening of political and cultural identity and a consolidation of local leadership (even if some power now had to be shared with the insurgents).

VI

Subsequent events proved that the creation of the tribal business committee in the aftermath of the Helen Grey affair marked something other than the Americanization of the Crows. It provided the community with an arena for focusing and articulating community-wide concerns. From the first tribal election in 1910, when the resident agent would not allow Jim Carpenter to take his seat because of his opposition to the government's policies, to its role in the succeeding decade as the chief opponent of further land sales, the business committee was a thorn in the government's side.

By 1920 the tribal business committee was operating as a forum for tribal complaints and as a vehicle for negotiating leases and other agreements with outsiders. It had also become an instrument for airing internal disputes and galvanizing community support for larger causes, such as hiring an attorney to file lawsuits before the U.S. Court of Claims or oppose continued attempts to acquire Crow land. Nevertheless, this arrangement could not prevent a final event in the development of a new political structure: the emergence in the middle 1920s of a general council form of government in which the entire tribe assembled to make and ratify important decisions.

The tribal business committee's success led to its replacement by a general council. The business committee defended the Crows' interests in Washington and curbed the autocratic tendencies of the resident agents. It also prevented the general opening of unallotted Crow lands to white settlement and publicized complaints against government officials and local farmers and ranchers. Business committee members even played a role in drafting the 1920 Crow Act, which divided the tribe's remaining unallotted lands among all Crows and provided for community control over subsurface resources. The result of these efforts was an economic boom for the tribe. In

1925, for example, the Bureau of Indian Affairs reported that the total income from all sources for tribal members was $694,804; $493,138— better than two-thirds—came from leases. This meant that the Crow tribe in 1925 enjoyed a per capita income of $390, slightly higher than the per capita income in Muncie, Indiana, at the same time (see U.S. Office of Indian Affairs 1925; Lynd and Lynd 1929:518). Even though a rising percentage of this lease income came from individual allotments rather than tribal lands, there was clearly a reason for individual Crows to see the business committee—the arena where lease agreements were negotiated and approved—as the source of their prosperity.

Not surprisingly, the business committee's work attracted a great deal of attention, and its meetings attracted an ever-increasing audience. As a result, one agent reported, "it has been difficult to prevent the [business] committee meetings from merging into a general council in which everybody takes part, and the actions of the voluntary council rather than of the business committee approved" (U.S. Office of Indian Affairs 1921:14–15).

During the latter 1920s, tribal income from leasing, land sales, and oil exploration dropped and per capita income declined, but rather than turn away from public gatherings, the Crows attended them with increased enthusiasm. The result of this process was the gradual replacement of the business committee with a general council. Leaders rose to prominence by promising court settlements or development schemes, and their supporters happily packed into the meeting rooms. Even as this process gained momentum, however, federal agents still watched for signs that the Crows would adopt an Anglo-American style of representative democracy. The superintendent who decried the trend of packing business committee meetings until they became general councils urged his superiors to be patient. "It is a new thing," he reported to Washington, "and we cannot expect them to grasp the full weight of their work at once" (U.S. Office of Indian Affairs 1921:15).

What had emerged by 1930 was a form of Crow politics adapted to the reservation environment. It operated within the fixed boundaries of the reservation and did not challenge the authority of the United States. The objective of tribal politics was the formation of politically active majorities within the Crow community and the successful promotion of those majorities as the decisive voice of "the Crow tribe." The agendas of the political interest groups reflected a mix of local concerns, personal rivalries, and cultural appeals.

Crow politics in the 1930s also reflected a new definition of tribal identity. In the nineteenth century, community leaders had sought complete independence from outside control. Individuals such as Crazy Head and Deaf Bull had hoped to keep their bands outside federal authority, while other leaders such as Plenty Coups and Medicine Crow cooperated with the government both to enhance their own standing and to minimize outside intrusion. Whatever their tactics, however, the "chiefs" of the 1880s wanted to maintain a community separate and apart from the non-Indian world. By 1930 it was clear that this older version of national identity was impossible to achieve. In its place tribal leaders sought to preserve a political structure that could operate with a minimum of outside interference. The "tribe" had come to be equated with a political structure that allowed freedom for local leaders while conforming to the requirements of life within the United States. In short, in 1930 the Crows equated their national existence with the political institutions they had developed during the era of reservation oppression.

In 1935 the Crows demonstrated their allegiance to their new national identity when they refused to accept the Indian Reorganization Act. Bureau of Indian Affairs Commissioner John Collier's scheme to "liberate" the tribes from the oppression of the past had no appeal for the Crows. In a special message circulated on the reservation, Collier, echoing the agent who preached patience with the tribe's inability to manage their business committee, predicted that tribes that rejected the democratic institutions provided for in the new law would "drift to the rear of the great advance open to the Indian race" (Collier n.d.: 16). Nevertheless, at a special election held on May 18, 1935, 86 percent of the ballots were cast in opposition to Collier's "new deal."

Writing to Collier a few weeks after the May vote, Crow Agency Super-intendent Robert Yellowtail—himself a tribal leader who had risen to prominence as an activist on the business committee in the 1910s—declared that while he was "most sorry that the Crows rejected the act," the commissioner would have to tolerate the fact that the tribe would not accept changes imposed on them from the outside: "I now feel, after having gone over the field at some expense and in asking the various tribes: 'why did you reject this bill when it offered you everything that you had lost, everything to gain and nothing to lose?' I invariably find that the old hostile feeling against the Indian Bureau, . . . is apparently the predominating motive." In the sixty years preceding their vote on the Indian Reorganization Act, the Crow people had retained an active political leadership and sustained a continuous set of political leaders. Traditional structures had been altered to accommodate the requirements of the reservation environment. When asked to abandon this new arrangement, the group felt compelled to refuse.

A brief review of one tribe's history indicates that its survival as a group and the transformation of its institutions were produced by more than a collective commitment to cultural conservatism. The Crow story reveals that like other racial and ethnic groups of the late nineteenth and early twentieth centuries, this Montana tribe used the political arena to confront a number of cultural issues. Before the reservation age, Indians were loyal to their band leaders and generally comfortable with a political system that rewarded traditional values such as bravery, military prowess, and religious power. To the extent that circumstances allowed, each community's leadership acted independently. To the extent that the various Crow bands acted as a unit—a tribe—they governed themselves.

Following the imposition of federal control, Crow self-government ended because the bands could no longer move or act freely. The community could not escape the power of the United States. Nevertheless, the Crows still desired leaders who could articulate common interests and mobilize a significant following. As the boundaries of the Crow lands shrank and were contested, these common interests were increasingly defined in terms of the reservation and its resources. The value of tribal leadership was demonstrated at the 1899 land sale no less than it was (for other ethnic Americans) at election time on Chicago's West Side. In the reservation era, therefore, tribal politics—like ethnic politics in general—became a struggle to control those forces which could mobilize a minority community and effectively communicate its preferences to outsiders.

The principal instruments of political power for reservation leaders like Plenty Coups were money, patronage, and influence with the Bureau of Indian Affairs. All of these commodities required an ability to deal with outsiders. Ironically, however, the most effective way to wield power outside the tribe was to mobilize the community itself by articulating and serving local concerns. Thus, as they engaged in contests for leadership and support in the reservation era, Native American politicians found themselves constantly shuttling back and forth between actions that stimulated community support (e.g., resistance to further land sales, opposition to the Indian Office) and those that fulfilled the government's expectations (e.g., agreeing to lease tribal lands). Successful leaders shrank from challenging federal power directly, but this did not mean that their actions or political agendas were defined by outsiders. Instead, the leaders' convoluted course through tribal councils, business committees, and agency offices produced an active political life in which community priorities and values became the stuff of tribal government. Maintaining the internal political life of the tribe became a way of maintaining the tribe itself.

The Crows' rejection of the Indian Reorganization Act was not an act of defiance so much as it was an act of loyalty. Divided by kin allegiance, reservation district, and interest group, the tribe was united in its conviction that its political leaders and institutions were a modern manifestation of their traditional values. The community's political leaders and political institutions played a leading role in shaping the group's identity long after most Americans thought they had been eradicated. Moreover, political activists could speak for "the Crow" and thus either defend or legitimize other reservation institutions such as churches, community organizations, and alliances of families. As was frequently the case for other embattled people in an oppressive age, the Crows found in politics a way of both transforming old structures and defending their particular cultural traditions. By extension, when one considers the immense scale of similar processes taking place among a wide array of ethnic groups across the United States, it is easy to see how the structural changes and cultural innovations taking place in eastern Montana contributed to the transformation of the entire nation.

NOTES

1. This essay is drawn from a larger work that benefited greatly from the advice and generous assistance of Timothy Bernardis, Joseph Medicine Crow, Barney Old Coyote, Mardell Hogan Plainfeather, Eloise Whitebear Pease, and Father Peter Powell. The view of Crow history presented here, however, is my own. The arguments contained herein have been sharpened and clarified in response to the excellent critical suggestions made by the University of Arizona Press's unnamed readers.

2. For the 1883 incident, see Arden Smith to Commissioner of Indian Affairs [hereinafter abbreviated CIA], February 13, 1883, Letters Received, Box 59, Letter 2545, Record Group 75, National Archives, Washington, D.C. [hereinafter abbreviated RG and NA]. For the arrest of Spotted Horse and Bear Wolf, see Armstrong to CIA, January 22, February 26, 1885, Item 3, Box 10, Records of the Crow Agency, Federal Records Center, Seattle.

Spotted Horse may also have had an old grudge against Plenty Coups for his involvement in the accidental death of his sister in the early 1870s. The woman picked up a pistol that Plenty Coups had laid near her fireplace; it went off and killed her. According to James Carpenter, Robert Lowie's principal Crow informant, Spotted Horse was prevented from exacting revenge against Plenty Coups because "he was his brother in law at the time." See Carpenter to Lowie, December

2, 1933, Incoming Correspondence, Robert H. Lowie Papers, University of California, Berkeley.

The arrest of Spotted Horse and Crazy Head may also have been connected with their refusal to sign a treaty agreement in January 1885. See H. J. Armstrong to CIA, January 13, 1885, Letters Received, Crow Agency, File 1249, RG 75, NA.

Interestingly, the army did not believe Spotted Horse and Crazy Head deserved incarceration. See Secretary of War to Secretary of the Interior, February 28, 1885, Letters Received, Crow Agency, File 4499, RG 75, NA.

3. Henry Williamson to CIA, September 27, 1886, Letters Received, Crow Agency, File 26353, RG 75, NA. See also the report of the resident allotting agents, J. G. Walker and James R. Howard, in their letter of the same date to the CIA. See Letters Received, Crow Agency, File 26352, RG 75, NA. Among other things, Walker and Howard reported that Sitting Bull

> has convinced the Crow chiefs that their influence with their people will be destroyed and lost in proportion as their people learn to look to their agent for guidance and control instead of to them. These chiefs were not astute enough to discover this fact until it was shown them by the wily Sioux. From his standpoint he is quite right, but from the civilized point of view, and in the true interest of the Indians, this is a result to be most desired, for it is certain that until this is accomplished, no material improvement of the Indians can be expected. The individual Indian must learn to look to the agent for guidance and control and not to their chief, who is naturally a thorough conservative and opposed to innovation.

4. During October 1887, when Sword Bearer was at large in the hills near Crow Agency, a band of ten Sioux warriors was intercepted en route to the Little Bighorn. The arrest set off fears of an intertribal outbreak. See Henry Williamson to CIA, October 12, 1887, Letters Received, Crow Agency, File 27077, RG 75, NA.

5. My compilations are based on the manuscript census returns for the 1900 federal census, the land sale agreement itself (filed as folder 45587-1899, Letters Received, Crow Agency, RG 75, NA), and the "List of Crow Allotments," Item 53, Box 199, Records of the Crow Agency, Federal Records Center, Seattle. The districts from which nonsigners came were Pryor (22), Black Lodge (36), Big Horn (22), Crow Agency (14), and Lodge Grass (25). The 1900 census lists 582 male heads of household; 420 appear on the 1899 document.

REFERENCES

ARMSTRONG, HENRY. 1882. Letter to Commissioner of Indian Affairs, December 6, 1882. Item 3, Box 9, Records of Crow Agency, Federal Records Center, Seattle.
——. 1885. Letter to Commissioner of Indian Affairs, February 26, 1885. Item 3, Box 10, Records of Crow Agency, Federal Records Center, Seattle.

BERTHRONG, DONALD J. 1976. "Legacies of the Dawes Act: Bureaucrats and Land Thieves at the Cheyenne-Arapaho Agencies of Oklahoma." In *The Plains Indians in the Twentieth Century.* Ed. Peter Iverson. Norman: University of Oklahoma Press, 1985.

CALLOWAY, COLIN G. 1986. "Sword Bearer and the 'Crow Outbreak' of 1887." *Montana, The Magazine of Western History* (Autumn 1986):38–51.

COLLIER, JOHN. N.d. "Facts About the New Indian Reorganization Act." Item 16, Box 119, Records of Crow Agency, Federal Records Center, Seattle.

COLSON, ELIZABETH. 1986. "Political Organization in Tribal Societies: A Cross Cultural Comparison." *American Indian Quarterly* 10(1):5–19.

DALBY, Z. LOUIS. 1908. *Hearings Before the Committee on Indian Affairs.* U.S. Senate, on S.2087 and S.2693, Senate Document 445, 60th Congr., 1st sess.

GIBSON, ARRELL MORGAN. 1980. *The American Indian: Prehistory to the Present.* Lexington, Mass.: D. C. Heath.

HAGAN, WILLIAM T. 1976. *U.S.-Comanche Relations: The Reservation Years.* New Haven: Yale University Press.

HALL, THOMAS D. 1987. "Native Americans and Incorporation: Patterns and Problems." *American Indian Culture and Research Journal* 11(2):1–30.

HOXIE, FREDERICK E. 1984. "Building a Future on the Past: Crow Indian Leadership in an Era of Division and Reunion." In *Indian Leadership.* Ed. Walter L. Williams, 76–84. Manhattan, Kans.: Sunflower University Press.

———. 1986. "Towards a 'New' North American Legal History." *American Journal of Legal History* 30.

LOUIS, ADRIAN C. 1989. *Fire Water World.* Albuquerque: West End Press.

LYND, ROBERT, and HELEN LYND. 1929. *Middletown: A Study of the Modern in American Culture.* Reprint. New York: Harcourt, Brace, and World, 1956.

PLENTY COUPS. 1927. Letter to Commissioner of Indian Affairs, February 11, 1927. Item 15, File 122-2, Box 79, Crow Agency Records, Federal Records Center, Seattle.

RECORDS OF CROW AGENCY. 1925. Farmer's Weekly Report, Big Horn District, August 3–8. Item 15, File 139, Box 87, Federal Records Center, Seattle, Washington.

RUGER, THOMAS H. 1887a. Letter to Assistant Adjutant General, November 30, 1887. Letters Received, Record Group 75, File 33393, 1887, National Archives, Washington, D.C.

———. 1887b. Letter, "To Whom It May Concern," November 8, 1887. Plenty Coups Papers, Montana Historical Society, Helena, Montana.

U.S. OFFICE OF INDIAN AFFAIRS. 1889. Proceedings of a Council, June 30, 1889. Special Case 133, Crow, Folder 21265, Record Group 75, National Archives, Washington, D.C.

———. 1899. Council Proceedings filed with Letter 45587-1899. Letters Received, Crow Agency, Record Group 75, National Archives, Washington, D.C.

——. 1921. Superintendent's Annual Narrative and Statistical Report, Crow Agency.

——. 1925. Superintendent's Annual Narrative and Statistical Report, Crow Agency.

U.S. SUPREME COURT. 1910. *Supreme Court Reporter* 221:315.

WALZER, MICHAEL. 1980. "Pluralism in Political Perspective." In *The Harvard Encyclopedia of American Ethnic Groups.* Cambridge: Harvard University Press, 1980. Reprinted in *The Politics of Ethnicity.* Cambridge: Belknap Press, 1982.

YELLOWTAIL, ROBERT. 1935. Letter to John Collier, June 13, 1935. Item 16, Box 148, "Education, 1935," Records of Crow Agency, Federal Records Center, Seattle.

PART II

THE NONRESERVATION EXPERIENCE

Utah Indians and the Homestead Laws

MARTHA C. KNACK

Reservations, as landed property, inevitably involve issues of land title and legal status.[1] Native Americans' rights to land have never been accorded the legal status of full title by the U.S. government; rather, they have been in a different conceptual category, called variously "Indian title" or "right of occupancy." Policymakers long assumed that natives' cultural perceptions of landownership and methods transferring land use rights were so different from Euro-American ones that, in order to protect their title from white men ever ready to exploit such unfamiliarity and lack of access to the legal system, Indians had to be paternalistically protected. This was reflected in the ideas of federal trust over Indian land and Indians as wards under federal tutelage, a condition presumably meant to continue until natives gained sufficient knowledge of American culture to effectively defend their own land title (U.S. Supreme Court 1831:16; Trennert 1975; Cohen 1982:50–58).

Such reservation policy, however, like all policy, was simply potential. It was actually applied in response to local economic circumstances and local political pressures, often after modification to accommodate those interests. While appearing to be uniform nationally, it was highly variable in practice. Not only must the creation of a general policy be explained historically, but then it must also be determined why that policy was activated in a particular place at a particular point in time and ignored at other times and places where it was apparently equally applicable. Thus, causes for the establishment of specific reservations may not be the same in all instances, nor need there be simple explanations; rather, one would expect them to be both multiple and variable since the situations in which their creation was rooted were neither simple nor uniform.

Most legal textbooks explain general reservation policy as an alternative to removal after Spanish colonial areas in the Southwest were acquired and the discovery of gold in California brought hordes of settlers who surrounded native tribes. If further westward American expansion was to proceed, natives would have to be restricted to small territorial "islands" of native occupancy; these enclaves were areas "reserved" from transfer to federal title when larger portions of the tribal territory were yielded by treaty (Getches et al. 1979:30–32, 143–52; Cohen 1982:471–507). Thus the treaty-generated reservation became archetypal, and other methods of reservation formation, such as executive order, act of Congress, administrative declaration, or lands assigned from beyond aboriginal territorial boundaries, were seen as variants on this model.

Although reservations were the standard method of Indian landholding by the mid-nineteenth century, a number of other legal options also existed (Sutton 1975). These were frequently used in the Great Basin, where native populations had always been thinly scattered and had stubbornly refused to leave local homelands for central reservations (Crum 1987). Their traditional hunting and gathering economies could not support prolonged military activity, and without military conquest there was no justification for treaties of submission or forceful collection of these bands in the name of public safety. The Bureau of Indian Affairs (BIA) viewed small reservations for each tiny band as impractical because of the expense of maintaining agency staff and buildings to oversee the few Indians at each site (Powell and Ingalls 1873:115–16). Therefore the bureau explored a variety of lesser-known nonreservation alternatives in this area during the late nineteenth and early twentieth centuries.

This essay compares the history of two small areas of Indian land in Utah. One of these, Kanosh, was held under mixed allotment and reservation status, and the other, Washakie, was held under a variety of homestead titles. These experiments with nonstandard reservation options may illuminate what we know about the more routine forms and help answer the questions Why then? Why there? and Why in that form? By reviewing such cases, in which federal supervision was at best slight and transient, we may also gain some insight into the federal role in Indian affairs by considering its inverse—absence.

Classic reservation title plays only a minor role in the cases I discuss here. Reservation land is held under federal trust in the name of the tribal group as a whole for a time period of unspecified duration. In contrast, these nonreservation land titles, while held in federal trust, were held so for only a short time and in the name of a specific individual, not the tribal group as a whole.

The most familiar alternative landholding method is the allotment. Resulting from the 1887 Dawes Act (24 Stat. 388) and its amendments, allotments were generally subdivisions of existing, jointly held reservation lands into small parcels which were then patented to individual Indians. Title remained under federal trust for twenty-five years, purportedly to allow Indians time to become familiar with American legal forms and methods and thus to be able to defend their title successfully after it was awarded to them in fee simple. During this time Indians could not sell the land, nor could states assess property taxes. The Dawes Act provided for extension of the trust period, which was done repeatedly, and trust status was not generally removed before the 1934 Wheeler-Howard Act rescinded allotment policy.

Section 4 of the Dawes Act provided that Indians without a reservation to divide could file for allotments of unoccupied public lands under the same trust arrangement. The U.S. Treasury paid the normal filing fees, so the entire transaction was free to the Indian allottee.

Another route to recognized land title for Indians was through the homesteading process. Although Native Americans were specifically barred from acquiring land under the original 1862 Homestead Act, in 1875 Congress passed a special bill for Indians. Any family head over the age of twenty-one who was willing to prove that he had "abandoned, or may hereafter abandon, his tribal relations" (18 Stat. 402, at 420) was eligible for a full-sized homestead of his own choosing from unclaimed public lands. Unlike the Dawes Act, no fee waiver was provided for, and unlike non-Indian homesteaders, after the Indian had met the residence and land improvement requirements, title to his land continued to be held under federal trust for five years, shielded from alienation and taxes.

Later, an 1884 rider to the BIA appropriations bill provided yet another homesteading alternative. Indians were allowed to locate on public lands and "avail themselves of the provisions of the homestead laws as fully and to the same extent as may now be done by citizens of the United States" after making the "necessary proofs" (23 Stat. 76, at 96). The federal government then held title to the land in trust for twenty-five years "for the sole use and benefit of the Indian by whom such entry shall have been made," or for his heirs. Thus the Indian was barred from selling or leasing this land, and the state was denied jurisdiction to tax it. Filing fees were explicitly waived.

At least theoretically, by 1887 Indians not living on reservations had no

Table 1. Legislation that allowed Indians to obtain title to land.

Year of Law	Initial Trust Period (in years)	Indians to Pay Fees
1875 Indian Homestead Act	5	Yes
1881 Winnebago Act	20	Yes
1884 Homestead Act, amended	25	No
1887 Allotment from public domain	25	No

fewer than two homestead options, plus allotment from the public domain, open to them as mechanisms to attain legally recognized land title (see table 1). Obviously, all of these resulted in individual title, not communal or tribal title, and all limited the amount of land that could be so claimed. None implied any recognition of tribal sovereignty or political rights. All required explicit renunciation of membership in the tribal social community and participation in the native cultural heritage before full title would be vested. Thus, although fees were waived in two of the three methods, the costs to Indians were still high.

WASHAKIE

Indian history in western Utah was driven less by incidents of military conquest than by those of agrarian settlement and religious history. For its first several decades Utah Territory remained under the control of the Church of Jesus Christ of Latter-day Saints (Mormons), which had settled the area in 1847. That church early established an active missionary program, arguing the importance of Indian conversion to the coming of the millennium (Book of Mormon, II Nephi 30:5–6; B. Young and Kimball 1856:204), as well as a more pragmatic goal of reducing raids on its own small agricultural villages. After the defeat of the Northwestern Shoshones at Bear River in 1863 (Madsen 1985), Mormons sent such a mission to encourage a remnant native group to attempt an agricultural settlement very near the northern Utah border. Citizens in nearby Corinne, the only significant non-Mormon town in the territory, objected violently to the proximity of the Indian colony (Madsen 1980a; Hill n.d.). When irrigation systems also proved more difficult than anticipated, the mission was relocated in 1877 to a site twenty miles farther north, which was named after the well-known, but never resident, Shoshone leader Washakie. Farming proved successful, and members of other scattered bands from southern

Idaho and Wyoming joined the group, which rose in population to 100 by 1880 and 144 by 1910 (U.S. Census 1880, 1910).

The Mormon missionaries, believing that the success of the project depended on secure land control, persuaded the Indians to file for land under the available homestead law options. They escorted groups to the federal land office in Salt Lake City, first in 1876 and then sporadically as the settlement grew over the next two decades. When the required public notification of these filings began to appear in the newspapers, citizens petitioned the commissioner of Indian affairs to get the Indians onto a reservation "where they belonged." The nearest BIA representative was sent two hundred miles from Uintah to investigate. He was pleased to find some Shoshone men in Euro-American dress farming in a businesslike way, in exact accord with BIA acculturation policy goals, but was less delighted with others out hunting in the mountains. In an era when many Indian agents were themselves missionaries of various sects, he was not overly concerned by the Mormons' plans to instruct the Indians. "I can see no reasonable objection to their doing so," he wrote, "and thus relieving the Gov't of their care and support." He recommended that the Indians be "encouraged in their efforts towards self-support," perhaps be given a few agricultural implements, but in general be left alone; that is exactly what the BIA did (Critchlow 1878).

So the mission proceeded undisturbed. The missionary retained actual title papers to the Washakie lands, ostensibly for safekeeping. Indian laborers drove an irrigation ditch over twenty miles from the Malad River to their property. With the proclaimed goal of creating a self-sufficient agricultural community, the church provided instruction, tools, and teams of plow oxen. Until 1890, farming and cattle herding were operated under what Mormons of the time called the United Order. In this socialist experiment, land title, farm equipment, and work stock were owned by the community as a whole, labor was performed cooperatively, harvests were pooled, and each household drew from the common store as needed. A passing federal observer praised this communal method as being compatible with Indian ethics, noting that the Shoshones "worked better for the tribe than they would for themselves individually" (Wright 1901:6–7).

Farming without irrigation was marginal in this dry northern climate. The irrigable land in the area was strictly limited and almost all claimed— much by the church itself. As the population grew on this inelastic land base, the missionaries began to subdivide the properties informally. "Gradually as these original entrymen died it was the policy to put other Indians to work upon the land, giving some of them 20 acres, and sometimes 60 acres. It was immaterial that these men were or were not the heirs of the original entrymen" (Elliot 1914:6–7).

By 1890 the United Order had proven a failure throughout Utah and the church had ordered all farming to be individualized, including that at Washakie. Some Indian families could not use their individual plots because of age or absence, so the missionaries, still the only significant Euro-American presence, undertook to lease that acreage and oversaw the collection and distribution of rents. In this area where successful farms were often hundreds of acres and successful ranches several thousand (J. Young and Sparks 1985), the small Indian farms could not provide adequate subsistence through either production or lease. Both Shoshone men and women supplemented their subsistence by continuing to hunt and gather and by engaging in migratory harvest wage labor (Hall 1916a, 1916b; Conner 1920; Sells 1921).

The BIA did not attempt to supervise Utah Indians other than the Utes on the large Uintah-Ouray reservation before 1911, when it opened a Salt Lake City office charged with overseeing the numerous small bands of Shoshones and Paiutes throughout the entire western half of the state. The new agent praised the Washakie Shoshones for achieving the government's policy goal of self-sufficient farming without federal assistance (Holderby 1916:393–94). Nevertheless, once it became aware of the community, the BIA tried to establish federal authority over Indian affairs at Washakie— increasingly to the exclusion of the missionaries, although for tactical reasons attempting to avoid a direct challenge to them. One of the first areas of contention became land title.

The local custom of informal land redistribution and intestate inheritance had led to serious problems. A number of Shoshones dissatisfied with the missionaries' handling of their affairs petitioned for BIA intervention (Estep 1913; Brown 1914). In 1914 a BIA probate examiner found that a number of families, although they had access to land for use, held no title in their own names because they had either failed to complete the required homestead proofs, arrived after all the land was claimed, or had their lands informally redistributed to others by the missionaries. The examiner questioned the ability of the federal government to interfere: "[O]n some of them [the Washakie homesteads] the Department [of the Interior] had lost its jurisdiction, owing to the fact that the 25 years [trust period] had expired. . . . and if the Department does not take immediate action, and assert its jurisdiction over these estates, it will only be a matter of six months to two years when it will lose jurisdiction of these remaining nine estates" (Elliot 1914:3–4).

Although probate hearings straightened out the immediate problems, the BIA did not get the General Land Office to do a general search on the Washakie title records until 1916. It then discovered that Washakie Shoshones had forty homesteads incorporating 6,400 acres of land. Fifteen initial filings had been made between 1875 and 1879, sixteen between 1880 and 1885, and the remaining nine between 1885 and 1895. Of these, twenty had been filed under the law of 1875, authorizing a five-year trust period, and eight under the law of 1884, which allowed a twenty-five-year trust; the remainder were filed under the Dawes Act. When the filings were "proved up" and final papers granted, the majority (thirty) were *actually issued* under yet another law, passed in 1881 and applicable only to the Winnebago Indians of Wisconsin, which carried a twenty-year trust period. Six more titles appeared under the law of 1884, with its twenty-five-year trust, and four were regular homestead patents that carried no federal trust protections at all.

The question then became which, if any, of these homesteads were still under federal trust restrictions from sale and state tax. Misapplication of the Winnebago law was apparently a nationwide problem, and the BIA pushed a test case through the courts. The Supreme Court decided that "the act under which a patent should issue governs, and not the instrument itself" (Hauke 1917:2, citing 241 U.S. 379). Issuance of a homestead to non-Winnebago Indians under the 1881 law would be considered an error, and rather than being automatically canceled, the homestead would be treated as coming under the 1884 law. Therefore the thirty Washakie titles mis-issued under the 1881 law were nevertheless recognized and awarded a twenty-five-year, rather than a twenty-year, trust period, calculated from the date of issue. This extra five years was just enough time to bring a few of the Washakie homesteads within federal trust protection, in several cases by a matter of a bare few weeks.

The issue involved in other Washakie titles was not the law under which they were filed but whether the nominal filing fees had been charged to the applicant. An opinion issued by the Department of the Interior's solicitor (D-40726) held that if an Indian had initiated homestead filings under the law of 1875 but had not completed proofs until after the more lenient 1884 law was in place, and if the patent was issued without payment of fees as provided for *only* under the latter law, then it should be assumed that the filing was in fact under the act of 1884; a twenty-five-year trust period would then apply (Hauke 1917:2). Thirty-five Washakie Shoshones had paid the initial $16 filing fee, but only nineteen of them had paid the additional $6 when final proofs were registered. The BIA argued that regardless of the law actually cited on the patent, the sixteen whose final fees had been waived were entitled to twenty-five years of federal trust protection under the 1884 law.

To further complicate the matter, an executive order issued on February 23, 1916, extended for one year the trust status of any Indian lands then under federal supervision. Subsequent annual extensions were made until 1923, when Congress (25 Stat. 1246) granted a further twenty-five-year period, thus retaining trust status over Indian homesteads and allotments until passage of the Wheeler-Howard Act in 1934. A few days or weeks in the exact date of filing determined whether some Washakie titles were brought under this chain of provisions.

By such tortuous calculations, in 1917 the United States claimed jurisdiction over thirteen of the original forty Washakie homesteads, encompassing 1,920 acres, or 30 percent of the original filings (Meritt 1917).

A number of efforts were made to exert this newly found federal jurisdiction against the authority of the Mormon church and the state of Utah. The BIA recruited the Department of Justice to bar Utah from settling the estates of deceased Washakie Shoshones under state probate laws. The BIA was totally unsuccessful in trying to wrest the actual homestead documents from the hands of the resident Mormon missionary, who saw their possession as his church's historical charge. Only after a federal lawsuit was threatened against both himself and the church, and his ecclesiastical superiors had ordered him to do so, did he deliver the papers to the federal district court (Evans 1918).

Meanwhile, land speculators were circling Washakie. When the trust period expired on a number of the holdings in 1919, five of the Indian homesteads containing over eight hundred acres were sold to non-Indians—two to the Mormon church itself. Another property was bought by a member of the Indian community, three had uncertain status, one was up for sale by the heir, and only three were being worked by titleholders. While federal officers were convinced that Shoshones received a quarter or less of the true value of their properties, they felt they could no longer legally interfere with Indians' choice to sell (Frank 1917; Evans 1918). The BIA did order its local agent to obtain notarized title abstracts and affidavits on all these transfers, with the view of possibly filing suit for fraud (Dortch 1920). At the same time, the state began assessing the land, raising the specter of tax sales (Conner 1919).

Land was lost even on plots still under federal trust. In 1905, for instance, the Oregon Shortline Railroad obtained a 100-foot-wide right-of-way across nine of the Washakie homesteads, for which it paid $40 per acre (Porter 1935). Western farmers generally favored the arrival of rail transportation for their products and recognized the increased property values that would result. Many Mormons in the Malad Valley donated their lands to the construction. A generation later, when the BIA began investigating these transfers, a number of Indians could not remember whether they had received any cash compensation (Donner 1925). The BIA eventually approved five of the railroad deeds but denied the two that crossed the lands bought by the Mormon church because those deeds did not list the right-of-way as a title encumbrance. Two more railroad deeds were challenged because, in the informal community realignment of land usage, they had been signed by persons other than the legal landowner and furthermore were still under federal trust (Burke 1928a).

Thus the BIA was reduced to a rearguard action, grasping at the trivia of title legalities to attempt to assert federal trust jurisdiction over the remaining scraps of Indian land at Washakie, in the firm conviction that Indian control would be lost if it should fail to do so.

As more of the original homesteaders died, estates remained in federal probate for periods of up to ten years, casting a cloud over use or lease by heirs (Burke 1928b). As Indian landholdings otherwise decreased, competition for these inheritances rose and internal dissension in the community escalated. The increasing population in the region and the arrival of the railroad had increased property values, so the pressure to sell increased. Loose and ineffective federal control led to large numbers of dubious transfers. Disputing Indian families repeatedly called on the BIA to step in (e.g., Pabawena 1927; Haas 1928).

Finally, in 1935, the Department of Justice filed suit against the Mormon church, the Oregon Shortline Railroad, Box Elder County, four banks, an irrigation company, a telegraph company in Wyoming, and over forty individuals, in order to determine title in the homesteads over which it still claimed jurisdiction. The government claimed that these parties had obtained Washakie homestead lands illegally. Declaring that at least thirteen homesteads had remained continuously in trust, the BIA claimed that the individual Indians had had no right to sell nor the county to levy taxes and foreclose for nonpayment. To reach its findings, as it would with any land title case, the lower court relied on the exact filing dates and laws under which the patents were issued. It viewed the BIA's logic regarding filings between 1881 and 1884 as pure chicanery; it refused to believe that the

administrative "error" of entering titles under the Winnebago law legitimized the application of another law which had not yet even been passed.
The court also thought that the nonpayment of final filing fees was more
likely a bureaucratic oversight than an indication of a policy change that
should bring the 1884 law, with its longer protection period, into effect. It
decided in favor of the non-Indians.

The court of appeals disagreed and sent the case back, ordering the
district court to reconsider the facts and reverse its decision. The lower
court then found that five Washakie Shoshones did retain title to their
homesteads, but in the remaining cases title had irrevocably passed out of
their hands and beyond federal jurisdiction (U.S. District Court 1936).

Even after federal jurisdiction was established, the practical benefits of
trust status appeared minimal. A state-administered grade school was subsidized, as was some emergency health care. For five years a field matron was
assigned—the only physical federal presence in the history of the community (Knack 1990). Any federal aid, such as purchase of agricultural equipment, ran afoul of the fact that so much of the Indian land was no longer in
trust and, as private land, was not the government's responsibility. The
homesteads remaining under federal jurisdiction were too few to warrant
major capital investment (e.g., Donner 1922).

The Washakie community of approximately forty families continued to
function on this severely reduced land base. In 1935 they accepted the
provisions of the Wheeler-Howard Act, although they never formally established a tribal council (Collier 1939). Then, arguing great need and with
the help of both their attorney and the Utah congressional delegation, they
asked that 6,400 acres be purchased under the land acquisition provisions of
the Wheeler-Howard Act. The BIA rejected the proposal because of limited
funds (Collier 1935).

During World War II, Salt Lake City was considered a secure inland site,
and extensive defense facilities and related industrial activities created an
economic boom in the valley. Nearly every Washakie family sent one or
more workers off to the city to supplement the income of the struggling
farms (Timbimbo n.d.). Of the 880 acres remaining under federal trust in
1954, only 41 were actually being used by the Shoshones for any purpose. A
congressional report found that of forty-one Washakie families, twenty were
self-supporting (all from off-reservation wage labor) while four were partially and five families were totally dependent on welfare support. None
could subsist totally by farming, and there was no income from farm
product sales. The lands the Mormon church had bought from the Indians
were still being operated as a cooperative farm, in which twelve Shoshone

families, along with other members of the church, participated (U.S. Congress, Joint Subcommittees 1954:12).

In 1952 the Washakie population was so small that the BIA discontinued its school subsidy, and in 1966 the Mormon church there closed, formally ending the missionary presence (Madsen 1980b:101–2). When the termination of federal supervision became official BIA policy, Washakie, with its long record of independence from federal administration, was evaluated as of "top priority for completing a withdrawal program" (Fort Hall Agency 1953).

In 1954 Congress considered general legislation to terminate all the small reservations in Utah, home state of the chairman of the Senate Indian Affairs Subcommittee and a strong supporter of the termination policy; Washakie was included in this highly political bill. The Washakie community promptly organized an informal representative body to protest this action, claiming it gave insufficient time for legal consultation into the potential effects on their pending land claims case (Neamon et al. 1954). Washakie was subsequently removed from the bill before it became law.

Although this success demonstrated that the dispersed Washakie community was still a functional political network, it was not and had not been for some time a viable economic unit. When the Northwestern Shoshone land claim was settled in 1972, federal investigators found that only 560 acres of the original homesteads still remained in federal trust. About one-third of the two hundred people listed on the 1964 revised census roles were living on the Fort Hall or Wind River reservations; "others left the area entirely to seek better employment and social opportunities than were availabel [sic] to them near the reservations or the public domain allotments"; almost half were in the metropolitan areas of northern Utah. Only two or three families still farmed at the Washakie site. About a third of the families registered to the group were self-supporting from wage labor, but 10 percent were totally dependent on welfare support and an additional 17 percent relied on public assistance to supplement insufficient income (U.S. Congress, House 1972:9–15).

KANOSH

Federal interest in title for the Kanosh community began in 1856 when a BIA agent set aside an area about twelve miles square along Corn Creek in central Utah for the so-called Pahvant Indians. This band was a transitional group along the border between the clearly equestrian Utes to the northeast and the pedestrian Paiutes to the south, maintaining kinship and political ties with both (Jones 1954). In addition, this, their traditional home, was directly on the Old Spanish Trail, which Mormons used extensively to reach their new villages and to carry trade goods into southern California. The Pahvant leader in early historic times, Kanosh, was careful to maintain close relationships with all three of these regional groups. The Pahvants themselves kept only a limited number of horses, took readily to farming, and had peaceful relationships with in-migrating non-Indians.

The original Corn Creek reservation fell victim to mismanagement, insufficient funding, a series of unsuccessful farming years, and increased pressure from Mormon settlers for irrigable farmlands. It was abandoned as a reserve in 1864 and returned to the public domain in 1878, after which federal interest in this group waned (Royce 1900:830, 892).

As with the case of Washakie, only in 1911 did the federal government become again concerned with the Kanosh band, as it was by then known, along with the other small groups in Utah that were not on the large Uintah Ute reservation. By then the Kanosh Indian community consisted of thirty-five people. The band still lived in the same spot where they had been found by the earliest historical observers, about three miles south of the small Mormon town also called Kanosh. They had about fifty acres of wheat land irrigated with a branch of that town's irrigation system, but they had no separate proven water right, a serious liability in this area. To supplement their incomes they performed seasonal agricultural labor for their non-Indian neighbors (Creel 1911a).

As had also occurred at Washakie, in about 1900 representatives of the Mormon church filed for six homestead entries on behalf of Kanosh Paiutes under the 1884 Indian homestead law. When the federal agent finally arrived, the time allowed for establishing settlement and development of the land had expired without any of the natives having "proven up." Consequently, at least one non-Indian had already filed a claim for land in the middle of the Indian settlement (Creel 1911b).

The BIA viewed such homestead title as less than reliable for Indians. As with all homesteads, land records were kept by the General Land Office, and the BIA was often unaware that filings had been made and could not easily monitor their completion. Upon learning of the homesteads at Kanosh, BIA headquarters asked its field agent for further information to "enable the Office to advise you specifically of the steps necessary to be taken in order to protect the interests of the Indians, particularly with a view of ascertaining whether it will not be advisable to suggest a change in the form of entry, where the tract has not already been patented from that of 'an Indian homestead' to 'an Indian allotment on the public domain' " under the Dawes Act, as amended (Hauke 1911a).

The BIA argued that allotments maximized the amount of land for Indians. Indian allotments, unlike Indian homesteads, did not require any fixed period of permanent occupation to qualify for final title, only a "reasonable degree of settlement . . . as an evidence of good faith." At the same time, minors and married women, who were ineligible for homesteads, could file for allotments on public domain lands if their parents/husbands actually made a settlement on their own plots. On the other hand, Indian homesteaders could claim 160 acres of land of whatever type. Under the Dawes Act they could receive an allotment this large only if it was grazing land; if the land was arable they could claim only 80 acres, and only half that amount if it was part of a federal irrigation project. With allotments, therefore, more people were eligible and requirements were more lenient, while with homesteads the amount of land might be larger. In both cases the federal trust period was twenty-five years (Hauke 1911b).

Because official Indian policy at this time favored individualized land title, the BIA strongly preferred one of these two options. It did consider the possibility of an executive-order reservation at Kanosh, but "[t]his should be done, however, in the event only that the interests of the Indians [specifically water rights] can not [sic] be fully protected under the Indian homestead and allotment laws" (Hauke 1912).

After considering these alternatives and arguments, the agent decided that allotments provided greater likelihood of retaining more land in Indian hands. He swiftly persuaded the six native homesteaders to change the nature of their title by going to Salt Lake City with him, relinquishing their homesteads, and immediately applying for the same lands under the allotment act. He engineered full applications for men who had originally requested only half homesteads, as well as sixteen additional first-time allotment applications, primarily for wives and minors. He justified this to protect water rights and to block out a contiguous piece of land for grazing presently owned horses and future cattle. By mid-1912 each member of the band had claimed a 160-acre allotment (Creel 1912a, 1912b, 1912c; McConihe 1915).

A new agent who arrived on the scene in 1919 was under the impression that the Kanosh lands were still claimed under homestead law. Without acknowledging that it had already been accomplished, the BIA repeated its 1911 advice to refile under the 1887 Dawes Act, as amended (Meritt 1920).

Nevertheless, early the following year, the General Land Office approved

six Kanosh allotment applications—those of the original homesteads converted to allotments in 1912. Many of the other allotment applications the
first agent had engineered, however, fell victim to bureaucratic regulations.
Contrary to what the BIA had told the agent, the General Land Office
rejected all allotments for wives "for the reason that the regulations made no
provision for allotments to Indian women whose husbands were entitled to
allotments. . . . In the event that the wives of the before mentioned
[approved] allottees can show two years of use or occupancy of the land
formerly covered by their allotment applications, upon receipt of corroborated affidavits to that effect, said applications will be reinstated" (Parrott
1920a). In two cases the agent had tried to "fill out" a 160-acre claim from
the available remaining land and had listed two noncontiguous parcels;
when, "although notified, the party failed to elect which tract he would
retain," the allotment applications were rejected. One of these, a father's,
was overlapped by another claim for his minor son, so the son's claim was
canceled too (Parrott 1920b). Eventually fifteen filings were approved under
the Dawes Act, making a total of 2,160 acres of allotted land to be held for
an initial twenty-five-year trust period (Sells 1920a, 1920b; Henderson
1931:25). Because of the rejected applications, these lands were no longer a
single contiguous block, although all the tracts were near each other.

As elsewhere in the arid West, questions of land title and water rights
were inextricably intertwined at Kanosh. In 1877 Mormon settlers had
founded the Corn Creek Irrigation Company and had diverted that stream
into their fields. They had donated twenty shares in the cooperative to the
Kanosh Indians. Local custom subsequently had allowed a small but steady
flow through their ditches, which they had become accustomed to use for
drinking water. As the regional population grew in the 1920s and agriculture expanded, the company wanted to establish a more efficient fixed-
rotation system of water flow among all users. The Kanosh Indians' twenty
shares would entitle them to eighteen hours of water once every sixteen
days, which was adequate for their farming needs. However, if they were
denied drinking water for the intervening fourteen days, they would have to
abandon their allotments (Fiske 1928a).

The only alternate source of household water was Rogers Spring, about a
mile and a half away, which local whites agreed the Indians had used
continuously since at least 1873. In 1928 a nonresident claimed she had
bought the land around the spring and its full water rights thirty-three
years earlier. She also claimed to have made an informal agreement with the
Indians in 1910 that they could use the spring in exchange for tending some
fruit trees for her (Ballerstein 1928). A government survey confirmed her

ownership of the spring site but found that the orchard was on an Indian allotment (Humphereys 1930). Agents and inspectors consistently recommended a lawsuit to acquire rights to this water and enable construction of a pipeline to deliver it to Kanosh. This would relieve dependence on irrigation ditches for drinking water, to the betterment of Indian health, and also ease relations with neighboring non-Indian farmers by allowing the rotation scheme to go into effect.

The pipe system could not be built because of the twenty-three 40-acre plots of public land still vacant within and adjacent to the Indian allotments. The worried agent pointed to the potential problems that non-Indian purchase of these properties might entail (Fiske 1928b). His forceful recommendation resulted in administrative withdrawal of 920 acres from the public domain, thus blocking their claim by non-Indians until further federal action could be taken. In justification, the BIA argued that "the principal benefit which will inure to them [Kanosh Indians] through the proposed withdrawal is that it will surround their present holdings with all protection possible against further controversies relative to the title and the use of water from Rogers' Spring" (Meritt 1928). On February 11, 1929, Congress approved this acreage as reservation land to be held in common (45 Stat. 1161). There were then 3,080 acres available to the five families of Indians living at Kanosh. About two-thirds of this was public-domain Indian allotments, and the other third was reservation land; there were still interspersed state sections and non-Indian landholdings.

When it came to actual development of these lands, a different set of considerations came into play. The noncontiguous scattered boundaries of these parcels meant that fencing the Indian-owned land would cost $188 per capita. This the BIA judged unacceptable, even though without fences the Indians could neither pasture their own stock nor protect growing crops from their neighbors' cattle (Scattergood 1929). When the agent suggested title consolidation as a preliminary step toward economic development, the commissioner of Indian affairs replied, "We fully appreciate the advisability . . . and the probable benefit that would accrue to the Indians therefrom. However, in view of the manner in which the lands involved are held, it is not believed that the matter could be carried to a successful conclusion" (Rhoads 1931).

The persistent and experienced agent, denied an overall solution, tried a piecemeal approach instead. An 80-acre parcel of public domain, a piece of one of the noncontiguous claims rejected by the General Land Office fourteen years earlier, was actually being used by Indians for grazing. Furthermore, it lay strategically below a small pond of impounded springwater which might be used for a simple gravity-fed irrigation system (Farrow 1934). The agent asked that this one parcel be reserved on grounds of utility and water access. The commissioner concurred with this modest proposal and the BIA prepared a bill approved by Congress on June 20, 1935 (49 Stat. 393). Encouraged by this small success, the process was repeated in 1937, and Congress added another 240 acres from the rejected allotment applications (50 Stat. 239) "to help block out the reservation so that it can be fenced and used to better advantage for grazing purposes" (West 1937). Both of these added tracts were then held in reservation trust for the band as a whole.

When the BIA under John Collier's administration began buying properties for Indians in the Great Basin under the Submarginal Lands Act, this same agent proposed purchasing 3,160 acres of privately owned non-Indian lands inside and adjacent to Kanosh. "The purchase of this land," he wrote, "is particularly desirable as it will make it possible to place a boundary fence around all the Indian holdings acquiring nearly all the available water from the local creeks and springs other than Corn Creek, and will make it possible for these Indians to be supplied with foundation herds to add to their present income sufficient to render them economically independent if they make the required effort" (Farrow 1935). The purchase was approved and later increased to 4,680 acres, of which 4,030 acres were actually acquired (Radcliffe 1936). When purchases were complete in 1945, Kanosh had increased in size by 150 percent, to a total of 7,730 acres (Stone 1945). Beginning in 1940 yet another bill for an additional 600 acres was introduced in Congress, but it repeatedly failed to pass.

Related to such questions of land title was the issue of land use. Although the BIA invested over $25,000 for irrigation construction during the 1930s and 1940s, the debate over fencing the reservation demonstrated how reluctant the bureau was to make capital investments at Kanosh. The Indians themselves lacked funds to buy tractors or livestock to make their land productive. Like the Washakie people, they had always engaged in seasonal wage labor on nearby ranches and towns to gain cash for simple household purchases. Even when the tribal land claims case was won against the federal government, their small population received a share so small as to make major investment impossible, so it was divided per capita and used for personal items (Knack 1986:578–79).

In 1945 the BIA considered a loan for a cooperative farm out of the revolving credit fund of the Wheeler-Howard Act, but it ran into the scattered allotment titles again. "[T]his group of allotments would seriously handicap such an effort until we could convert titles back to Tribal ownership," the agent wrote. "[O]ne of our first efforts should be to secure relinquishments from the owners to deed the land back to Tribal owner- ship" (Stone 1945). The BIA Land Division promptly sent out a field agent who "discussed the matter of having them convey their land to the tribe without compensation, and they all agreed to this." However, eight of the original allottees had died and the Kanosh people had informally rearranged land use without wills, probate, or agency supervision. The BIA required long probate hearings which delayed conversion of land title to tribal status for over a year (Sallee 1946).

Eventually, in 1950, the BIA made a $25,000 loan to the Kanosh Paiutes for a cooperative wheat-farming and cattle-ranching enterprise, and encour- aged them to use the then-consolidated reservation lands for their joint economic support. A series of informal community arrangements and what the BIA viewed as bookkeeping irregularities later violated the terms of this loan and earned the wrath of the agency (Stone 1951). Because of unre- alistically optimistic planning, a series of poor crop years, and casual super- vision from the distant Uintah-Ouray agency now in charge of Kanosh, the band fell seriously behind in their repayment schedule (J.E.W. 1953). The remaining debt from this loan was finally canceled when the band was terminated from federal supervision in 1954.

Kanosh Paiutes were caught up in the bill to terminate the small Paiute and Shoshone communities in Utah. BIA records show that the Kanosh community voted in favor of termination, but at the last minute a small faction protested unsuccessfully (U.S. Congress, Joint Subcommittees 1954: 84). Given the choice between individual title to parcels and com- mon ownership under a corporation charter, the Kanosh people elected to continue joint operation of the land. The BIA pressed efforts to have the additional 600 acres of grazing land transferred to them, arguing that this would create a viable economic base for the group so they could move into the general economy without further government support (Greenwood 1955). Congress was persuaded in July 1956 (70 Stat. 528), and upon termination of federal supervision the seventeen Kanosh adults had title to 8,830 acres of land.

Meanwhile, heirs to the original allotments had continued to consider these properties their own, despite the fact that formal title rested with the band. Late in the termination proceedings, ten decided they would prefer to sell their lands rather than continue in a cooperative. The small Kanosh community decided that it would be better to give them their wish than to fight a prolonged and ugly legal battle to keep the joint-use plan alive. The BIA administered the bid and subsequent sale of nine of these properties (Bobo 1956; Ring 1956).

In the end, Kanosh decided to separate out the traditional town site, where each person would retain a homesite; the remaining common reservation lands were divided into individual parcels ranging from 120 to 180 acres, depending on land quality, right-of-way deductions, and other considerations (Commissioner of Indian Affairs 1956). Each band member, including minors, received a piece, and in January 1958 the BIA asserted that "the Federal Government has no further interest in the lands patented to members of the Kanosh Band" (Noyes 1958).

By 1973 no one lived at Kanosh; everyone had moved to non-Indian towns to seek wage employment (Knack, unpublished notes, 1973–74). When the Utah Paiutes petitioned successfully for reinstatement of federal recognition in 1980 (94 Stat. 317), the Kanosh Paiutes had lost title to all but 55 acres of their land through private sales and taxes (U.S. Department of the Interior 1982:17, 40).

DISCUSSION

These cases illustrate that while policy can exist on the national level, it is shaped in application to the land and labor needs of the particular locale, as well as to the specific political context (Bee 1981). In Utah, settlement was more reminiscent of early New England than of the later, more individualized westward-moving American frontier. Here a highly organized, preexisting religious community made an intentional mass migration. Mormons were committed agriculturalists. Arriving in family units, often very large as a result of polygyny and high fertility rates, they had little need for Indian labor; in fact, they had sufficient manpower to construct the extensive irrigation systems demanded by the arid and unpredictable environment. Such projects stretched beyond both the property boundaries and the financial means of any single individual and were, in Mormon areas, built by and for the community.[2] Such intensive labor investments reinforced Mormons' beliefs in the differential value of particular plots of land and developers' rights to exclusive use. At the same time, the Indians in this area did not produce any goods Mormons much desired for internal or external trade. Lacking utility as producers of any valued commodity, Indians were viewed primarily as threats to the property interests of the closed corporate communities (Wolf 1957).

Early Mormon settlers' concern with private property included household goods and livestock. For pragmatic reasons they were willing to share their food with Indians, acceding to Brigham Young's oft-quoted injunction, "It is cheaper to feed the Indians than to fight them." This dole was a financial drain on the small communities, which they tried to keep in check by punishing natives found "sharing" without permission. The obvious solution was to get the Indians to produce these same foods and goods for themselves; in other words, to eliminate their cultural distinctiveness (Alter 1944; Brooks 1944; Arrington 1970).

This could be done if Indians became members of the closed corporate communities and participated in the religious faith, economy, and labor for the common good (Nelson 1952). This solution conformed to both economic expediency and religious dictate, for Mormonism defined Indians as of the House of Israel, and their conversion played a fundamental role in the anticipated millennium. Church authorities considered incorporation of Indians practical, however, only on an individual basis and only after profound cultural change, which was both more difficult and slower than initially anticipated. Furthermore, the idea of interracial communities met serious resistance from both Mormons and natives (B. Young 1854). The solution was mission colonies, which permitted non-Indian communities to proceed with their own developments while Indians acculturated at a slower pace (e.g., Jenson 1926; Brooks 1972). Despite the sectarian phraseology justifying the motivation, the segregationist and overtly acculturative purpose of these missions marked them as fundamentally identical to the BIA's own interpretation of reservations (Trennert 1975:194–95).

As a private group, the Mormon church could not establish actual reservations, so it needed a different legal mechanism. Congress provided the Indian homestead option at a time when missions were already well established in Utah. Homesteads were fully compatible with strongly held Mormon concepts of property. By helping Indians get their own private lands, Mormon ownership would be protected, since this would reduce the area used by still-mobile natives. It would also place all land titles, both Indian and non-Indian, under a uniform legal system, thus facilitating the exchange or sale of property from one group to the other.

Beyond such regional economic motivations, Mormons filed homesteads for Indians at a few places, such as Washakie and Kanosh, for reasons that seem to have been local and political. The Washakie filings followed the military defeat of the Northwestern Shoshones in 1863. The potential for continued hostilities so close to the Salt Lake City heartland pressed for an immediate solution. Along with new Mormon settlements, the Washakie community was an attempt both to neutralize Shoshones on the northern frontier and to counterbalance the only significant non-Mormon, non-agricultural presence in the territory, the adjacent boomtown of Corinne (Madsen 1980a). Furthermore, during this period Mormons were intensely suspicious of outsiders, particularly the federal government, and they still smarted from what they saw as an invasion by the U.S. Army in 1858. Local citizens sought to avoid any increased federal presence in the form of the BIA if there was any chance of local containment of the "Indian problem."

Missionary records justify the choice of the specific Washakie site by the juxtaposition of unclaimed water and reasonably fertile, unclaimed public land capable of gravity irrigation. The sequence of preliminary relocations does tend to confirm this explanation.

Kanosh was not homesteaded until a generation later, again for local reasons. The church authorities cultivated the friendship of this group strategically located on the Mormons' route to California. The Kanosh Pahvants were only minimally active in early armed resistance to white settlement by neighboring Utes and showed a willingness to expand their traditional horticultural sector to become semisedentary. The headman, Kanosh, rapidly perceived the advantages of an alliance with Mormons, regularly extracted gifts from local settlers, and even joined Brigham Young's party as he traveled up and down the roadway. Not offering a physical threat requiring military containment, and sheltered by the patronage of the highest church officials, the Kanosh community coexisted peacefully until regional agricultural expansion caused pressure on the land base and water resources about the turn of the century. Then local settlers made efforts to regularize Indian land title through the already proven strategy of homesteads.

The Bureau of Indian Affairs, having once checked into the situation at Washakie, found that this homesteading conformed with its own efforts to individualize Indian relations with the government and encourage Indians to farm privately owned land parcels. Ever aware of limited budgets, the BIA decided to let the missionaries proceed at the church's expense and then ignored the area for forty years. During that time the bureau actively encouraged other Great Basin Indians to file for allotments from the public domain under the Dawes Act, in a self-conscious effort to avoid the expense of reservation buildings and personnel for small, isolated groups.

Indian affairs in Utah changed substantially when improved communication—especially roads, telephones, and automobiles—made it possible for a single agent to be responsible for a number of small, scattered reservations. Beginning with the Salt Lake City office in 1911, and continuing through a variety of aggregate administrative arrangements, a number of small Southern Paiute and Shoshone communities were drawn into BIA oversight for the first time. Unlike reservations with resident agents, this central office–outliers network resulted in very minimal federal supervision. Nevertheless, once established, the bureaucracy tried to perpetuate itself by asserting control over Indian affairs to the exclusion of both church and state. In the case of Washakie, where a missionary had been resident for more than two generations and would continue for another two, this distant BIA posturing was never very effective.

Kanosh was another matter. Never a formal mission and receiving only intermittent beneficial interest from local churchmen, it gradually acquired the character of a reservation after the BIA took control. Initially, the Dawes Act was the prevailing federal policy, and the bureau promptly converted homestead titles to allotments. Then, after the Collier administration renewed the tribe as the unit of policy application and community economic development became a programmatic goal, Kanosh allotments were reverted to the tribe, communal reservation lands were added, and capital for a cooperative farming enterprise was provided. Again, as termination became national policy, both Kanosh and Washakie were targeted, one to completion and the other not. Finally, once termination had been publicly proclaimed "morally unacceptable" (Nixon 1971) and restoration of tribal status became possible, the Kanosh community actively led Utah Paiutes back into federal recognition (Knack, unpublished notes, 1973–74).

The history of particular reservations, then, cannot be explained by appeal to uniform federal policy alone. That policy is rooted in the nature of the national economy and in general historical trends often encompassing far more than simply Indian affairs. National policy is not in and of itself determinant, for it is activated or evaded in particular areas for purely local reasons. These reasons lie in the needs and goals of the local white and Indian communities operating within the limits and opportunities of the regional physical environment. These groups argue ideological justifications for their actions, which are otherwise based on pragmatic necessity and self-interest. They attempt modifications of that national policy to serve their own local interests, creating variation from one tribal case to the other, as is so clear in the historical record illustrated in this volume.

A second source of variation between tribal histories is the role of the BIA itself. The BIA is a bureaucracy and as such has its own political existence (Porto 1974; Bee 1982). At times it is caught up in competition for power and resources in the seething broil of Washington; when it loses, its Indian clients also often lose (Knack, in press). At other times, as the record clearly shows, the BIA has stood by and allowed rampant and blatant exploitation of the very Indian resources it is charged to protect, either through ignorance, incompetence, or outright collusion (e.g., Knack and Stewart 1984). The history of numerous Southern and Northern Paiute groups shows that even in remote desert areas of the Great Basin there are always avid local interests able and willing to use all the resources of any reservation left unguarded.

It does not, however, follow from the oft-times shabby record of the BIA that such illicit exploitation would necessarily have been any less without the bureau's presence. Other political power brokers would have been readily available to serve local constituencies.

In the cases of Washakie and Kanosh, federal presence did give some degree of protection to the formal land title of these native communities. The BIA sued in federal court to wrest physical possession of the title papers from the hands of church agents. It prevented the state of Utah from probating heirship. For Kanosh, it engineered significant expansion of the land base.

What it did *not* do was ensure that Indian owners would be the ones actually to use and benefit from the land, for that would have required economic resources that the government did not provide; here as elsewhere (e.g., Nybroten 1964:6, 40; Jorgensen 1972:102, 147, 165), non-Indians leased land that Indian owners could not afford to operate themselves. BIA presence did *not* ensure that Indians would obtain control over their own land; missionaries at Washakie continued to distribute and assign use rights to Indian homesteads. It did *not* ensure any permanency of Indian owner-ship; in each case, because of the extreme weakness of the native economy, the land base dwindled as soon as federal trust protection was removed.

The Bureau of Indian Affairs is far from a benevolent force in Indian life. It is clearly an agent of the power of the nation-state, and it can exercise force against the will of both the native community and avaricious local competitors. The particular circumstances existing on both the national and local levels determine how that power is used at a particular time and place, or even whether it is used at all. By examining off-reservation (Knack 1980) and marginally controlled Indian communities such as the two cases described here, we can begin to envision alternatives to the BIA, an absence of the federal role.

NOTES

1. Previous versions of this paper were read at the Arizona-Nevada American Academy of Sciences meetings at Las Vegas, April 15, 1989, and at the South-western Anthropological Association meetings at Riverside, California, April 28,

1989. I am grateful to the following organizations for partially funding my research and writing: University of Nevada, Las Vegas, Sabbatical Committee; Wenner-Gren Foundation for Anthropological Research; National Endowment for the Humanities; Phillips Fund of the American Philosophical Society; Rockefeller Foundation; and the Newberry Library.

2. This contrasts sharply with the later, non-Mormon West where large-scale irrigation was provided by the federal government. See Worster 1985.

REFERENCES

ALTER, J. C. 1944. "The Mormons and the Indians." *Utah Historical Quarterly* 12:49–67.

ARRINGTON, LEONARD. 1970. "The Mormons and the Indians: A Review and Evaluation." *The Record* (Friends of the Library of Washington State University) 31:5–29.

BALLERSTEIN, ALICE. 1928. Letter to Commissioner of Indian Affairs, January 28, 1928. Bureau of Indian Affairs Central Classified Files [hereinafter abbreviated BIACCF] 1907–1939, File 56602-1919, Goshute 341, U.S. National Archives.

BEE, ROBERT L. 1981. *Crosscurrents Along the Colorado: The Impact of Government Policy on the Quechan Indians.* Tucson: University of Arizona Press.

———. 1982. *The Politics of American Indian Policy.* Cambridge, Mass.: Schenkman.

BOBO, WESLEY. 1956. Letter to Commissioner of Indian Affairs, July 9, 1956. Phoenix Area Office General Classified Files, 1932–1948, File Uintah Ouray—Sale of Allotments, U.S. National Archives Branch, Los Angeles.

BROOKS, JUANITA. 1944. "Indian Relations on the Mormon Frontier." *Utah Historical Quarterly* 12:1–48.

———, ed. 1972. *Journal of the Southern Indian Mission: Diary of Thomas D. Brown.* Western Text Society no. 4. Logan: Utah State University Press.

BROWN, CHARLEY. 1914. Letter to [Commissioner of Indian Affairs], May 25, 1914. BIACCF, 59756-1914, Scattered Bands in Utah-311, U.S. National Archives.

BURKE, CHARLES H. 1928a. Letter to George H. Smith, June 9, 1928. BIACCF, File 113,732-1915, Scattered Bands in Utah-150, pt. 2, U.S. National Archives.

———. 1928b. Letter to Joseph Gibbs, August 31, 1928. BIACCF, File 113,732-1915, Scattered Bands in Utah-150, pt. 2, U.S. National Archives.

CHURCH OF JESUS CHRIST OF LATTER-DAY SAINTS. 1970. *Book of Mormon.* Salt Lake City, Utah: Church of Jesus Christ of Latter-day Saints.

COHEN, FELIX S., et al. 1982. *Handbook of Federal Indian Law.* Rev. ed. Charlottesville, Va.: Michie Bobbs-Merrill.

COLLIER, JOHN. 1935. Letter to Fred A. Gross, October 15, 1935. BIACCF, File 41297-1935, Fort Hall 310, U.S. National Archives.

———. 1939. Letter to Fred Gross, July 22, 1939. BIACCF, File 34233-1939, Fort Hall 310, U.S. National Archives.

COMMISSIONER OF INDIAN AFFAIRS. 1956. Memorandum to Director of Bureau of Land Management, August 30, 1956. BIACCF, File 11,674-1956, Uintah and Ouray 312, U.S. National Archives.

CONNER, NICK. 1919. Letter to Commissioner of Indian Affairs, November 13, 1919. BIACCF, File 113,732-1915, Scattered Bands in Utah-150, pt. 2, U.S. National Archives.

———. 1920. Letter to Commissioner of Indian Affairs, June 21, 1920. BIACCF, File 113,732-1915, Scattered Bands in Utah-150, pt. 2, U.S. National Archives.

CREEL, LORENZO. 1911a. Letter to Commissioner of Indian Affairs, October 16, 1911. BIACCF, File 90091-1911, General Service 341, U.S. National Archives.

———. 1911b. Letter to Commissioner of Indian Affairs, December 15, 1911. Uintah and Ouray Miscellaneous Correspondence, Box 5, U.S. National Archives Branch, Denver.

———. 1912a. Letter to Commissioner of Indian Affairs, January 27, 1912. BIACCF, File 90091-1911, General Service 341, U.S. National Archives.

———. 1912b. Letter to Commissioner of Indian Affairs, May 9, 1912. BIACCF, File 90091-1911, General Service 341, U.S. National Archives.

———. 1912c. Letter to Commissioner of Indian Affairs, September 6, 1912. BIA Special Agent Files, File 88261-1912-Creel 313, U.S. National Archives.

CRITCHLOW, J. J. 1878. Letter to E. A. Hayt, May 8, 1878. Letters Received, Microfilm M234, Roll 906, Letter Utah-1878-C-322, Enclosure 1, U.S. National Archives.

CRUM, STEVEN. 1987. "The Skull Valley Band of the Goshute Tribe—Deeply Attached to Their Native Homeland." *Utah Historical Quarterly* 55:250–67.

DONNER, WILLIAM. 1922. Letter to Commissioner of Indian Affairs, March 18, 1922. BIACCF, File 113,732-1915, Scattered Bands in Utah-150, pt. 2, U.S. National Archives.

———. 1925. Letter to Commissioner of Indian Affairs, July 15, 1925. BIACCF, File 113,732-1915, Scattered Bands in Utah-150, pt. 2, U.S. National Archives.

DORTCH, J. H. 1920. Letter to Nick Conner, May 4, 1920. BIACCF, File 113,732-1915, Scattered Bands in Utah-150, pt. 2, U.S. National Archives.

ELLIOT, STUART. 1914. Letter to Commissioner of Indian Affairs, June 12, 1914. BIACCF, File 59756-1914, Scattered Bands in Utah-311, U.S. National Archives.

ESTEP, AGENT OF FORT HALL. 1913. Telegram to Indian Office, May 14, 1913. BIACCF, File 60093-1913, Fort Hall 313, U.S. National Archives.

EVANS, ISAAC. 1918. Letter to Commissioner of Indian Affairs, May 29, 1918. BIACCF, File 113,732-1915, Scattered Bands in Utah-150, pt. 1, U.S. National Archives.

FARROW, E. A. 1934. Letter to Commissioner of Indian Affairs, January 24, 1934. BIACCF, File 41753-1928, Paiute 307.4, U.S. National Archives.

——. 1935. Statement Concerning the Proposed Kanosh Project, June 10, 1935. Phoenix Area Office Files, Land Operations–Land Acquisition 1935–1938, File Kanosh Project, U.S. National Archives Branch, Los Angeles.

FISKE, H. H. 1928a. Letter to Commissioner of Indian Affairs, August 11, 1928. BIACCF, Inspection Division, Inspection Files—Paiute, U.S. National Archives.

——. 1928b. Letter to Commissioner of Indian Affairs, August 14, 1928. BIACCF, File 41753-1928, Paiute 307.4, U.S. National Archives.

FORT HALL AGENCY. 1953. Document D, September 10, 1953. BIA Accession 68A-4937, File 17210-1952, Fort Hall 077, U.S. National Archives.

FRANK, AMOS R. 1917. Letter to Commissioner of Indian Affairs, March 29, 1917. BIACCF, File 113,732-1915, Scattered Bands in Utah-150, pt. 1, U.S. National Archives.

GETCHES, DAVID, DANIEL ROSENFELT, and CHARLES WILKINSON. 1979. *Cases and Materials on Federal Indian Law.* St. Paul: West Publishing.

GREENWOOD, W. B. 1955. Memorandum to Legislative Counsel, November 25, 1955. Accession 68A-4937, Box 126, File 17,200-1952, Uintah and Ouray 077, U.S. National Archives.

HAAS, R. P. 1928. Letter to Commissioner of Indian Affairs, June 12, 1928. BIACCF, File 113,732-1915, Scattered Bands in Utah-150, pt. 2, U.S. National Archives.

HALL, PHILENE. 1916a. Field Matron's Weekly Report, November 4, 1916. Uintah and Ouray Miscellaneous Correspondence, File 52.1, U.S. National Archives Branch, Denver.

——. 1916b. Field Matron's Weekly Report, November 11, 1916. Uintah and Ouray Miscellaneous Correspondence, File 52.1, U.S. National Archives Branch, Denver.

HAUKE, C. F. 1911a. Letter to Lorenzo Creel, December 15, 1911. BIACCF, File 90091-1911, General Service 341, U.S. National Archives.

——. 1911b. Letter to Lorenzo D. Creel, December 18, 1911. BIACCF, File 90091-1911, General Service 341, U.S. National Archives.

——. 1912. Letter to Lorenzo Creel, January 3, 1912. BIACCF, File 90091-1911, General Service 341, U.S. National Archives.

——. 1917. Letter to Amos R. Frank, January 4, 1917. BIACCF, File 113,732-1915, Scattered Bands in Utah-150, pt. 1, U.S. National Archives.

HENDERSON, EARL Y. 1931. Report to the Board of Indian Commissioners, February 24, 1931. BIACCF, File 16,454-1931, Paiute 150, U.S. National Archives.

HILL, GEORGE WASHINGTON. n.d. Account of the Labor & Travels of G. W. Hill While Engaged in a Mission to the Lamanites. G. W. Hill Papers, ca.

1872–1882, Historian's Office, Church of Jesus Christ of Latter-day Saints, Salt Lake City, MS 8172.

HOLDERBY, LAURA B. 1916. Report to the Commissioner of Indian Affairs, June 27, 1916. Superintendents' Annual Narrative Reports for 1916. Microfilm series M 1011, Roll 129, Frames 378–394, U.S. National Archives.

HUMPHEREYS, GERAINT. 1930. Letter to Commissioner of Indian Affairs, August 8, 1930. Uintah and Ouray Miscellaneous Correspondence, 1916–1952, Box 7, File 341 Paiute, U.S. National Archives Branch, Denver.

JENSON, ANDREW, ed. 1926. "History of the Las Vegas Mission." *Nevada State Historical Society Papers* 5.

J. E. W. 1953. BIA internal memo, April 6, 1953. BIACCF, File 277-1946, Uintah and Ouray 259, U.S. National Archives.

JONES, J. A. 1954. "A Reinterpretation of the Ute-Paiute Classification." *Anthropological Quarterly* 27:2:53–58.

JORGENSEN, JOSEPH G. 1972. *The Sun Dance Religion: Power for the Powerless*. Chicago: University of Chicago Press.

KNACK, MARTHA C. 1973–74. Unpublished field notes. In possession of the author.

——. 1980. *Life Is with People: Household Organization of the Contemporary Southern Paiute Indians*. Ballena Press Anthropological Papers, no. 19. Socorro, N.M.: Ballena Press.

——. 1986. "Indian Economics, 1950–1980." In *Great Basin*. Ed. Warren d'Azevedo, 573–91. Vol. 11 of *Handbook of North American Indians*. Gen. ed. William Sturtevant. Washington, D.C.: Smithsonian Institution Press.

——. 1990. "Philene T. Hall, Bureau of Indian Affairs Field Matron: Intentional Culture Change of the Washakie Shoshone Indian Community." *Prologue: Quarterly Journal of the U.S. National Archives* 22:150–67.

——. In press. "Interethnic Competition at Kaibab in the Early Twentieth Century." *Ethnohistory*.

KNACK, MARTHA C., and OMER C. STEWART. 1984. *As Long as the River Shall Run: An Ethnohistory of Pyramid Lake Reservation*. Berkeley: University of California Press.

MCCONIHE, W. W. 1915. Report of Inspection to Commissioner of Indian Affairs, October 19, 1915. BIACCF, File 113,732-1915, Scattered Bands in Utah-150, pt. 1, U.S. National Archives.

MADSEN, BRIGHAM D. 1980a. *Corinne: The Gentile Capital of Utah*. Salt Lake City: Utah Historical Society Press.

——. 1980b. *The Northern Shoshoni*. Caldwell, Ida.: Caxton Printers.

——. 1985. *The Shoshoni Frontier and the Bear River Massacre*. Salt Lake City: University of Utah Press.

MERITT, E. B. 1917. Letter to Secretary of the Interior, April 2, 1917. BIACCF, File 113,732-1915, Scattered Bands in Utah-150, pt. 1, U.S. National Archives.

——. 1920. Letter to Nick Conner, January 19, 1920. BIACCF, File 101,296-1919, Goshute 723, U.S. National Archives.

——. 1928. Letter to Secretary of the Interior, October 22, 1928. BIACCF, File 41753-1928, Paiute 307.4, U.S. National Archives.

NEAMON, LEE, WALLACE ZUNDEL, and MAE PERRY. 1954. Letter to Alexander Lesser, February 9, 1954. Reprinted in U.S. Congress, Joint Subcommittees 1954, p. 82.

NELSON, LOWERY. 1952. *The Mormon Village: A Pattern and Technique of Land Settlement.* Salt Lake City: University of Utah Press.

NIXON, RICHARD M. 1971. "Special Message to Congress on Indian Affairs." In *Public Papers of the Presidents of the United States: Richard Nixon, 1970.* Washington, D.C.: Government Printing Office. Pp. 564–74.

NOYES, JOSEPH. 1958. Memorandum to Fredrick Haverland, February 13, 1958. BIACCF, File 11829-1956, Uintah and Ouray 311, U.S. National Archives.

NYBROTEN, NORMAN, ed. 1964. *Economy and Conditions of the Fort Hall Indian Reservation.* Idaho Bureau of Business and Economic Research Report no. 9, Moscow, Idaho.

PABAWENA, THOMAS. 1927. Letter to the Commissioner of Indian Affairs, May 26, 1927. BIACCF, File 113,732-1915, Scattered Bands in Utah-150, pt. 2, U.S. National Archives.

PARROTT, D. K. 1920a. Letter to Commissioner of Indian Affairs, April 29, 1920. BIACCF, File 37460-1920, Goshute 313, U.S. National Archives.

——. 1920b. Letter to Commissioner of Indian Affairs, April 29, 1920. BIACCF, File 28730-1920, Goshute 313, U.S. National Archives.

PORTER, ROBERT. 1935. Letter to Knox Patterson, August 1, 1935. BIACCF, File 44559-1935, Fort Hall 371, U.S. National Archives.

PORTO, BRIAN. 1974. "Policy Processes in American Indian Affairs: Patterns of Interaction Between American Indian Interest Groups, the Bureau of Indian Affairs, and the Indian Affairs Committees of Congress." Ph.D. diss., Miami University, Miami, Ohio.

POWELL, JOHN WESLEY, and GEORGE W. INGALLS. 1873. "Report to the Commissioner of Indian Affairs," June 18, 1873. Reprinted in *Anthropology of the Numa.* Ed. Don D. Fowler and Catherine S. Fowler, 97–119. Smithsonian Contributions in Anthropology, no. 14. Washington, D.C.: Smithsonian Institution, 1971.

RADCLIFFE, MARK. 1936. Indian Reorganization Act Land Acquisition: Kanosh Project, October 27, 1936. Phoenix Area Office, Land Operations–Land Acquisitions, 1935–1948, File Kanosh Project, General, U.S. National Archives Branch, Los Angeles.

RHOADS, C. J. 1931. Letter to Edgar A. Farrow, June 6, 1931. BIACCF, File 41,753-1928, Paiute 307.4, U.S. National Archives.

RING, JAMES. 1956. Letter to Commissioner of Indian Affairs, May 9, 1956. BIACCF, File 8044-1954, Uintah and Ouray 317.2, U.S. National Archives.

ROYCE, CHARLES. 1900. *Indian Land Cessions in the United States*. Eighteenth Annual Report of the Bureau of American Ethnology. Washington, D.C.: Government Printing Office.

SALLEE, ERNEST. 1946. Letter to Commissioner of Indian Affairs, April 12, 1946. BIACCF, File 10969-1946, Uintah and Ouray 313, U.S. National Archives.

SCATTERGOOD, J. HENRY. 1929. Letter to E. A. Farrow, October 14, 1929. Uintah and Ouray Miscellaneous Correspondence, 1916–1952, Box 7, File 342, U.S. National Archives Branch, Denver.

SELLS, CATO. 1920a. Letter to Nick Conner, July 3, 1920. BIACCF, File 00-1922, Goshute 307, U.S. National Archives.

———. 1920b. Letter to Nick Conner, December 14, 1920. BIACCF, File 00-1922, Goshute 307, U.S. National Archives.

———. 1921. Letter to C. V. Safford, March 17, 1921. BIACCF, File 113,732-1915, Scattered Bands in Utah-150, pt. 2, U.S. National Archives.

STONE, FORREST. 1945. Letter to Commissioner of Indian Affairs, December 27, 1945. BIACCF, File 10969-1946, Uintah and Ouray 313, U.S. National Archives.

———. 1951. Letter to Commissioner of Indian Affairs, July 10, 1951. Uintah and Ouray Miscellaneous Correspondence, Box 1, U.S. National Archives Branch, Denver.

SUTTON, IMRE. 1975. *Indian Land Tenure*. New York: Clearwater Publishing.

TIMBIMBO, MORONI. n.d. Oral History of Moroni Timbimbo. Manuscript Collections, Brigham Young University Library, OH 133.

TRENNERT, ROBERT A. 1975. *Alternative to Extinction: Federal Indian Policy and the Beginning of the Reservation System, 1846–1851*. Philadelphia: Temple University Press.

U.S. CONGRESS, HOUSE OF REPRESENTATIVES. 1972. *Report 92-701 to Accompany* HR 10846. 92d Congr., 1st sess. Washington, D.C.: Government Printing Office.

U.S. CONGRESS, JOINT SUBCOMMITTEES ON INDIAN AFFAIRS. 1954. *Termination of Federal Supervision over Certain Tribes of Indians, Part I—Utah*. Joint Hearing of Subcommittees of the Committees on Interior and Insular Affairs, February 15, 1954. 83d Congr., 2d sess. Washington, D.C.: Government Printing Office.

U.S. DEPARTMENT OF COMMERCE, BUREAU OF THE CENSUS. 1880. Tenth Census of Population. Microfilm roll 1335, Utah, Box Elder County, West Portage Precinct, frames 100–101.

———. 1910. Thirteenth Census of Population. Microfilm roll 1602, Utah, Box Elder County, West Portage Precinct, sheets 1A–5B, no frame numbers.

U.S. DEPARTMENT OF THE INTERIOR. BUREAU OF INDIAN AFFAIRS. 1982. "Proposed Paiute Indian Tribe of Utah Reservation Plan." Typescript.

U.S. DISTRICT COURT FOR NORTHERN UTAH. 1936. *United States v. Corporation of the Presidency of the Church of Jesus Christ of Latter-day Saints et al.* 1936. RG 21, Records of the U.S. District Courts—Utah, Civil Case Files, File 12881, U.S. National Archives Branch, Denver.

U.S. SUPREME COURT. 1831. *Cherokee Nation v. Georgia.* 30 U.S. (5 Pet.) 1.

WEST, CHARLES. 1937. Letter to the President of the Senate, March 10, 1937. BIACCF, File 36,353-1935, Paiute 310, U.S. National Archives.

WOLF, ERIC. 1957. "Closed Corporate Peasant Communities in Mesoamerica and Central Java." *Southwestern Journal of Anthropology* 13:1–18.

WORSTER, DONALD. 1985. *Rivers of Empire: Water, Aridity, and the Growth of the American West.* New York: Pantheon Books.

WRIGHT, A. O. 1901. Letter to Commissioner of Indian Affairs, February 14, 1901. BIA Letters Received 1881–1907, 1901-10294, U.S. National Archives.

YOUNG, BRIGHAM. 1854. "Proper Treatment of the Indians," April 6, 1854. In *Journal of Discourses.* Vol. 6, *Liverpool, 1854–1886.* Pp. 327–29.

YOUNG, BRIGHAM, and HEBER C. KIMBALL. 1856. "Fourteenth General Epistle." December 10, 1856. In *Messages of the First Presidency of the Church of Jesus Christ of Latter-day Saints, 1833–1964.* Ed. James Clark, 2:192–211. Salt Lake City: Bookcraft, 1965.

YOUNG, JAMES A., and B. ABBOTT SPARKS. 1985. *Cattle in the Cold Desert.* Logan: Utah State University Press.

The Enduring Reservations of Oklahoma

JOHN H. MOORE

A recurring myth of Anglo-American society is that Indians live on reservations; if there are no reservations in an area, then there are no proper Indians. It is therefore disappointing to read a statement like the following in official U.S. government publications: "The Indian land status in Oklahoma is unique in comparison with Indian lands elsewhere. Because of special laws related to Indian-owned land in Oklahoma, there are no reservations in that State, insofar as the term generally applies to Indian lands in other parts of the United States" (U.S. Department of Commerce n.d.:439).

The consequent conclusion—that there are no "proper" Indians in Oklahoma—has not been missed by various members of the dominant society. At a recent professional meeting of anthropologists, for example, a colleague from an Eastern university told me that she was trying to discourage a student from doing a dissertation in Oklahoma because there are no reservations there and, consequently, "very little Indian culture left in the state." Another colleague, after visiting the Chickasaw tribal complex and seeing no phenotypical Indians there, commiserated with me that it must be depressing to work in an area where the reservations are gone and all the Indian culture has disappeared. Even Angie Debo, the historian who championed Indian legal causes in Oklahoma, spoke mournfully about the end of the Creek people, who, she felt, "disappeared" about 1903 when Indian Territory was being legally dissolved for the creation of the state of Oklahoma (Debo 1941).

But thousands of ordinary tourists, especially foreigners, visit Oklahoma each year fully expecting to find lots of Indian culture—and, of course, reservations. The pattern of these expectations was brought home to me a few years ago at the annual Colony pow-wow. I had arrived early to set up a genealogical booth for the Sand Creek Descendents Association, to enroll claimants for the Sand Creek Massacre lawsuit. About noon on Friday a family of tourists from Philadelphia arrived and parked next to me, with much bustle and clanking of tent poles as they set up their camp. I heard the young son ask his father if there were going to be any Indians there with their tipis. "No," said the father thoughtfully, "Indians don't live in tipis anymore."

By suppertime about fifty Indian families had arrived and set up their camps, including ten or twelve tipis, one of which was erected right next to the family from Philadelphia. Recovering from his earlier gaffe, the father had reorganized his thoughts and at the supper table made the following speech to his family, which exhibits, I think, the continued strength of the racist and patronizing *reservation cosmology* that has plagued Indian people for such a long time: "Here on the reservation," he said, "some of the Indians still live in tipis. Over there you see an old man, he is the medicine man; the middle-aged man is the chief, and the young men are the braves." I braced myself as he added, "The women are called squaws and the children are called papooses." So here was the complete stereotypical picture—the Indian family, complete with pidgin English social descriptions, living in a tipi on the reservation.

One point I wish to make in this essay is that some of my colleagues in anthropology and history, and apparently many legal scholars as well, are not far emancipated from the views of the man from Philadelphia. Upon hearing the folklore that there are no reservations in Oklahoma, some scholars do not expect to find any Indian languages or cultures still extant in the state. And when they discover that traditionalist, native-speaking communities still exist, they sometimes have peculiar reactions.

As an academic host, I sometimes take visiting scholars and prominent people to esoteric Indian ceremonies and meetings where they can witness for themselves the continuing richness of Oklahoma Indian cultures. On the way to such meetings they often ask, "Are we on the reservation yet?" After meeting traditional Indians and getting acquainted, they sometimes ask me why the tribe doesn't "organize their own reservation" or try to "get recognition from the federal government." Such is the pull of the Anglo-American myth of the Reservation, the idea that Indianness is something bestowed by the federal government, in some mysterious way, when a reservation is created, and thus something withdrawn when a reservation is dissolved.

As I show in this essay, however, it is not true legally that there are no Indian reservations in Oklahoma (with the eternal caveat, "except for the Osage"), despite the fact that such statements bear the weight of "common knowledge" about Oklahoma and are heard continually from federal officials, politicians, and "Indian experts" of various stripe. But I document here the fact that such beliefs are mythic and were invented for selfish and anti-Indian purposes by a combination of Oklahoma state officials and federal bureaucrats at about the time Oklahoma became a state, in 1907.

To begin with, it is exceedingly strange that the ethnocentric and self-serving fiction that Oklahoma reservations have been dissolved still bears the weight of truth in official circles. For example, the current maps of "Indian Land Areas" published by the Bureau of Indian Affairs (BIA) still perpetuate the myth by showing Osage County colored yellow as the only official Indian reservation in the state, and showing a yellow outline around much of the rest of the state labeled "Former Reservations in Oklahoma" (BIA 1971). The same government line is followed in the statement I quoted at the beginning of this essay, from the official Department of Commerce guide entitled *Federal and State Indian Reservations* (n.d.:439).

The Bureau of the Census has been influenced by the same body of myth and has gone to extraordinary lengths to differentiate between "reservations" and the "historic areas of Oklahoma." The bureau offers the following explanation for making this distinction: "The historic areas of Oklahoma . . . consist of the former reservations which had legally established boundaries during the period 1900 to 1907. These reservations were dissolved during the two- to three-year period preceding the statehood of Oklahoma in 1907" (U.S. Bureau of the Census 1986:viii).

But as is so often the case with myths and apocryphal stories, references are vague regarding actual times and places, and allusions are made to certain indefinite "special laws," never mentioned by name but allegedly enacted by some governmental power just before Oklahoma statehood. As Indian attorney and legal scholar Browning Pipestem noted, "The detractors of tribal powers always make vague references to something that happened in this era that eliminated tribal sovereignty and jurisdiction" (Pipestem 1978:15). But what are these special laws which supposedly prevent Oklahoma Indians from having the same "reservation" status as Indian people elsewhere?

If one consults the BIA itself about these special laws, it is very difficult to find an official statement in print about exactly how Oklahoma reservations came to be "dissolved." The official, semiofficial, and sympathetic histories of the BIA simply don't mention anything about the reservation status of Oklahoma Indian land (Taylor 1972, 1983; Jackson and Galli 1977; Stuart 1978). This leads one to believe that BIA assertions about the dissolution of reservations will not stand up against even the slightest scholarly scrutiny. But the nonexistence of documents also leads to a logical dilemma in historical methodology: when something did happen, the search ends when the evidence is found. But when something didn't happen, how does one know when the search is finished? Perhaps someday a BIA official will emerge with an old presidential proclamation or federal statute that explicitly dissolved the reservations. But I haven't seen it yet.

Despite this lack of documentary evidence, just about any experienced BIA official will be glad to relate the "oral history" of how the present situation came into being.[1] They consistently take the position that when the allotment of Indian land was carried out in Oklahoma, it was done by reference to certain congressional acts that applied only to Oklahoma, and which had the effect of abolishing reservations there, whereas allotment did not have that effect elsewhere. So what are these acts that differentiated Oklahoma from other states and territories? The acts mentioned most frequently by BIA officials—and in fact it is a comprehensive list of the major legislation of that period—can be listed chronologically as follows: the 1887 General Allotment Act, the 1890 Oklahoma Organic Act, the 1897 Curtis Act, and the 1906 Oklahoma Enabling Act. These acts, I should note, specifically exempted the Osage reservation, which is why, according to the legal reasoning of the Bureau of Indian Affairs, the Osage reservation still persists. Of course, the underlying reason for Osage exemption was that even before allotment the tribe had signed oil and land leases with important sectors of the dominant society, who then undertook to prevent Osage allotment as a way of preserving their leases (Baird 1972:66–73). The continuation of the Osage reservation, then, exhibits the same logic as the alleged dissolution of the other reservations: it was the play of allotment against these other congressional acts that caused all the other reservations to be dissolved, but not the Osage reservation. But what is the true content of these acts? Do they in fact state that reservations shall cease to exist? To examine this issue more carefully, perhaps we should begin at the beginning, looking at the original texts with some strict legal definitions in mind.

WHAT IS A RESERVATION?

The legal definition of *reservation* cited most often is probably the one given in *United States* v. *Martin* (Murchison 1901, 1, sec. 73): "An Indian reservation is a part of the public domain set apart by proper authority for the use and occupation of a tribe of Indians. It may be set apart by treaty, act of Congress, or Executive order." Note that this definition says that reservations arose as the result of federal action. It does not state that reservation land is necessarily "owned" by a tribe or nation of Indian people. And in historic fact, reservation land has normally been "owned" by the federal government.

As a complement to this definition, the courts also decided, very early on, that since reservations are creations of the federal government, only the federal government can *dissolve* a reservation. In the pivotal case, *United States* v. *Celestine* (1909, 215 U.S. 278), we find the following definitive language, which is reflected in other important cases as well: "Only Congress can disestablish, diminish, or alter the boundaries of an Indian reservation. The Court has ruled that when a reservation has once been established, all tracts included within it 'remain a part of the reservation until separated therefrom by Congress'" (1909:278, 287–91).

In applying the legal definition of *reservation* to the historical situation in Oklahoma, we must recognize that the legal histories of the eastern and western halves of the state are somewhat different. In the east, which was called Indian Territory, the legal situation was defined by early treaties and legal precedents that explicitly pertained only to groups removed as part of the Indian Removal Act—such large nations as the Cherokees, Creeks, Choctaws, and Chickasaws, and smaller tribes such as the Kickapoos and Shawnees (Cohen 1982:770–97). These tribes in eastern Oklahoma were consistently excepted from the federal laws applied to the Plains Indian tribes that were later settled on reservations in the western part of the state. In the west, which was designated Oklahoma Territory, the same reservation status pertained and the same laws applied as those that governed Indian groups outside Oklahoma. That is, the legal situation of Indians in Oklahoma Territory was simpler because these groups had not been in contact with the U.S. government for such a long time and there was no huge and complex body of law in existence concerning their particular tribal affairs, as was the case with the Eastern nations.

Looking chronologically at the laws and statutes that supposedly dissolved the reservations in Oklahoma, we should first consider the two laws that created allotment in severalty, the most devastating blow to the physical integrity of reservation land. "Allotment in severalty" means that each Indian citizen of a tribe or nation was personally assigned a small plot of land from the reservation area, and the excess, or "surplus," land was sold to non-Indians. In the western part of the state, Oklahoma Territory, the law creating allotment in severalty was the General Allotment (Dawes) Act of 1887 (*U.S. Statutes* 1888:388–91). In the east, the document used to accomplish the same end was the Curtis Act of 1897 (Dale and Rader 1930:648–61). Let us examine these documents for any language that abolishes reservations.

The text of the General Allotment Act, entitled "An Act to Provide for the Allotment of Lands in Severalty to Indians on the Various Reservations," first of all recognizes that the land to be allotted is in fact reservation land. Not only is there no language abolishing reservations, but parts of the act imply that the reservation would *not* cease to exist after allotment was accomplished. For example, section 5 refers to "portions of [the tribe's] reservation not allotted." The same implication is contained in section 7, which provides for a planned distribution of water among the allotted Indians "within any Indian reservation." That is, in the entire document there is no statement that even implicitly dissolves reservations, and there are several explicit indications to the contrary.

If the General Allotment Act did not itself dissolve the reservations, perhaps subsequent agreements, ratifications, and proclamations did. But here we must consider that each reservation or group of Indian people had its own agreement and proclamation. For present purposes, I examine the case of one reservation I am familiar with, that of the Southern Cheyennes and Arapahoes in western Oklahoma. Even leaving aside the fact that this particular agreement was obtained by naked fraud, as Donald Berthrong and I have amply demonstrated (Berthrong 1976:148–81; Moore 1987: 210–13), it contains nothing threatening the reservation status of the federal land remaining after the "surplus" land was opened to non-Indians. Even so, the dramatic opening language of the agreement seems to imply that some momentous change has occurred in the reservation status of the land (*U.S. Statutes* 1891, sec. 13): "The said Cheyenne and Arapahoe tribes of Indians hereby cede, convey, transfer, relinquish, and surrender forever and absolutely, without any reservation whatever, express or implied, all their claim, title, and interest of every kind and character, in and to the lands embraced in the following described tract of country."

But all of this high-sounding language is quite irrelevant to the *reservation* status of the land, which derives not from Indian title but from federal title, as the legal definitions cited above clearly state, and as federal courts have decided time and time again from 1887 until the present day (Cohen 1982:770–97). In the case of the Cheyenne and Arapahoe reservation, substantial portions of land remained in federal hands—land in trust not only for individual Cheyennes and Arapahoes, but also for the agency offices, schools, for Fort Reno, and for other purposes. And it is important to note that despite all the trauma of allotment and the entry of thousands of non-Indians onto the reservation, all of the federal administrative agencies—offices, schools, and so on—continued their activities unabated, right through the allotment period to modern times, with no interruption (*Congressional Reports* 1952:1584–92). That is, the actual physical arrangements of the Cheyenne and Arapahoe reservation in Oklahoma after allotment were indistinguishable from the situations of reservations outside Oklahoma that were allotted in the same period and likewise invaded by non-Indians. Anyone visiting the Cheyenne and Arapahoe reservation in 1910, 1930, 1950, or right now would find the same constellation of federal, especially BIA, activities as anywhere else in the country.

But even if the agreement between the government and the Cheyennes and Arapahoes says nothing about dissolving the reservation, perhaps something in the presidential proclamation that resulted from the agreement can be construed as undermining the reservation status of trust and other lands remaining under federal control after allotment. In October 1890 the Jerome Commission concluded its work with the Cheyennes and Arapahoes and forwarded the agreement to Washington. In 1891 Congress approved the agreement without modification, and on April 12, 1892, a proclamation was issued by President Benjamin Harrison (*U.S. Statutes* 1892:1018–21). The proclamation, which quotes at length from the ratified agreement, merely specifies when and how the land will be opened to settlement, and also explicitly preserves the federal trust status of "the lands allotted to the Indians . . . or otherwise reserved in pursuance of the provisions of said agreement and the said act of Congress." There is nothing at all in the proclamation about reservation status, much less about any alleged dissolution of it. In sum, the whole body of documents generated by the General Allotment Act for the Cheyennes and Arapahoes merely allows the sale and settlement of "surplus" lands, and has nothing at all to say about disestablishing the reservation. And in general outline, the Cheyenne and Arapahoe documents are not much different from those generated by the allotment of other reservation lands, both inside Oklahoma Territory and elsewhere.

For Indian Territory, the eastern part of Oklahoma, the instrument of allotment was the Curtis Act, generalized from the Atoka Agreement, which concerned only the Choctaws and Chickasaws (Dale and Rader 1930:641–52). In the Curtis Act, as in earlier treaties and documents concerning Indian Territory, the term *reservation* is not the most popular word for describing the status of Indian land, although it is used. Just as often, reference is made to "Indian territory," the "Indian nation," or "the reserve." Nevertheless, whenever the federal courts were consulted in the nineteenth century about the "reservation" status of Indian Territory, they responded that the area constituted "reservations," and they did not hesitate to use the word and concept in their deliberations and decisions, wherever appropriate. The cases regarding the Choctaws, especially, established that Indian Territory constituted the combined reservations of the Eastern Indians who had been removed to what is now eastern Oklahoma (Murchison 1901:452–54).

The Curtis Act was passed in June 1897. Once again, far from explicitly dissolving the reservations of Indian Territory or removing federal authority, section 10 of the Curtis Act explicitly states that "nothing herein contained shall in any way affect any vested legal rights which may have been heretofore granted by act of Congress" (Dale and Rader 1930:656). In brief, like the General Allotment Act and its derivative documents, the various sections of the Curtis Act simply allot land, retaining some in trust status for individuals or other purposes, as in western Oklahoma; nothing at all is said about an end to reservations.

Another important federal act of this period was the Oklahoma Organic Act, passed in 1890, which was intended to ameliorate the legal differences between Oklahoma Territory and Indian Territory, thereby paving the way for the two areas to enter the Union as a single state. Here we have one of the magic documents of that period in which laws were allegedly passed to abolish reservations. But here again we look in vain for even a reference to reservations, particular tribes, or the issue of how the collective status of tribes and nations might change under the act or when statehood was achieved (Hill 1910, 1:276–90). And in this case, in the collateral documents there is an explicit statement that the Oklahoma Organic Act is not supposed to have *anything at all to do with the status of Indians and their reservations.* We shall see in a moment that such statements from U.S. congressmen during the course of debate carried considerable weight in subsequent court decisions that Oklahoma reservations did in fact persist after statehood. In any event, the *Congressional Record* quotes Congressman Charles Harley Mansur: "as this bill expressly declares, this Territorial government or organization is not for any Indian reservation whatever; it does not apply to Indian reservations. . . . I would like to have it understood, that the first twenty-four sections of this bill do not relate to a red man or to a tribe, do not relate to the Indians in any manner whatever" (*Congressional Record* 1890:2104, 2176). (The last part of the Oklahoma Organic Act, sections 24–44, also does not address itself to Indian people, but has to do with a rearrangement of judicial authority.)

The last important document from the statehood period that deserves our attention is the act of Congress that created the state of Oklahoma, the Oklahoma Enabling Act, passed in June 1906 (Dale and Rader 1930:707–22). Here again we find that the act does not dissolve reservations. In fact, it does the opposite; it guarantees that federal reservations will continue to exist. Speaking of the requirements for the new state's constitution, section 1 of the Oklahoma Enabling Act says that "nothing contained in the said constitution shall be construed to limit . . . or affect the authority of the Government of the United States to make any law or regulation respecting such Indians, their lands, property or other rights by treaties, agreement, law or otherwise which it would have been competent to make if this act had never been passed."

And in section 3 it is made even more explicit: the new state must "agree and declare that they forever disclaim all right and title in or to . . . all lands lying within said limits owned or held by any Indian, tribe, or nation; and that until the title to any such public land shall have been extinguished by the United States the same shall be and remain subject to the jurisdiction, disposal and control of the United States." Translated into ordinary language, these sections simply repeat the same long-standing principle stated in the definition of *reservation* I quoted earlier. The state government of Oklahoma was explicitly told at its inception that it could not legally intrude on reservation land or resources in any manner at all. Any legislation the state might pass in its legislature and any decisions that might be made in state courts were all irrelevant to the status of reservations in Oklahoma. Only the federal government, the creator of the reservations, could dissolve them.

Soon after the passage of the Oklahoma Enabling Act, a constitutional convention was called in Guthrie, Oklahoma, to design the governmental framework of the new state. Apparently following the instructions of the enabling act, the delegates to the state constitution inserted the following long sentence in Article 1, section 3, of the new constitution: "The people inhabiting the State do agree and declare that they forever disclaim all right and title in or to any unappropriated public lands lying within the boundaries thereof, and to all lands lying within said limits owned or held by any Indian, tribe or nation; and that until the title to any such public land shall have been extinguished by the United States, the same shall be and remain subject to the jurisdiction, disposal and control of the United States" (Bunn and Bunn 1907).

But even as the delegates to the constitutional convention were writing this language, they were involved in grand conspiracies to undermine Indian title, avoid interference from Congress, and gain direct access to Indian resources. That is, they conspired to "dissolve" the reservations in fact while upholding reservation status in principle. In designing a network of collusions, the conspirators counted on powerful support not only from others interested in gaining access to Indian resources in Oklahoma but also from certain wealthy citizens of Indian nations, and from the Department of the Interior, of which the Bureau of Indian Affairs is a part. During this period it became increasingly difficult to find anyone at all who was willing to advocate federal authority over the remaining reservation land or support the legal and especially property rights of ordinary Indians. Here, then, is the genesis of the mythology that "special laws" had dissolved the Oklahoma reservations.

CREATING THE MYTH

If the Bureau of Indian Affairs, upon reading the pertinent legislation passed by Congress to protect reservation status, had nevertheless decided administratively to do the opposite, it would not have been the first time. From Indian removal to *Harjo* v. *Kleppe,* the bureau has often operated contrary to the wishes of other branches of the federal government, the courts, and the Congress, and has sometimes even been described as a "rogue" or "outlaw" agency (Nickeson 1976; Moore 1988:182–88). The BIA has been investigated and reprimanded by Congress many times—as early as 1843 for its management of affairs in Indian Territory, and notably again in 1910, 1929, and 1952 (*Congressional Reports* 1843, 1910, 1952; *Senate Resolution* 1929).

So if we are to understand why the myth that Oklahoma reservations had been dissolved was created, we must begin with the idea that the bureau has never felt particularly obliged to do what Congress or the courts desire. The BIA has always had its own agenda and priorities. And we should also note, as a preface, that during the period in question—from 1887 to about 1920—the employees of the BIA in Oklahoma, the politicians of the state, and the non-Indians who lusted after Indian land and minerals were not three different and discrete self-interested groups; they were largely the same people. Just as there is now said to be a "revolving door" between the

Department of Defense and defense industries, or between the State Department and multinational corporations, so was there a revolving door at the turn of the century among (1) those who worked for the BIA selling and leasing Indian resources, (2) those who were actively buying land and prospecting for minerals, and (3) those who served in state offices. As Angie Debo so masterfully showed, the conspiracies to defraud Indians cut across the ordinary boundaries of private enterprise and officialdom (Debo 1940, 1941, 1970). In general, this was a dark and terror-filled period in Oklahoma history, a period in which those who merely stole from Indians were regarded as upright citizens when compared with those who kidnapped, tortured, or killed Indian people to get their way.

One episode from the constitutional convention well illustrates the general atmosphere of greed and disregard for law in Oklahoma at that time, as well as showing most of the essential components of the strategies for getting at Indian resources. Although it may seem strange in the recounting, it actually happened that some entrepreneurs who were entrusted with writing the new state constitution got together during mid-convention and conspired to use the activities of the convention itself to gain access to Choctaw and Chickasaw coal resources, which were then in federal trust status.

Devised under the leadership of Delegate John Leahy, the plan was to create a committee of the convention to travel to the Choctaw and Chickasaw reservations and offer to buy the subsurface rights to coal deposits which were worth, according to Leahy, "a hundred million dollars" (*Oklahoma Constitutional Convention* 1907, reel 1). Leahy said further that he knew of several delegates who were willing to make the trip and undertake the negotiations without compensation, and that if the Indians were unwilling to sell their lands to the still-nonexistent state of Oklahoma, he was sure these men of means would be willing themselves to "take the risk."

Concerning the possible objections of the Bureau of Indian Affairs and the Department of the Interior, another member of the proposed committee, Henry Cloud, assured the convention that he had heard unofficially that there would be no problems. The chairman of the convention, the legendary "Alfalfa Bill" Murray (later governor of Oklahoma), who claimed periodically to represent the Chickasaw Nation despite having no Indian ancestry at all, pointed out that the secretary of the interior had already agreeably reduced the royalties that must be paid to Indians from fifteen cents to eight cents.

When a delegate pointed out that the plan was patently illegal and contrary to the Atoka Agreement, the Curtis Act, and the Oklahoma Enabling Act, Delegate Cloud undertook to reassure the convention. He

had checked, he said, and their plan would not "cause a disturbance by the
Interior Department or by the Congress of the United States." Murray
added that he had talked with the leaders of the two tribes, some of whom
were delegates at the convention, and they were very anxious to make a deal
and distribute the money before statehood was approved: "I say to you
gentlemen, you can't appreciate the importance of getting control of those
lands. You have the opportunity; you have the people on the other side
willing to negotiate direct, and they are willing to go more than half way."
Delegate W. A. Ledbetter added that the deal had better be struck quickly
because "the Indian tribes, so far as their political autonomy is concerned,
are practically disintegrated."

In the end, the plan designed by Leahy, Murray, and others was only
partly successful (Debo 1940:79–85). But my purpose in recounting the
episode here is not so much to review the substance of the plan as to point
out the manner in which it was accomplished. The prime movers were
Oklahoma entrepreneurs who wanted cheap access to Indian resources.
Their allies were certain tribal officials, drawn from the "mixed-blood
elite," who wanted cash for their collusion and intended thereafter to
assimilate into the general white population of the new state. The major
opponent to these plans was Congress itself, which represented at least two
constituencies alluded to in the convention debate: those who truly wanted
to protect Indian land, many of them under the influence of the Indian
Rights Association; and those who were in competition with Oklahoma
entrepreneurs for Indian resources, the dastardly "Eastern syndicates" so
often denounced in convention proceedings (Miner 1976; Hagan 1985).
The Oklahoma interests finally prevailed by relying on regional and other
friendly congressmen to pressure the Department of the Interior and especially the Bureau of Indian Affairs to do administratively what could not be
done by reference to statute. They took the coal and the land, and later they
took the oil. To justify their disregard for federal law and Indian governments, they created the myth that the reservations had not merely been
allotted and diminished but "disintegrated" and "dissolved."

Just as the BIA, administratively, went far beyond its legal authority in
"abolishing" reservations, it also illegally abolished tribal governments,
creating a legal mess that has taken decades even to begin to resolve (Pipestem 1978). Here again, the motives of the group Miner called the "Territorial Ring" were essentially the same. They wanted to remove another
barrier to free access to Indian resources. With recognition administratively withdrawn from tribal governments, another avenue of Indian appeal
would be closed. The only alternative for Indian people was to appeal to the

state and federal courts, which were mostly controlled by the very people who wanted the Indians out of the way.

Even though the BIA in Oklahoma was steadily abolishing reservations and tribal governments in this period, the Washington headquarters of the BIA was frequently ambivalent, in the years just before and after the constitutional convention, concerning the issue of whether the Oklahoma reservations had in fact been disestablished by allotment in severalty. For example, even though the Cheyenne and Arapahoe reservation disappeared from the "Oklahoma Territory" section of the *Report to the Commissioner* after allotment of the reservation in 1891, it was included on an official list of reservations in 1896 and intermittently thereafter. But in 1906, with planning under way for the constitutional convention and with statehood imminent, an emboldened bureau contemplated the coming allotment of the Sac and Fox reservation and exulted that "another reservation will soon cease to exist" (*Annual Report* 1896:77). But in 1915 the Sac and Fox holdings and the Cheyenne and Arapahoe holdings, as well as the other Oklahoma areas, were mentioned once again as "reservations" (*Annual Report* 1915:157).

A few decades later, however, after the actual overseers of allotment had died or retired from the bureau, an event occurred that brings to mind Socrates' famous exchange with Glaucon in *The Republic of Plato*. After the two have decided that it would be necessary to create a body of convenient lies to tell to the people in their planned "Republic," Socrates asks, "Now, how may we get this fiction to be believed?" Glaucon's response is that "there is no way with the men who are in at the start of our state. But maybe their sons and those who come after will have some belief in it" (Richards 1942:71).

In the same way, those who created the myth that Oklahoma reservations had been dissolved had no belief in it, but it was easy to perpetuate the myth after its creators had retired or died. Beginning about 1930, all official references to Oklahoma "reservations" were dropped. From this point on, there is the increasing "certainty" that something definitive *must* have happened at the turn of the century to dissolve the Oklahoma reservations; and from this point reservations were omitted from maps and other government documents, with the vague and inaccurate "official statements" quoted earlier.

Most ironic of all, and totally in keeping with Glaucon's prediction, in 1953 the son of Alfalfa Bill Murray, Johnston Murray, himself now the governor of Oklahoma, made the following statement regarding the applicability of federal law to Oklahoma Indians (Murray 1953, October 31): "When Oklahoma became a State, all tribal governments within its boundaries became merged in the State and the tribal codes under which the tribes were governed prior to statehood were abandoned and all Indian tribes . . . came under State jurisdiction." And that is that, or is it?

JUDICIAL AUTHORITY

The apparent certainty about the dissolution of reservations that has been circulating in Oklahoma and in the administrative branch of the federal government since the turn of the century has never been shared by the federal courts. For a long time, however, the courts were not asked to rule on such issues. The people who might have asked embarrassing questions—the tribal governments—had been administratively dissolved, in part to prevent just this occurrence. It may also be that ordinary Indian people and their neighbors had come to believe the myth simply because it was said so often and with such certainty.

Still, there is some evidence that in the language and perceptions of ordinary Oklahomans, the reservations have never ceased to exist. For example, in my conversations with rural Indians since 1970 I have continuously heard references to local reservations, although sometimes these references are corrected by "educated" Indians who have been taught in public schools that there are no longer any reservations in Oklahoma "except for the Osage." But even in 1937 folk musician Woody Guthrie, who was raised in the town of Okemah in eastern Oklahoma, wrote the following lines in his song "Oklahoma Hills" (Klein 1980:97):

Way down yonder in the Indian Nation
Ride my pony round the reservation
In them Oklahoma Hills where I was born . . .

And although certain vestiges of the idea of Oklahoma reservations continued in the popular mind throughout the twentieth century, the continuation of reservations as a legal issue was simply not tested. With the encouragement of tribal governments after the passage of the Oklahoma Indian Welfare Act in 1936, however, and especially with the enactment of the 1948 Indian Country statute, Oklahoma Indians increasingly have been asking the courts whether they are living on reservations (Pipestem 1978; Cohen 1982). So far—in addition to the Osages—the Iowas, the Sac and Foxes, and the Cheyennes and Arapahoes have all established the reservation status of land under their control. Apparently, all they need to do to establish that they still have a "reservation" is go into court and ask.

But in some cases the court says no, when the historical context clearly indicates that abolition was the intent of Congress, as with certain lands of the Kickapoos, Cheyennes and Arapahoes, and Kiowas, Comanches, and Apaches. Both Pipestem and Cohen, however, feel that even these negative decisions can be remedied. In 1977, as these court decisions began to accumulate, the American Indian Policy Review Commission reported to Congress that "Congress has never specifically extinguished the reservation boundaries of many of the tribes, and it is not to be assumed that the various allotment acts constituted such an action." The commission said further that during the period of Oklahoma statehood and allotment in severalty "Congress knew exactly how to extinguish reservation boundaries" for Oklahoma tribes but did not choose to do it (American Indian Policy Review Commission 1977:521).

In summarizing the status of Oklahoma reservations, legal scholar Felix Cohen concluded:

> Whether a statute or agreement providing for cession or allotment of a reservation terminates, diminishes, or merely opens the reservation depends on the intent of Congress and the understanding of the Indians. A few court opinions have held or assumed that certain reservations in Oklahoma were terminated by such laws. There has been no judicial interpretation for many of the reservations in the state, and the Supreme Court has held that each statute or agreement should be examined individually. Whether tribal lands reserved from cessions constitute diminished reservations also has not been addressed. (Cohen 1982:775–76)

Pipestem added that "the question of whether the boundaries of Indian reservations in western Oklahoma have been disestablished by the various allotment agreements is complex and will, in most cases, require litigation to finally settle the issue" (Pipestem 1978:75–76).

So if the courts have decided that certain Oklahoma lands *are* reservations, and if the leading authorities on Indian law say that the status of other federal and Indian lands in Oklahoma has yet to be determined, how can the Bureau of Indian Affairs be so certain that the reservations have been disestablished, and why does it continue to perpetuate these old myths? The answers to these questions can be found in the continuing struggle between the BIA and modern organized Indian political entities—the various councils, incorporated tribes, and business committees formed in modern times, as well as the traditional Indian polities in Oklahoma that are older than the U.S. government, such as the Confederacy of Mvskoke Creek Tribal Towns and the Cheyenne Council of Forty-Four.

Everyone who works among Indian people knows that the struggle to preserve Indian resources is far from over. Native American polities on one side, and the BIA, pushed by various non-Indian political constituencies, on the other side, wage daily warfare over issues of sovereignty and access to Indian resources. The continuing refusal of the dominant society and its agencies to use the word *reservation* to describe Oklahoma Indian lands is only part of the continuing propaganda aspect of this war. The BIA's intention, evidenced by its stubborn refusal to use the word, is to discourage and demoralize the Indian side of controversies in Oklahoma. The term implies the existence of that whole cosmology of proper Indians, traditional communities, native language, and sovereignty that are part of Anglo-American expectations about "reservations." The disuse of the word implies that an Indian group has no leaders, no government, no land, and no rights. And that is why the BIA and its allies remain adamant; they do not want to concede that part of the ideological struggle.

In 1981 I served as a consultant to the Kiowas, Comanches, Apaches, Cheyennes, and Arapahoes in Oklahoma as they reenacted the events of their Grand Alliance of 1840. They had organized the affair to show their solidarity as the BIA began its efforts to close the Indian schools at Concho and Fort Sill. At an interlude in the proceedings I was standing with then-chairman of the Kiowas, Pressley Ware. Talking about the BIA, he said, "You know, there are two words which I use when I want to bring fear to the faces of BIA officials. One word is *nation*. When I say 'Kiowa Nation,' they know I am talking about treaties and sovereignty. And the other word is *reservation*. When I refer to the 'Kiowa Reservation,' they know I am talking about land rights and oil royalties. It makes them scared." Perhaps the time has come to rekindle an interest in the use of the word *reservation* to describe Indian land in Oklahoma. The word provides a legally correct and historically accurate description of the status of this land, from the creation of the first reservations in Oklahoma in 1816 until now, and it re-creates an ideological barrier which the dominant society must surmount in order to intrude further into Indian resources and Indian culture.

NOTES

For their comments and suggestions I thank Professor Kirke Kickingbird and Eddie V. Edwards of the Oklahoma City University School of Law, who are now looking in detail at the reservation status of Oklahoma Indian lands.

1. For example, in my interviews on October 19, 1989, with Terry Bruner, tribal government services officer, Anadarko Area Office, and with Rose Garbow, tribal operations specialist, Muskogee Area Office.

REFERENCES

AMERICAN INDIAN POLICY REVIEW COMMISSION. 1977. *Final Report*. 2 vols. Washington, D.C.: Government Printing Office.

BAIRD, W. DAVID. 1972. *The Osage People*. Phoenix: Indian Tribal Series.

BERTHRONG, DONALD J. 1976. *The Cheyenne and Arapaho Ordeal*. Norman: University of Oklahoma Press.

BUNN, CLINTON, and WILLIAM C. BUNN. 1907. *Constitution and Enabling Act of the State of Oklahoma*. Ardmore, Okla.: Bunn Brothers.

BUREAU OF INDIAN AFFAIRS. 1971. "Indian Land Areas." Foldout map. Washington, D.C.: Government Printing Office.

COHEN, FELIX S. 1982. *Felix S. Cohen's Handbook of Federal Indian Law*. Ed. Rennard Strickland. Charlottesville, Va.: Michie.

CONGRESSIONAL RECORD. 1890. 51st Congr., 1st sess. Vol. 21, pt. 3.

CONGRESSIONAL REPORTS. 1843. "Frauds in Indian Territory." Report 271.

———. 1910. "Investigation of Indian Contracts." Report 2273.

———. 1952. "Report with Respect to the House Resolution Authorizing the Committee on Interior and Insular Affairs to Conduct an Investigation of the Bureau of Indian Affairs." Report 2503, 82d Congr., 2d sess.

DALE, EDWARD EVERETT, and JESSE LEE RADER. 1930. *Readings in Oklahoma History*. New York: Row, Peterson.

DEBO, ANGIE. 1940. *And Still the Waters Run*. Princeton: Princeton University Press.

———. 1941. *The Road to Disappearance*. Norman: University of Oklahoma Press.

———. 1970. *A History of the Indians of the United States*. Norman: University of Oklahoma Press.

HAGAN, WILLIAM T. 1985. *The Indian Rights Association*. Tucson: University of Arizona Press.

HILL, LUTHER B. 1910. *A History of the State of Oklahoma*. 2 vols. Chicago: Lewis Publishing.

JACKSON, CURTIS E., and MARCIA J. GALLI. 1977. *A History of the Bureau of Indian Affairs and Its Activities Among Indians*. San Francisco: R & E Associates.

KLEIN, JOE. 1980. *Woody Guthrie*. New York: Ballantine Books.

MINER, H. CRAIG. 1976. *The Corporation and the Indian*. Columbia: University of Missouri Press.

MOORE, JOHN H. 1987. *The Cheyenne Nation*. Lincoln: University of Nebraska Press.

———. 1988. "The Mvskoke National Question in Oklahoma." *Science and Society* 52(2):163–90.

MURCHISON, KENNETH S. 1901. *Digest of Decisions Relating to Indian Affairs*. Washington, D.C.: Government Printing Office.

MURRAY, JOHNSTON. 1953. Correspondence. Oklahoma Bureau of Libraries Archives, Oklahoma City, Oklahoma.

NICKESON, STEVE. 1976. "The Structure of the Bureau of Indian Affairs." In *American Indians and the Law.* Ed. Lawrence Rosen, 61–76. New Brunswick, N.J.: Transaction Books.

PIPESTEM, BROWNING. 1978. "The Journey from *Ex Parte Crow Dog* to *Littlechief:* A Survey of Tribal Civil and Criminal Jurisdiction in Western Oklahoma." *American Indian Law Review* 6(1):1–80.

PROCEEDINGS OF THE OKLAHOMA CONSTITUTIONAL CONVENTION. 1907. Oklahoma Historical Society, Microfilm Document A-5, 3 reels.

RICHARDS, I. A. 1942. *The Republic of Plato.* New York: W. W. Norton.

SENATE RESOLUTION NO. 79. 1929. 70th Congr., 2d sess.

STUART, PAUL. 1978. *The Indian Office: Growth and Development of an American Institution, 1865–1900.* Ann Arbor: University of Michigan Research Press.

TAYLOR, THEODORE W. 1972. *The States and Their Indian Citizens.* Washington, D.C.: Bureau of Indian Affairs.

———. 1983. *American Indian Policy.* Mt. Airy, Md.: Lomond.

U.S. BUREAU OF THE CENSUS. 1986. *American Indians, Eskimos, and Aleuts on Identified Reservations and in the Historic Areas of Oklahoma.* Vol. 2, pt. 2, sec. 1. Washington, D.C.: Government Printing Office.

U.S. DEPARTMENT OF COMMERCE. n.d. *Federal and State Indian Reservations.* Washington, D.C.: Government Printing Office.

U.S. STATUTES AT LARGE. 1888. 49th Congr., vol. 24, chap. 119.

———. 1891. 51st Congr., vol. 26, sec. 13.

———. 1892. 52d Congr., vol. 27.

Without Reservation

Federal Indian Policy and the

Landless Tribes of Washington

FRANK W. PORTER III

Geographically defined communities of distinct ethnic origin throughout the United States have attracted the attention of social scientists for many years. Chinatown, Little Italy, Spanish Harlem, the black ghettoes—each invokes an image of a tightly knit, racially distinct, and ethnically similar community. Correspondingly, communities of American Indians have usually been associated with federal reservations located west of the Mississippi River. The Samish, Snohomish, Snoqualmie, Duwamish, Steilacoom, Cowlitz, and Chinook Indians of western Washington, however, do not convey such an image. Their status as American Indian tribes has been legally challenged, historically questioned, and anthropologically misunderstood.

Ethnohistorians studying the Indians of the Puget Sound area of western Washington have suggested three general categories of communities: (1) *reservation,* or *recognized,* Indians, who moved onto reservations and remained there; (2) *off-reservation* Indians, who either did not move onto reservations or moved on and then quickly left because of unfavorable conditions; and (3) *Indian descendants* of the many early marriages between non-Indian pioneers and Indians. The federal government, and specifically the Bureau of Indian Affairs (BIA), has incorrectly used these categories to establish the degree of Indianness and to determine the existence and maintenance of tribal identity of the landless tribes of western Washington. The possession of trust landholdings remains the main issue.

The United States has never adhered to a consistent policy in fulfilling its trust relationship with the landless tribes of western Washington. Nevertheless, the landless tribes have persistently battled to secure the treaty rights of their ancestors. Although the landless tribes have not been formally and legally recognized by the federal government, they have maintained their tribal identity, fought legal battles in both state and federal courts over treaty rights, and in recent years have petitioned the BIA for federal acknowledgment. The vicissitudes of federal Indian policy explain how and why the landless tribes have been denied recognition and their treaty rights.

TREATIES AFFECTING PUGET SOUND INDIANS

Isaac Ingall Stevens was appointed governor of Washington Territory in 1853. In addition he served as superintendent of Indian affairs, and the Indians of Washington were put on reservations through treaties concluded with Governor Stevens during the 1850s. Stevens and his commissioners adopted nine principles as guidelines in the treaties with the Indians of Puget Sound: (1) to concentrate the tribes as much as possible; (2) to encourage agriculture and other non-native economic activities; (3) to pay for the land they had taken from the Indians with annuities consisting of useful commodities instead of cash; (4) to provide teachers, doctors, farmers, blacksmiths, and carpenters; (5) to prohibit war between the tribes; (6) to end slavery; (7) to terminate the liquor trade; (8) to allow the Indians to continue to hunt, fish, and gather berries; and, eventually, (9) to allow division of the reservation land in severalty (Kappler 1904:661–64, 669–77).[1] Some argue that this was an enlightened policy because it allowed for a period of transition and a process of gradual assimilation, but the treaty negotiators erroneously assumed that these changes could be realized by the economic shift from hunting, gathering, and fishing to farming; that the federal government would honor the treaties; and that all of the tribes could be persuaded that the treaties were in their best interests (Richards 1979).

These treaties—Point Elliott, Medicine Creek, and Point No Point—established eighteen reservations. Four were in the Neah Bay Agency, nine were under the Puyallup consolidated agency, and five were under the Tulalip Agency. The sole purpose of these treaties, according to Commissioner of Indian Affairs Charles E. Mix, was to extinguish Indian title to large tracts of land "which were needed for the extension of our settlements, and to provide homes for the Indians in other and more suitable locations, where they could be controlled and domesticated." Even before the treaties had been negotiated, strong inducements were held out to white settlers to emigrate and settle in Washington Territory, and a considerable amount of Indian land was already occupied by whites before the treaties were ratified by Congress. The Indians firmly believed that "they were to be dispossessed of it without compensation or any provision being made for them."[2]

The federal government's failure to promptly ratify the treaties and to protect the Indians' land created the framework for the future development of Indian policy in the state of Washington. Indians in the Puget Sound area quickly became disaffected with the federal government, and Commissioner of Indian Affairs William P. Dole urged the immediate fulfillment of the treaties in order to restore the tribes' confidence. In 1861, goods were for the first time distributed to the Duwamish, Suquamish, and Clallam tribes, who relocated on reservations. The Chehalis, Chinook, and Cowlitz tribes, who had refused to sign treaties in 1855, now indicated their willingness to enter into agreements with the federal government as well. Dole pointed out that "a tract of land on the Chehalis river, at the mouth of Black river, which has been surveyed, is deemed a suitable reservation for the Upper Chihalis and Cowlitz bands; and it is believed that the Lower Chihalish and the Chinooks may, without difficulty, be associated with the Qui-nai-elts and Qui-leh-utes upon their reservation."[3]

At the same time Indian officials in Washington Territory were recommending increases in the number and size of reservations, the Department of the Interior was developing a plan to consolidate the existing reservations. In 1858 Commissioner Mix complained that the major problem with the management of Indian affairs in Oregon and Washington was "the insufficiency of one superintendent for the great extent of country, and the numerous tribes and large number of Indians in the two territories."[4] Commissioner Dole remarked in 1861 that it would have been "fortunate if some territory had been reserved in the northwest, as is the case in the southwest, upon which these and all other tribes of that State could be congregated. There is, however, no unorganized territory remaining."[5] This was a critical point because there were many tribes and bands with whom no treaties had been negotiated, and several tribes and bands had been promised reservations that had not yet been created.

As early as 1863, Commissioner Dole had suggested the creation of only two reservations for all the Indians in Washington Territory, one located in the interior and the other on the Pacific coast. Dole also recognized a problem attendant to such a situation: "It is said to be a fact, notorious to all observers, that Indians reared in the interior, and accustomed from childhood to its products, cannot be induced to remain upon the coast; and that those raised on the coast, and accustomed to sea-fish and weed, cannot be induced to remain in the interior."[6]

POLICY OF CONCENTRATION

In the 1870s there was a steady stream of migrants to the Pacific Northwest, and white settlers rapidly occupied the desirable land. As the population of settlers continued to increase, the Indians were crowded into smaller and smaller areas. To ease friction between Indians and emigrants in the Northwest Territory, the Department of the Interior intensified its program of concentration and resettlement. The original treaties contained provisions anticipating the consolidation of all the bands in Washington Territory onto a single reservation. Numerous small bands of Indians were forced to live on reservations, while at the same time many of the reservations were reduced in size to provide more land to white farmers. J. Q. Smith, commissioner of Indian affairs at this time, thought that the reservations that should be consolidated were the Indian Territory, the White Earth Reservation in northern Minnesota, and a reservation in the southern part of Washington. Although he admitted to knowing very little about southern Washington, he singled out the Yakima Reservation as the most likely candidate for consolidation "because it is well known that the Indians there . . . have made remarkable progress."[7]

E. C. Watkins, the U.S. Indian inspector, proposed for geographic and ethnographic reasons the continuance of only two reservations. Oregon and Washington are naturally divided by the Cascade Mountains, which range north and south from British Columbia to southern Oregon. The only natural passageway connecting the two regions is the Columbia River. These physical features created a natural boundary between tribes along the coast and those in the interior. More significant, the tribes in each of these distinct ecological zones possessed very different cultures. Watkins observed that those "of the coast are accustomed to water; are skillful in constructing and managing canoes, and subsist mostly on fish; while those of the interior are more athletic, skillful horsemen, and subsist on game, berries, and the products of the soil." Watkins gave very little consideration to Indians residing along Puget Sound, believing that only the Skykomish and a few other tribes "would prefer to remove to a reservation along the coast." Watkins identified a second category of Indians, those who were adopting agriculture as their way of life. These Indians, he argued, could be consolidated on the Puyallup Reservation, which was centrally located, contained sufficient arable land, and offered access to a branch of the Northern Pacific Railroad, which ran through it. Watkins believed that four thousand Indians could be placed on the Puyallup Reservation, thus vacating eleven reservations in the Puget Sound area.[8]

THE DAWES ACT

The attempt to consolidate the reservations in Washington was never implemented. The Dawes Act, passed in 1887, sought to break up the reservation system by providing individual allotments to each adult Indian. Commissioner of Indian Affairs Hiram Price stated that "the allotment system tends to break up tribal relations. It has the effect of creating individuality, responsibility, and a desire to accumulate property. It teaches the Indian habits of industry and frugality, and stimulates them to look forward to a better and more useful life, and, in the end, it will relieve the government of large annual appropriations."[9]

"It has become the settled policy of the Government to break up reservations, destroy tribal relations, settle Indians upon their own homesteads, incorporate them into the national life, and deal with them not as nations or tribes or bands, but as individual citizens," declared Commissioner of Indian Affairs T. J. Morgan in 1890. "The American Indian is to become the Indian American." Morgan noted that the Puyallups, because of the operation of the land-in-severalty law, were quickly becoming citizens and slowly moving away from governmental supervision.[10]

The Dawes Act aimed to break up tribal life and establish the Indians on private farms. The act also stated that every "Indian born within the territorial limits of the United States to whom allotment shall have been made under the provision of this Act, or under any law or treaty, and every Indian born within the territorial limits of the United States, who has voluntarily taken up, within said limits, his residence separate and apart from any tribe of Indians therein, and has adopted the habits of civilized life, is hereby declared to be a citizen of the United States and is entitled to all the rights, privileges and immunities of such citizens" (St. John 1914:12). This did not necessarily make these Indians citizens of the states in which they resided, however. In Washington, for example, the state constitution declared that Indians not taxed could not vote.

Charles M. Buchanan, superintendent in charge of the Tulalip Agency, was highly critical of the Dawes Act: "I know of instances where allotments have been made to an Indian without his application, without his knowl-

edge, and without his desire—where in twenty-five years he has never set
foot upon his alleged land, does not know where it [is] and does not want it.
He is in possession of land that he does not want and citizenship that he does
not know, much less understand" (St. John 1914:12).

Allotment was a radical departure from the Indian concept of land
tenure. To Indians the land was a whole; individual parcels were unknown.
The allotments were supposed to be sufficient to allow a family to make a
living by farming, but in reality little attention was given to the quality of
the land or the interests and abilities of the families. "The real aim of this
bill is to get at the Indian lands and open them up to settlement," stated a
House committee minority report. "The provisions for the apparent benefit
of the Indians are but the pretext to get at his lands to occupy them. . . . If
this were done in the name of greed, it would be bad enough, but to do it in
the name of humanity, and under the cloak of an ardent desire to promote
the Indian's welfare by making him like ourselves, whether he will or not, is
infinitely worse."[11]

Admittedly, some Indians readily occupied their allotments and became
successful farmers. These were, however, the exceptions. Indian Agent
Daniel C. Govan, in his annual report for the Tulalip Indian Agency,
observed that the Indians were not, as a rule, systematic farmers. "Farming
is with them the incident and not the business of every-day life," he noted.
"Some of them, the more thrifty and industrious, have well-cultivated
farms and comfortable houses and are anxious to have their children educated; they generally live like white people." But most Indians in the latter
part of the nineteenth century continued to practice traditional subsistence
activities. During the salmon season, many Indians spent most of their time
fishing. In the fall, both young and old went to the hop fields. During these
outings they met old friends from Puget Sound and spent time gambling
and drinking.[12]

Govan believed that this seasonal round of activities was extremely
detrimental to the Indians, but he depicted only one side of the situation.
Life on the reservations was frequently strained by the inability of the agents
to meet the subsistence needs of the resident Indian population. One observer remarked in 1877: "These Sound Indians go in the old style, in
canoes, taking along whole families—men, women and children, dogs and
chickens, guns, fishing lines, gambling utensils, and every other conve-
nience, luxury and article of property incident to Indian life."[13] Most of the
families so described were en route to the hop fields. The consequences of
this exodus were both good and bad. On the one hand, the Indian agents

were relieved that their charges could earn money to reduce subsistence costs on the reservations. Conversely, the agents worried about the adverse influences the Indians would be exposed to in the hop fields; even worse, whites could trespass on or take possession of Indian land not being used or occupied during hop-picking season.

Because most of the reservations were not suited for agriculture, the Indians were forced to seek food and employment off the reservation. In 1899 Edward Mills, reporting from Tulalip, stated that he could only estimate the statistics for the annual report because of the "migration of the Indians to the fish canneries, the berry patches, the hop fields, etc. etc."[14] Many of these families, while retaining their affiliation with their tribes, ultimately purchased land and remained off the reservation.

Life on the reservations in the late nineteenth century was complicated by several factors. Charles Buchanan pointed out that the progress of the Indians "has not been large, it has been slow and painful. By white standards it has been pitiful; by Indian standards it has been remarkable." He identified the major obstacles to progress as insufficient educational facilities, vicious and meddlesome white men, the inherent conservatism of the older Indians, the prevalence of liquor, and the common lack of fair play in business dealings between whites and Indians.[15]

Federal Indian policy focused primarily on those Indians associated with reservations. As early as 1870 it became evident that a considerable number of Indians throughout the Puget Sound area would not, and in many instances could not, live on the reservations. C. C. Finkbonner stated that the "Sahmish and No-Wha-At, two small remnants of tribes, persistently refuse to come and live on the reservation. They would rather live and roam at will in all their ancient and nomadic grandeur."[16] In time, the members of these tribes, bands, and families came to be commonly known as "unattached Indians." W. F. Dickens, superintendent at Tulalip, observed that "the so-called unattached Indians are very scattered from Tacoma on the south to Canada on the north and from the west coast back to the Cascade Mountains. It is these unattached Indians that have received so little attention in my opinion from the local authorities and this is because of their scattered condition and isolation, and the difficulty of reaching them." Although the unattached Indians were located throughout Washington, the largest concentration was in Clallam County.[17] Other identifiable settlements were noted in the Nooksack River and Skagit River valleys. A considerable number of unattached Indians were also living in King County near Tolt, Snoqualmie, and Auburn. These unattached Indians became the present-day landless and nonrecognized tribes of Washington.

By the close of the nineteenth century, federal authorities had identified three "classes" of Indians on the reservations in Washington:

There are the old Indians sixty-five and over who have had practically no schooling, no training of any sort and live much in the customs of the past. These Indians are generally honest, industrious in their own way, and until they are very aged are independent. The second class are those from forty to sixty who have had a little training in school, have lost much of the more worthy characteristics of the aborigine and are generally rather shiftless, lack interest in home making and are more or less a drawback to progress. Their homes are not well kept and they lack the qualities of either Indian or White. Not all by any means of this age are so backwards, but it is at this age that we find the most shiftless of the Indian people. Those under forty have nearly all had some schooling and show the advantages.[18]

Such was the situation in 1900. Indians residing on the reservations demonstrated various stages of assimilation into white society. Indians living off-reservation, while maintaining close ties with their kin, were gradually integrating into the mainstream of white society. The landless Indians also retained close ties with kinfolk living on the reservations, maintained a political relationship with Bureau of Indian Affairs personnel, and persevered in their efforts to realize the promises made to their ancestors in the treaties signed by Governor Stevens. Before 1914 these activities were individual tribal efforts. The time had come for the presentation of a unified demand to the federal government.

NORTHWESTERN FEDERATION OF AMERICAN INDIANS

The Northwestern Federation of American Indians was created in 1914 to pursue claims to the treaty rights of the unattached and unallotted Indians throughout western Washington. Under the leadership of Thomas G. Bishop, a Clallam Indian, author, and political lobbyist in the nation's capital, a constitution and by-laws were approved on February 23, 1914. In the succeeding years the federation devoted most of its attention to the pursuit of Indian claims. As one member succinctly stated, the federation had been created "for the purpose of digging into our treaty rights which had been neglected and for the purpose of getting the value of the land paid to us either by allotment or cash."[19]

On May 20, 1916, Bishop, as president of the federation, submitted to the BIA a large number of applications for enrollment and allotment with the Indians of Quinault Reservation in Washington. More than forty tribes were represented in these applications; furthermore, a significant number of these tribes had been previously provided with reservations and had received allotments on them.

Bishop stated that between two and three thousand such applicants belonging to the various tribes in northwestern Washington were eligible to share in the lands and funds of the Indians of Quinault Reservation under the provisions of the executive order of November 4, 1873, which had enlarged the reservation for the Quinaults, Quillehutes, Hohs, and Quits, and "other tribes of fish-eating Indians on the Pacific Coast." The Department of the Interior requested a decision as to just which tribes were to be included as "fish-eaters on the Pacific Coast."[20] On September 16, 1916, the solicitor for the Department of the Interior rendered an opinion that limited the tribes entitled to enrollment and allotment on the Quinault Reservation to those "fish-eating Indians" south of Neah Bay or the Makah Reservation to the mouth of the Columbia River. This did not include all unattached Indians as far east as the Cascades. Furthermore, only those Indians whose tribes or bands had been party to the Treaty of 1855–56, who were members of the tribes or bands named in the Executive Order of November 4, 1873, and the Act of March 4, 1911, and those found to be in affiliation with the Indians on Quinault Reservation were to be eligible.[21] The solicitor required a separate eligibility showing for each individual applicant.

On May 16, 1912, the superintendent at Quinault submitted more than five hundred applications for enrollment. A careful examination, however, showed that the superintendent's investigation had been unsatisfactory. Many applicants did not submit any evidence in support of their claim, although they "appeared to be persons of Indian blood." Apparently the Quinault Tribal Council had passed the applicants en masse without offering any explanation for "adopting" nearly all of those who had applied. No attempt was made to demonstrate that the applicants were "poor or homeless or belonged to the fish-eating tribes of the Pacific Coast."[22]

On October 12, 1912, the Office of Indian Affairs remanded the cases to the superintendent and ordered a thorough investigation. The cases were returned with the superintendent's report of August 12, 1913, but the applications were still found to be unsatisfactory. Cato Sells, commissioner of Indian affairs, asked BIA special agent Charles Roblin to carefully examine "each application and aid the applicant so far as practicable in furnishing the evidence indicated to the end that you may be in a position to make a definite recommendation for or against enrollment with the Indians of Quinault Reservation."[23] In instances in which the tribal council had failed to demonstrate that an applicant met all the criteria, a new tribal council was to be convened in order to supply the additional information.

It was obvious that many of the applications submitted by Bishop would have to be denied. The Office of Indian Affairs requested that separate enrollment be made of all the applicants who could not be enrolled or allotted at Quinault and that a full report be made about the unattached and homeless Indians who had not previously received any benefits from the federal government.[24]

Cato Sells believed that many of the applicants to be included in the separate enrollment actually belonged to tribes for whom reservations had already been created. These individuals would have to submit formal applications to Roblin with accompanying substantiating evidence or testimony. "It is probable that many unattached Indians, especially of the Puget Sound region, who have not submitted applications through Mr. Bishop, will ask enrollment," Sells informed Roblin. "These are to be included in the separate enrollment and report to be made by you."[25]

The unattached and unallotted Indians of the Puget Sound area increasingly became a major point of discussion because of the enrollment issue at Quinault. Bishop continued to represent these Indians as they sought to establish their treaty rights. Tulalip superintendent W. F. Dickens informed the commissioner of Indian affairs in 1921 that the BIA was in a "position of technical guardianship, possible donor and 'Big Brother' to the unattached and unallotted Indians."[26] Dickens noted that if Roblin "could have remained on the job as tenaciously as [Bishop], or if your local agent had the clerical force to compile this data and force it all to an end, it would be far better and less expensive than to permit the Indians, in self defence, to organize into a headless council where they can be dominated by unscrupulous and dishonest leaders."[27]

Representatives of the Northwestern Federation of American Indians prepared a lengthy document outlining the claims of the Indians who had been signatories to the Treaty of Point Elliott. They noted that western Washington was "one of the very few places where the white people have ever been permitted to move onto Indian country to settle and occupy the same without the Indians' rights having been settled for and extinguished." At Dickens's request, a meeting of the federation was held on December 10, 1921, at the Potlatch House on the Tulalip Reservation. The Indian representatives at this meeting drafted and approved a resolution stating their position. Bishop introduced the historical documents that resulted in the legislation allowing the landless tribes of Washington to present their case to the Court of Claims.[28]

The United States cannot be sued without its consent, but it may be sued with its consent in any court or tribunal that Congress creates or designates for this purpose, with such terms or conditions and regulations as Congress sees fit to prescribe. This rule applies to claims by Indians against the United States because "the moral obligations of the Government toward the Indians, whatever they may be, are for Congress alone to recognize, and the courts can exercise only such jurisdiction over the subject as Congress may confer upon them" (Cohen 1942:373–78; Rosenthal 1976).

In 1925 Congress passed a law permitting the aboriginal tribes of Puget Sound to sue the federal government for injustices stemming from the Point Elliott, Point No Point, and Medicine Creek treaties. The U.S. Court of Claims did not reach a decision in *Duwamish et al. Tribes of Indians* v. *United States* until 1934, and the findings offered little satisfaction to the Indians because of the court's strict adherence to limitations placed on its jurisdiction by Congress. For example, the court determined that the Oregon Donation Act of 1850 had cost the Lower Skagits about 15,000 acres but ruled not to compensate this claim. The court argued that it could only pass judgment compensating claims growing out of treaties, not claims based on acts of Congress. A similar decision was made for the Upper Chehalis, Muckleshoot, Nooksack, Chinook, and San Juan Island tribes, none of which had signed treaties. The court ruled it was without jurisdiction when the federal government had given the Indian owners of the land no formal recognition by signing a treaty or passing an act acknowledging their title by right of occupancy.[29]

The Court of Claims recognized the "marked and irrefutable" failure of the federal government to honor the treaties made with the Puget Sound Indians. Nevertheless, no award was given because of the difficulty in appraising the value of the lost lands. It was the Indians' responsibility to demonstrate the monetary value of the loss, and the court believed their proof was inadequate. Furthermore, the 1925 claims law stipulated that the Court of Claims must deduct the government's counterclaims from the total amount granted to the Indians. These included treaty annuities, post-treaty moving fees, school administration costs, and health care expenditures accumulated during the seventy-five years following the treaties. These counterclaims amounted to over $2 million, substantially more than the amount the court decided that the Indians deserved for their claims. Consequently, the court dismissed the case without giving the Indians anything. Twenty years of hard work had resulted in little more than an education in U.S. law (Rosenthal 1976).

INDIAN REORGANIZATION ACT

The Indian Reorganization Act (IRA) of May 15, 1934, also known as the Wheeler-Howard Act, provided a means by which tribes could become recognized. Section 19 of the act included definitions of *Indians, tribes,* and *adult Indians.* The act specifically applied to "all persons of Indian descent who were members of any *recognized* [my emphasis] tribe now under Federal jurisdiction." A tribe was defined as "any Indian tribe, organized band, pueblo, or the Indians residing on one reservation."[30] John Collier, commissioner of Indian affairs at this time, instructed his superintendent to report unrecognized tribes because the BIA was "particularly anxious to get information on 'lost' or homeless bands of Indians."[31] Although the IRA was not perceived as a means of expanding federal trusteeship, several previously unrecognized tribes did in fact gain federal acknowledgment.

Many tribes throughout the United States did attempt to gain recognition through the IRA. Despite these efforts, the BIA did not always follow through administratively with promises made to nonrecognized tribes. This was particularly true for the landless tribes of Washington. All the nonrecognized tribes in Washington tried to obtain official federal acknowledgment by organizing under the IRA. Their futile efforts help to illustrate the continuing and growing dilemma of nonrecognition.

Snoqualmie

In the late 1930s, under the leadership of Chief Jerry Kanim, the Snoqualmie tribe tried to organize under the IRA. Because the tribe had never been given a reservation and had never identified itself to the satisfaction of the BIA with any of the tribes that had reservations administered by the Tulalip Indian Agency, the Snoqualmies were informed by George LaVatta, field agent for the BIA, that it would be necessary to establish a reservation or landholdings for the tribe before organization could take place. LaVatta strongly urged officials at the BIA to secure suitable and sufficient land for the Snoqualmies.[32]

On March 20, 1937, H. D. McCullough, the credit agent, outlined to E. M. Johnson, the land field agent, the necessary steps to secure a reservation for the Snoqualmie tribe. The establishment of new reservations was a matter for administrative determination. According to circular L.A. 3077, which related to the land acquisition program for the Tulalip jurisdiction, the BIA recommended the purchase of a tract of land in Townships 25 and 26, watered by the Tolt River and other small streams. This tract, the circular noted, could be "designated for all homeless Washington Coast Indians not otherwise provided for, but to be governed by the unallotted Snoqualmie band."[33] Superintendent O. C. Upchurch at the Tulalip Reservation declared in his *Report of Planning Committee of Tulalip Indian Agency* that the "only recommendation for the next Ten-year period of this band of Snoqualmie Indians is the acquisition of such a reservation."[34] Unfortunately, the Snoqualmie band under the leadership of Chief Kanim was not asked to vote to implement the IRA because they had no reservation or community property.

The creation of a Snoqualmie reservation eventually became a dead issue. Although no specific reason was given to Chief Kanim, it seems that by 1945 the BIA had completely changed its position. With regard to land purchases under the IRA, the BIA recommended the immediate abandonment of long-standing cases and use of the money on other lands. These funds could no longer be encumbered for purchases that could not be completed.[35] H. M. Critchfield, director of lands in the Department of the Interior, provided a more specific reason why no Snoqualmie reservation was created. In a letter to Douglas Clark he explained that the lands purchased had to be able to produce the revenue for repayment, or the tribe had to prove that it possessed other funds with which to repay the loan.[36] Clark, in turn, notified Upchurch that any land acquisition projects from the proposed revolving credit fund would have to be submitted by August 15, 1944. This gave the Snoqualmies less than two weeks to comply. Surprisingly, Upchurch informed Clark that "because of unfavorable market at present for the purchase of land, I do not believe it advisable at this time to urge any such purchases for the Tulalip jurisdiction."[37] The Snoqualmies are still awaiting the creation of their reservation.

After 1944 the tribe became less active. William Martin, chairman of the Snoqualmie tribe, informed BIA officials that the lapse of annual meetings was due to the gasoline shortage. At the last meeting, the tribe had voted to turn their remaining funds into war bonds. Significantly, the Snoqualmies also voted "to continue their organization and continue to work for a reservation and an allotment of land."[38] The Snoqualmies continue as a tribe, but the BIA has never fulfilled its promise to create a separate reservation for them.

Steilacoom

The Steilacoom tribe also decided to organize under the IRA. George La-Vatta and Superintendent Nicholson agreed that approximately half of the tribe satisfied the requirements of the IRA. After considerable deliberation with their attorney, the Steilacooms decided to join with the Nisquallys in their attempt to organize. This would allow them to retain members who had less than one-half Indian blood. On October 8, 1936, the subject of reorganization and joining with the Steilacooms was discussed with Willie Frank and George Bob of the Nisquallys. Both men favored the proposition but thought that the majority of the Nisquallys would oppose the idea. Many believed that "the Steilacoom would eventually take over all offices and dominate over the Nisquallys should they join up with them under a Constitution and By-Laws."[39] Bob and Frank, however, viewed the situation from a different perspective: "The Nisqually tribe have nothing in the way of tribal property or even a reservation, . . . they are backward and do not have the education that is possessed by the Steilacoom, so therefore, by joining with the Steilacoom group, they could profit to a great extent and would have nothing to lose."[40]

LaVatta notified the Steilacooms that if the Nisquallys were unwilling to accept them into their organization, then it would be necessary for them to submit affidavits to the Office of Indian Affairs. The commissioner of Indian affairs made a direct inquiry to LaVatta about the status of the Steilacoom tribe. In response, both Nicholson and LaVatta concluded that the Steilacooms should continue to pursue organization under the IRA. In fact, the BIA proposed transferring the Steilacooms to the Ozette Reservation.[41]

It was at this particular juncture that the Nisquallys became embroiled in a fishing rights case in the U.S. District Court for the Western District of Washington Southern Division. All attention became riveted on this case, *Peter Kalama et al. v. B. M. Brennan et al. and State of Washington*. The next official mention of the Steilacooms' efforts to organize was on April 9, 1941, when Binns & Cunningham, attorneys at law, contacted Superintendent Phillips at the Indian Agency in Hoquiam. Cunningham stated that some Steilacooms had contacted him with the "proposition of perfecting a tribal organization." He had investigated the matter and "found that there had been some attempts and lack of unity."[42] Phillips responded "that some steps were had several years ago to organize this tribe but little or nothing was then accomplished in the way of organization mostly because of the disunion among the persons concerned and their failure to present the Department proof of their Indian ancestry."[43] In a final letter to the chairman of the Steilacoom tribe, LaVatta explained that "these benefits are somewhat limited at the present time due to the national emergency, however, your people might want to establish their identity as Indians under the law."[44] Nothing more was done.

The IRA was a complete failure as far as the other landless tribes of

Washington were concerned. In every single instance the BIA failed to carry out the intent and purpose of the act. Furthermore, several of the tribes—the Snoqualmie in particular—had received promises of federal recognition, reservations, and services from the BIA. The outbreak of World War II, the shortage of gasoline, and another major change in federal Indian policy closed this chapter of the landless tribes' quest for recognition.

FORMALIZING THE POLICY OF NONRECOGNITION

In 1947 Kenneth R. L. Simmons became the attorney for the Snoqualmie tribe after Arthur E. Griffin, the tribe's former attorney, died in an automobile accident. Simmons, whose law firm was located in Billings, Montana, continued the land claims cases initiated by Griffin. Simmons immediately contacted F. A. Gross about the status of the Snoqualmies. Gross responded that "the Snoqualmie Tribe of Indians has never received any benefits to speak of from the Government. They occupied the territory in the vicinity of Seattle and have never been given a reservation nor have very many of them ever received homestead allotments on the Public Domain."[45] Chief Kanim had asked Gross the previous year whether the Snoqualmies had any right to land on the Tulalip Reservation. Gross acknowledged that the Snoqualmies had a legitimate claim but added that "the Tulalip Tribes of the Tulalip Reservation, incorporated under the [IRA], would contest the rights of any other Indians not duly enrolled on said reservation, and . . . what rights the Snoqualmie tribe might have had on the Tulalip Reservation in the past, these rights were extinguished at the time these Indians accepted the provisions under the Act of June 18, 1934."[46] After 1948 the Snoqualmies and the other landless tribes became increasingly involved in fishing rights issues and suits under the Indian Land Claims Commission.

Simultaneously, the Department of the Interior developed an administrative policy of nonrecognition of the landless tribes. In September 1951 the Samish tribe notified Raymond H. Bitney, superintendent of the Western Washington Agency, that it intended to close its enrollment. Bitney responded that it would be necessary for the Samish to secure legislation through Congress to establish the necessary machinery for the tribe to do that. Appended to the bottom of this letter, however, was the following note: "I would appreciate hearing from you on the above matter as this is another case of where a group of Indians, or group of people who have some Indian blood, are now attempting to establish themselves as a Tribe, when to my knowledge, they have no restricted property and only a few with a small amount of Samish blood may have been the recipients of a trust patent on public domain allotments. Frankly, I think we should have *some policy* on the handling of matters of this type of case."[47] Bitney initiated an inquiry to determine the identity of the Indians in the Tulalip band or group known as the Tulalip Tribes, Incorporated.

At this critical juncture Bitney began to question the rights and authority of the Tulalip Tribes, Inc. He noted that in the Treaty of Point Elliott the "so-called Tulalip Indian Reservation was to be set aside for *all* of the members of the various tribes that participated in the making of the treaty. Yet, the Tulalip tribes of the Tulalip Reservation are apparently reserving for themselves the exclusive right to manage and handle any and all tribal property on the Tulalip Reservation, regardless of the fact that a number of the members of the other tribes reside off the Tulalip Reservation."[48] The landless tribes asked Bitney to determine "whether the fact that they live off the Tulalip Reservation has extinguished these rights to the use and benefit of any tribal property or the proceeds of any tribal property."[49] Bitney agreed to examine the situation. In the meantime, he made one critical observation: "there are no Tulalip Indians appearing in the treaty."[50]

The legal status of the landless tribes became an increasingly significant question. Bitney realized that dual enrollment and confusion in the tribal rolls were problems that had plagued both the recognized and nonrecognized tribes. Bitney directed Wilfred Steve, chairman of the Tulalip Tribes, Inc., to investigate the census rolls. Steve reported that he had visited the Swinomish Reservation and contacted Tulalip enrollees residing there. He had also visited the Snoqualmies and found a great number of Tulalip Indians residing there. Sebastian Williams stated at a meeting of the Tulalip Board of Directors that his attempt to bring the different tribes together for a census roll meeting had failed because they were not interested. Steve agreed to visit these tribes and to contact individuals and families enrolled at Tulalip.[51]

On May 15, 1953, the Committee on Interior and Insular Affairs of the House of Representatives distributed a "Questionnaire on Tribal Organizations." Although this questionnaire was seeking information to support the federal government's withdrawal of services from tribes, it also provided detailed summaries of the status of the landless tribes. Shortly after the questionnaire was distributed there appeared a "Summary Statement of Withdrawal Status" for the tribes under the jurisdiction of the Western Washington Agency.

The questionnaire afforded Bitney the opportunity to prepare detailed reports about each of the landless tribes. Bitney's report was an accurate and sympathetic account of the landless tribes. Unfortunately, his information fell on deaf ears, and nothing was done to alleviate the plight of these tribes. The report not only recognized the tribal status of the landless tribes but also emphasized their legal right to the benefits promised in the treaties negotiated with Governor Stevens. Bitney cautioned the commissioner of Indian affairs to obtain a solicitor's opinion from the BIA about the rights of the landless tribes before pursuing withdrawal legislation. D. C. Foster, area director, was opposed to an omnibus termination bill covering all of the tribes of western Washington. "A general termination bill now would unleash such a storm of protest from the Indians, their attorneys, and many elements of the general public that we would have an almost impossible climate to work in," he cautioned the commissioner. "Conditions are so varied, rivalries between some of the tribes so serious that an omnibus bill would, in our opinion, cloak the Bureau in the role of a villan and destroy the friendly relations which we have now generally re-established."[52]

Foster also urged that grouping the western Washington area for BIA planning purposes be on the basis of trust land ownership patterns, and not on the basis of tribes, treaty tribal groupings, or other broad categories not connected directly to land. "We see little or no purpose in the Bureau concerning itself with tribes who have no trust real property (or government real property held for their use)," Foster argued, "and whose only special connection with the Federal Government is the settlement of their claims."[53] Included in this group were the Samish, San Juan Island, Satsop, Skagit, Snoqualmie, Steilacoom, and other landless groups. On the basis of trust land ownership patterns, Foster suggested that BIA planning be directed at the eighteen reservations and the public domain allotments, and not on the thirty-five or thirty-six tribes previously considered. This was the first time the BIA stated a policy of disengagement from the landless tribes. It was directly related to the tribes' lack of trust land.

INTER-TRIBAL COUNCIL OF WESTERN
WASHINGTON INDIANS

The Northwestern Federation of American Indians disbanded in 1949. The Inter-Tribal Council of Western Washington Indians was eventually created to take its place, and it immediately assumed responsibility to represent the status and needs of the landless tribes. On February 9, 1954, representatives from ten western Washington tribes met formally to organize the council. Wilfred Steve, from the Tulalip Reservation, and Joe Hillaire tried to get the delegates to accept the proposed constitution and by-laws, but several delegates were reluctant. George Adams, chairman of the Skokomish Tribal Council and dean of the House of Representatives of the Washington State Legislature, was urged to speak on their behalf. Adams was not sympathetic "to the folks there who were looking for a dollar, but he was sympathetic to the old Indians and [said] that they should try to get the old Indians a bit of comfort." He also urged them to "cooperate with the Indian officials to bring about these things as regards education, health, welfare, hospital services and a program for tomorrow and not sit there and talk about the past."[54] Martin Sampson, who claimed to be chief of the Swinomish tribe, stated that "the treaty was the only law that the Indians had—that they had to hang on to the treaty—that they must have that treaty." He further declared: "Regardless of what these tinhorn lawyers say and do about your property, don't betray that treaty, because as long as the treaty is in effect, the Indians can't lose their rights whether they live on or off the reservation—so hang on to that treaty."[55]

At the next meeting, on February 18, 1954, Lyman Kavanaugh directed attention to the recognition of the nonreservation Indians, expressing his opinion that they should be recognized in the Inter-Tribal Council and in the proposed termination bill. Several delegates from the landless tribes forcefully urged that the nonreservation Indians be given more recognition and a greater role in the proceedings. Wilfred Steve, as president of the Inter-Tribal Council and a leader of the Tulalip Tribes, Inc., expressed his belief that "the non-reservation Indian should have recognition as well as the reservation Indian."[56]

A second set of the February 18, 1954, minutes of this meeting record a different and more heated version of the discussion. Kavanaugh remarked that "too little was said for the non-reservation Indian . . . , they should be given more consideration." McDermott noted that "all non-reservation Indians were treated as poor relations." The issue of nonreservation Indians almost prevented the formation of the Inter-Tribal Council. McDermott asked that the word *property* at the heading of the proposed bill be stricken. Kavanaugh took the floor and declared that if that word was not stricken, the Samish tribe might withdraw from the Inter-Tribal Council. The word was removed from the bill.[57]

Raymond Bitney questioned the authority of the Inter-Tribal Council to represent all of the Indians in the Western Washington Agency. "We should be very careful about recognizing any such group as having the authority to speak for or represent the Indians under the Western Washington Agency jurisdiction," he cautioned the commissioner of Indian affairs.[58] What Bitney failed to realize was that the Inter-Tribal Council was the legal successor to the Northwestern Federation of American Indians, an organization that had been representing and pressing for Indian rights in Washington since 1914.

In a confidential letter to E. Morgan Pryse, area director, Bitney offered a completely different reason for Steve's desire to create the Inter-Tribal Council. He stated that for over two years Wilfred Steve, Joe Hillaire, Sebastian Williams, and Tandy Wilbur had been carrying on an active campaign to force him to follow their interpretation of the regulations regarding the cutting of timber on restricted Indian allotments on the Tulalip, Swinomish, and Lummi reservations, and on restricted Indian land, formerly the Tulalip Agency Reserve. Steve had even been placed under a $500 bond for timber trespass.[59]

The controversy between Bitney and Steve was quickly coming to a head. Pryse reiterated his position to the commissioner of Indian affairs on February 11, 1954, noting that the controversy concerned ownership of lands and the authority of the various tribes to manage their resources without federal intervention. There was more to this controversy than meets the eye. As early as 1952, Bitney had been deeply concerned about the Tulalip Tribes, Inc., issuing and transmitting certain funds drawn on the treasurer of the United States. Under direct orders from Pryse, Bitney sequestered the funds and credited them to "Special Deposits" until he received instructions for their final and legal disposition. If the Tulalip Tribes, Inc., were legally recognized as a tribe, he would deposit the funds in the treasury to the credit of the "Revolving Funds for Loans." On August 11, 1952, Bitney wrote to the attorney general of the United States about the treaty rights conferred by the treaties of 1855 on the descendants of the various treaty tribes. "First, I should like to repeat that there is no Tulalip Tribe nor has there been one of record before January 24, 1936. That one was created under the Indian Reorganization Act of June 18, 1934."[60] The IRA was the only source of authority, said Bitney, for "exercising [power] over tribal property and tribal rights created under the Point Elliott Treaty and which the other tribes' descendants claim that these people do not possess."[61]

On July 7, 1952, Bitney wrote to G. Warren Spaulding, director of programs in Washington, D.C., and outlined the developing controversy. Steve, former chairman of the Tulalip Tribes, Inc., had demanded that the old Tulalip Agency site and buildings be turned over to the Tulalip Tribes, Inc., because the site had always been tribal property and was occupied by the Tulalip Indians. Bitney's research demonstrated that the agency and school grounds had been purchased by the government in May 1860 from non-Indian owners who had acquired the property through the Donations

Claim Act at Tulalip before the reservation was created by executive order on December 23, 1873. Bitney further stated that the Point Elliott treaty embraced "some 22 bands, groups or tribes and that these people still claimed a share of the properties at Tulalip." Referring to *Duwamish et al.* v. *United States,* Bitney concluded that the "Tulalip Tribes, Inc. have no claim on the site and further, their present title on a portion of it is invalid since the true facts were not presented to the Department when it was turned over to them as there is no Tulalip Tribe and the other Indians' rights under the Treaty have not been extinguished so they would have a share in any reservation properties." The identity of the Tulalips lay at the heart of the controversy.[62]

The argument of the Tulalip Tribes, Inc., was somewhat tenuous. On August 9, 1951, the Tulalip Tribes, Inc., had petitioned the Indian Claims Commission for payment of damages because of the alleged failure of the United States to act in their interest. The assistant attorney general stated in part: "Defendant alleges that if any of the petitioner Indians or ancestors or predecessors in interest of the members of the Tulalip Tribes, Inc. constituted a separate and distinct Tribe, band or group of Indians (which is denied) any territory used by them was used and occupied only in common with other Tribes, bands, or groups of Indians, and the exclusive 'possession' of said territory was not recognized by other Tribes, bands or groups of Indians, or by the United States." Significantly, the findings declared it "would appear that the Tulalip Tribes, Inc. is not a tribe, but a community organization."[63] Ironically, the landless and nonrecognized tribes won their claims cases but saw them dismissed because the counterclaims of the federal government exceeded the award.

Wilfred Steve used the Inter-Tribal Council to further his assault on Bitney and to establish recognition for the Tulalip Tribes, Inc., as the only legal successor to the Point Elliott treaty. At a meeting of the council on February 6, 1954, Steve accused L. P. Towle (assistant area director) of bias in the matter and of supporting Bitney. Steve sought the support of the landless tribes to remove Bitney from office, but they refused because Bitney supported their treaty rights.[64] As soon as Steve realized that he had lost the support of the landless tribes, he directed all of his attention to establishing the Tulalip Tribes, Inc., as the sole successor to the Treaty of Point Elliott.

The year 1955 became a critical one for the landless tribes. The Snoqualmies adopted a resolution on October 20, 1955, requesting "that any income that the Tulalip Tribes, Inc. received from the Government buildings located at the former Agency reserve and recently turned over to the

Tulalip Tribes, Inc. under a Use Permit, be impounded until the Solicitor
has rendered a decision as to which Indians are entitled to an interest in the
unreserved tribal lands on the Tulalip Reservation." "Although it is the
opinion of this office that the Snoqualmie Tribe does not have any rights
insofar as the buildings, located on the former Tulalip Agency Reserve, are
concerned, we wish to call your attention to the fact that they feel quite
strongly about the Tulalip Tribes, Inc. 'running' the affairs on the reservation," stated C. W. Ringley to Don C. Foster. "We believe this is a continuation of their efforts to prove their 'treaty rights' in the unreserved tribal
lands on the Tulalip Reservation."[65] The Tulalip Tribes, Inc., sought to
terminate certain supervisory powers reserved to the secretary of the interior
in the Tulalip Corporate Charter. In Solicitor's Opinion M-36181, "it was
concluded that the Indian title to the unallotted lands on the Tulalip
Reservation is now vested in the Tulalip Tribes, Inc."[66]

This solicitor's opinion sealed the fate of the landless tribes of Washington. The BIA had taken a firm stand that the absence of trust land
holdings among the landless tribes prevented them from receiving any
services and being accorded recognition. A series of decisions made by the
BIA when the landless tribes attempted to prepare enrollment lists in the
1960s further articulated the government's position. In 1967, Sammy Kay
Landover attempted to enroll in the Nez Perce tribe, but the question of
whether she was enrolled as a Snoqualmie delayed her application. Fred H.
Claymore, acting superintendent of the Western Washington Agency, informed the Nez Perce tribal chairman that "the Snoqualmie Indians have no
reservation and are scattered through Western Washington. The tribe as it
existed at the time of the Treaty of Point Elliott *is no longer a recognized tribe,*
and the United States government considers the Snoqualmie Indians only
descendants of members of the Tribe as it existed at the time of the Treaty."
"Therefore," Claymore concluded, "Mrs. Landover cannot be considered a
member of the Snoqualmie Tribe because the Tribe is not recognized to be
an entity."[67] In 1968, Chester J. Higman, the enrollment officer, informed
Isaac Kinswa of the Cowlitz tribe: "There are some very limited exceptions
for Indians who are recognized members of a reservation tribe, but these do
not apply to the Cowlitz who are not a reservation group and who are not
presently recognized as an organized tribe by the United States."[68]

The 1960s marked the entrenchment of nonrecognition as a means of
denying services to the landless tribes. In the absence of any official procedure for a tribe to achieve federal recognition, the landless tribes continued to exist in a no-man's-land. Not until the creation of the Federal
Acknowledgment Project in 1978 would there be another opportunity to

achieve federal recognition. Significantly, the Samish and Snohomish petitions for federal recognition were turned down, while the Jamestown Clallams were recognized. The major distinction between the three tribes was that the Jamestown Clallams maintained possession of a very small parcel of trust land.

The creation of reservations in Washington Territory was an attempt by the federal government to extinguish the Indians' right of possession. From the outset the federal government—and specifically the BIA—failed to honor the treaties and fully implement the reservation system. Federal officials sought various stopgap measures throughout the late nineteenth and early twentieth centuries to satisfy the needs and demands of those tribes and bands that had been promised reservations that were either never created or were substantially reduced in size. The legal quagmire of the landless tribes of Washington exemplifies the failure of the reservation system.

NOTES

1. The history of Indian-white relations in Washington has not been well documented. For a general background see Charles F. Coan, "The Federal Indian Policy in the Pacific Northwest, 1849–1870" (Ph.D. diss., University of California, 1920); Douglas D. Martin, "Indian-White Relations on the Pacific Slope, 1850–1890" (Ph.D. diss., University of Washington, 1969); and American Friends Service Committee, *Uncommon Controversy: Fishing Rights of the Muckleshoot, Puyallup and Nisqually* (Seattle: University of Washington Press, 1970).

2. Commissioner of Indian Affairs, *Annual Report* (Washington, D.C.: Government Printing Office, 1858), pp. 354–59.

3. Commissioner of Indian Affairs, *Annual Report* (Washington, D.C.: Government Printing Office, 1861), pp. 639–43.

4. Commissioner of Indian Affairs, *Annual Report,* 1858, pp. 354–59.

5. Commissioner of Indian Affairs, *Annual Report,* 1861, pp. 639–43.

6. Commissioner of Indian Affairs, *Annual Report* (Washington, D.C.: Government Printing Office, 1863), pp. 133–46.

7. *Proposed Consolidation of Reservation.* Senate Executive Document 20 (Washington, D.C.: Government Printing Office, 1877); Commissioner of Indian Affairs, *Annual Report* (Washington, D.C.: Government Printing Office, 1876), pp. 384–91.

8. *Letter from the Secretary of the Interior.* Senate Executive Document 20 (Washington, D.C.: Government Printing Office, 1877), pp. 1–2. See Erna Gunther, "The Indian Background of Washington History," *Pacific Northwest Quarterly* 41 (July 1950):190.

9. Commissioner of Indian Affairs, *Annual Report* (Washington, D.C.: Government Printing Office, 1881), pp. 1–7, 13–19.

10. Commissioner of Indian Affairs, *Annual Report* (Washington, D.C.: Government Printing Office, 1890), p. iii.

11. Quoted in Harold E. Fey and D'Arcy McNickle, *Indians and Other Americans* (New York: Harper and Brothers, 1959), p. 73.

12. Annual Reports, Tulalip Indian Agency, RG 75 BIA, Tulalip Indian Agency, Boxes 311–17; Sand Point Regional Archives, Seattle, Washington. Unless otherwise specified all documents cited are from the Sand Point Regional Archives in Seattle, Washington.

13. *Weekly Pacific Tribune,* August 31, 1877, p. 3.

14. Annual Reports, Tulalip Indian Agency, RG 75 BIA, Tulalip Indian Agency, Boxes 311–17.

15. Ibid.

16. C. C. Finkbonner, Annual Report for 1870, Lummi Reservation, RG 75 BIA, Tulalip Indian Agency, Boxes 311–17.

17. Annual Reports, Tulalip Indian Agency, RG 75 BIA, Tulalip Indian Agency, Boxes 311–17.

18. Ibid.

19. Minutes of a meeting held by W. F. Dickens, superintendent, at the Potlatch House, Tulalip Agency, Tulalip, Washington, December 10, 1921, RG 75 BIA, Western Washington Agency, Tribal Operations Branch, General Correspondence (Old Tahola/Tulalip) ca. 1914–1951, Box 258; Constitution of the Northwestern Federation of American Indians, Western Washington, February 23, 1914, at Tacoma, Washington, RG 75 BIA, Tulalip Indian Agency, Tribal Operations Branch, Box 259.

20. Cato Sells, Commissioner of Indian Affairs, to Charles E. Roblin, November 27, 1916, RG 75 BIA, Western Washington Agency, Tribal Operations Branch, General Correspondence, (Old Tahola/Tulalip) ca. 1914–1951, Box 259.

21. Ibid.

22. Ibid.

23. Ibid.

24. Ibid.

25. Ibid.

26. Dickens to Commissioner of Indian Affairs, July 30, 1921, RG 75 BIA, Western Washington Agency, Tribal Operations Branch, General Correspondence, (Old Tahola/Tulalip) ca. 1914–1951, Box 258.

27. Ibid.

28. "Claim of the Indians Embraced Within the Pt. Elliott Treaty," RG 75 BIA, Tribal Operations Branch, Box 259. Minutes of a meeting held by W. F. Dickens, Superintendent, at the Potlatch House, Tulalip Agency, Tulalip, Washington, December 10, 1921. RG 75 BIA, Western Washington Agency, Tribal Operations Branch, General Correspondence, (Old Tahola/Tulalip) ca. 1914–1951, Box 258.

29. "Federal Claims Courts to Get Indian Suits," *Seattle Post-Intelligencer,* January 19, 1926; *Duwamish et al. Tribes of Indians* v. *United States* (79 Court of Claims 530) 1934.

30. See also Kenneth R. Philp, ed., *Indian Self-Rule: First-Hand Accounts of Indian-White Relations from Roosevelt to Reagan* (Salt Lake City: Howe Brothers, 1986).

31. John Collier, Commissioner of Indian Affairs, Circular 3022 to Superintendents, on "Information on Non-enrolled landless Indians of one-half or more Indian blood, pursuant to Section 19 of the Wheeler-Howard Act," September 7, 1934.

32. George P. LaVatta to E. M. Johnson, March 16, 1937, RG 75 BIA, Tulalip Indian Agency, Boxes 311–17.

33. Circular L.A. 3077, Bureau of Indian Affairs, Department of the Interior.

34. O. C. Upchurch, Report of Planning Committee of Tulalip Indian Agency Washington 1944–1954.

35. Walter V. Woehlker to Douglas Clark, May 25, 1945, RG 75 BIA, Tulalip Indian Agency, Boxes 473–75.

36. H. M. Critchfield to Clark, August 1944, RG 75 BIA, Western Washington Agency, General Correspondence, 1952–68, Decimal 103.3-109, Box 0017.

37. Clark to O. C. Upchurch, August 1944, RG 75 BIA, Western Washington Agency, General Correspondence, 1952–68, Decimal 103.3-109, Box 0017.

38. H. M. Critchfield, Director of Lands, to Commissioner of Indian Affairs, July 2, 1944, RG 75 BIA, Portland Area Office, Realty Division, Jurisdiction Files, 1935–61, Instructions 1935–37, Box 178.

39. William Martin to F. A. Gross, May 16, 1945, RG 75 BIA, Tulalip Indian Agency, Records of Tribal Councils 1925–52, Snoqualmie, Box 4.

40. Frank D. Beaulieu to N. O. Nicholson, October 13, 1936, RG 75 BIA, Tahola Indian Agency, Decimal File 100.3, Box 90.

41. LaVatta and N. O. Nicholson to Commissioner of Indian Affairs, June 10, 1937, RG 75 BIA, Tahola Indian Agency, Decimal File .064, Nisqually and Quileute, Box 85.

42. Nicholson to Commissioner of Indian Affairs, August 9, 1938, RG 75 BIA, Tahola Indian Agency, Decimal File .064, Nisqually and Quileute, Box 85.

43. Binns & Cunningham to Floyd H. Phillips, April 9, 1941, RG 75 BIA, Tahola Indian Agency, Decimal File .064, Nisqually and Quileute, Box 85.

44. Floyd H. Phillips to LaVatta, April 14, 1941, RG 75 BIA, Tahola Indian Agency, Decimal File .064, Nisqually and Quileute, Box 85.

45. LaVatta to Joe Eskew, July 3, 1941, RG 75 BIA, Tahola Indian Agency, Decimal File .064, Nisqually and Quileute, Box 85.

46. Gross to Kenneth R. L. Simmons, May 11, 1947, RG 75 BIA, Tulalip Indian Agency, Records of Tribal Councils 1925–52, Snoqualmie, Box 4.

47. Gross to Chief Jerry Kanim, April 1947, RG 75 BIA, Tulalip Indian Agency, Records of Tribal Councils, 1925–52, Snoqualmie, Box 4; my emphasis.

48. G. S. Myer to Russel V. Mack (House of Representatives), November

1951, RG 75 BIA, Western Washington Agency, General Correspondence, 1952–68, Box 11; my emphasis.

49. Raymond H. Bitney to E. Morgan Pryse, October 17, 1950, RG 75 BIA, Tulalip Indian Agency, Records of Tribal Councils, 1925–52, Box 479.

50. Ibid.

51. Bitney to Pryse, October 13, 1950, RG 75 BIA, Tulalip Indian Agency, Records of Tribal Councils, 1925–52, Box 479.

52. Regular Meeting of the Tulalip Board of Directors, January 10, 1950, RG 75 BIA, Tulalip Indian Agency, Records of Tribal Councils, 1925–52, Box 479.

53. Ibid.

54. Bitney to Pryse, February 9, 1954, RG 75 BIA, Western Washington Agency, Tribal Operations Branch, General Correspondence, 1953–70, Decimal File .060, Box 260.

55. Ibid.

56. "Recommendations Prepared by the Executive Board of the Inter-Tribal Council of Western Washington Indians, February 13, 1954 at Seattle," RG 75 BIA, Western Washington Agency, Tribal Operations Branch, General Correspondence, 1953–70, Decimal File .060, Box 260.

57. "Minutes of Meeting of Inter-Tribal Council of Western Washington Agency, February 18, 1954, RG 75 BIA, Western Washington Agency, Tribal Operations Branch, General Correspondence, 1953–70, Decimal File .060, Box 260.

58. "Inter-Tribal Council Meeting 2/18/54," RG 75 BIA, Western Washington Agency, Tribal Operations Branch, General Correspondence, 1953–70, Decimal File .060, Box 260.

59. Bitney to Commissioner of Indian Affairs, February 19, 1954, RG 75 BIA, Western Washington Agency, Tribal Operations Branch, General Correspondence, 1953–70, Decimal File .060, Box 260.

60. Pryse to Commissioner of Indian Affairs, February 11, 1954, RG 75 BIA, Portland Area Office, Tribal Council Minutes, 1952–65.

61. Bitney to Attorney General of the United States, August 11, 1952, RG 75 BIA, Portland Area Office, Tribal Council Minutes, 1952–65.

62. Bitney to G. Warren Spaulding, July 7, 1952, RG 75 BIA, Portland Area Office, Tribal Council Minutes, 1952–65.

63. Ibid.

64. "Minutes of Meeting of Inter-Tribal Council of Western Washington Indians, February 6, 1954, RG 75 BIA, Portland Area Office, Tribal Council Minutes, 1952–65; Mary M. Hansen to L. P. Towle, February 6, 1954, RG 75 BIA, Portland Area Office, Tribal Council Minutes, 1952–65; Chief Jerry Kanim to Pryse, January 11, 1954, RG 75 BIA, Portland Area Office, Tribal Council Minutes, 1952–65.

65. C. W. Ringley to Don C. Foster, October 25, 1955, RG 75 BIA, Portland Area Office, Tribal Council Minutes, 1952–65.

66. Ibid.; Vincent Little to Samuel H. Koenig, December 30, 1964, RG 75 BIA, Western Washington Agency, Tribal Operations Branch, General Correspondence, 1953–70, Decimal File .063.

67. Fred H. Claymore to Nez Perce Tribal Chairman, July 28, 1967, RG 75 BIA, Western Washington Agency, Tribal Operations Branch, General Correspondence, 1953–70, Decimal File .063; my emphasis.

68. Chester J. Higman to Isaac Kinswa, September 27, 1968, RG 75 BIA, Western Washington Agency, Tribal Operations Branch, General Correspondence, 1953–70, Decimal File .063.

REFERENCES

COAN, CHARLES F. 1920. "The Federal Indian Policy in the Pacific Northwest, 1849–1870." Ph.D. diss., University of California.

COHEN, FELIX. 1942. *Handbook of Federal Indian Law.* Washington, D.C.: Government Printing Office.

GUNTHER, ERNA. 1950. "The Indian Background of Washington History." *Pacific Northwest Quarterly* 41:189–202.

KAPPLER, CHARLES J. 1904. *Indian Affairs, Laws and Treaties.* Vol 2. Washington, D.C.: Government Printing Office.

MARTIN, DOUGLAS D. 1969. "Indian-White Relations on the Pacific Slope, 1850–1890." Ph.D. diss., University of Washington.

PHILP, KENNETH R., ed. 1986. *Indian Self-Rule: First-Hand Accounts of Indian-White Relations from Roosevelt to Reagan.* Salt Lake City: Howe Brothers.

RICHARDS, KENT D. 1979. *Isaac I. Stevens: Young Man in a Hurry.* Provo, Utah: Brigham Young University Press.

ROSENTHAL, HARVEY D. 1976. "Their Day in Court: A History of the Indian Claims Commission." Ph.D. diss., Kent State University, Kent, Ohio.

ST. JOHN, LEWIS H. 1914. "The Present Status and Probable Future of the Indian of Puget Sound." *Washington Historical Quarterly* 5:12–21.

Uncommon Controversy: Fishing Rights of the Muckleshoot, Puyallup and Nisqually. 1970. Seattle: University of Washington Press.

WASHBURN, WILCOMB E. 1975. *The Assault on Indian Tribalism: The General Allotment Act (Dawes Act) of 1887.* Philadelphia: J. B. Lippincott.

PART III

POWER AND SYMBOLS

Riding the Paper Tiger

ROBERT L. BEE

For years accepted analytical practice has tried to fit reservation-federal relations into a series of general models or types: colonialism throughout the nineteenth century and into the twentieth; assimilation as a fellow traveller after the mid-1800s and extending into today's vocational training and urban relocation programs; "development," both as heavy-handed paternalism and client-centered therapy, for Indians as a special group and as part of the growing underclass; and the metropolitan-satellite model as a distinctive subset of both the colonial and "development" models.

Yet the past three decades, 1960–90, seem the most difficult to portray with a single analytical model or theory. One of the reasons is the increasing complexity of the issues, partly a residue of both intended and unintended effects of past policies. But there is also a lack of policy focus compared with earlier periods. The various components of the Indian policy apparatus leap from issue to issue, and policy has become increasingly ad hoc (Deloria 1985b:254).

This is not necessarily an unhappy situation for Indian rights. The most disastrous policy periods have featured a single-minded policy cant: removal, termination, assimilation. But although most Indian communities are relatively better off now than in 1960, the 1987 revelations in the *Arizona Republic* and the ensuing congressional investigations underscore two urgent needs: a comprehensive, informed, systematic rearticulation of basic policy; and a major effective effort to implement and enforce it. [1]

Ironically, the period since 1960 has not wanted for informed recommendations for policy overhaul.[2] And basic policy concepts have also been reaffirmed or developed: tribal sovereignty, federal trust protection, the government-to-government relationship, and Indian preferences. But such reaffirmation and development have come mostly from adversarial confrontations before the law, not from innovative, comprehensive, and informed policy overhaul (Barsh and Henderson 1980:256; Wilkinson 1987:9). Policy action caroms off one concept only to bash into another, and then another, keeping the policy play in motion without much apparent refinement of basic concepts or resolution of perennial issues. In fact, the most basic of the policy concepts—tribal sovereignty and the federal trust responsibility—remain logically and operationally contradictory regardless of the semantic gymnastics they are put through (Bee 1982:25; Prucha 1984, 2:1205–6). This scarcely helps to dissipate the aura of policy ad-hoccery.

I think it is pushing materialist-oriented models too hard to see all this as a product of capitalist economics (cf. Jorgensen 1971). Policy ad-hoccery has abetted the exploitation of Indian resources, and Indian economic poverty and the commercial interests of non-Indians are key factors in any analysis of Indian-federal relations (see Weiss and Maas, *this volume*). But an analytical model that focuses more specifically on relations of domination between individuals and groups lends another necessary dimension to understanding the recent past of policy dynamics and the structure of Indian-federal relations. The model is based on the work of Max Weber, in particular the ideal types and dynamic relationships he drew from analysis of nineteenth-and early twentieth-century German politics. It proceeds from Weber's declaration that "without exception every sphere of social action is profoundly influenced by structures of dominancy. . . . [T]he structure of dominancy and its unfolding is decisive in determining the form of social action and its orientation toward a 'goal' " (Weber 1968, 3:941).[3]

Superficially, some Weberian notions strike us now as commonsensical: nobody needs to tell folks in Washington that power matters, for example; and everyone knows something—typically unpleasant—about bureaucracy. So the challenge here is to take a well-worn analytical approach and impose it on a situation familiar to most readers in order to offer systematic insight and the possibility of comparison with other cases and other times.

I have assumed that most readers are generally acquainted with the events of the past three decades, and I do not dwell on detailed descriptions except as necessary for illustration or substantiation (see Officer 1971; Tyler 1973; Barsh and Henderson 1980; Deloria 1985a, Deloria and Lytle 1984; Prucha 1984; Taylor 1984).

ON DOMINATION

Key to Weber's analytical technique is the careful description of ideal types of social structures and belief systems (*ideal* in this essay meaning "what is expected," not "what is most desirable"). Once developed, these ideal types are then compared with actual structures and belief systems. The discrepancies between the ideal and the real draw attention to important causal variables and provide a means for comparing one case with another.

The concept of domination is a subset of the broader concept of power. Power is simply "the possibility of imposing one's will upon the behavior of other persons" (Weber 1968, 3:942). Weber described two basic types of domination: *domination by authority*—that is, the power of command and obedience[4]—and *domination by constellations of interest,* in which parties not bound together by coercion or statute voluntarily agree to follow orders or an agenda because they perceive it is in their best interest or advantage to do so (Weber 1968, 3:943). For our purposes it is more helpful to view the two as referring generally to "official dominance" and "dominance by influence," respectively. Congress, for example, is officially endowed with plenary power over Indian affairs and is capable of issuing "commands" that are binding on other elements in the policy apparatus. Within the executive, the official hierarchy of domination is helpfully drawn out on flowcharts that grace office walls—lest someone forget. Indian tribes, of course, are not in an official position to "command" any federal office to do anything. Instead they, along with (but decidedly not in concert with) private corporations and the various states, attempt domination through influence. Policy analysts have described "power clusters" that subordinate their separate interests to the larger one of influencing the legislative process to some common end (Ogden 1971:5; cf. Taylor 1984:123).

Both of these pure types of domination are involved in actual policy dynamics, and the distinction between them becomes blurred in the behavior within and between the various groups or components of the policy process. Each component uses both the official structure of power relations and the informal leverage of common interest to obtain the upper hand in making decisions that affect the others.

Weber subdivided domination by authority into three subtypes: *traditional domination, charismatic domination,* and *legal domination.* Each rests on a different principle of justification or legitimation for the exercise of power. The most relevant for considering relations between the tribes and the government is the legal type of domination, whose legitimation is based on written laws, statutes, and regulations (Weber 1968, 3:954).[5] But I will argue later that the traditional basis of authority and legitimacy has had an important effect on those relations as well (cf. Nelson and Sheley 1985:182, 187).

Within the legal type of domination by authority Weber distinguished two basic traditions: the *formal* (or bureaucratic) and the *substantive* (or political; Weber 1968, 3:960). Their relationship is dialectical. Each depends on the other's existence in the complexity of modern state governance; but within the legal system each struggles with the other for ascendancy in the power hierarchy, even though the official relations between them may be spelled out by statute—as is the case between the executive branch and Congress in handling Indian affairs. The interests of each come from different bases and involve distinctive behavior patterns. The best interests of those in the bureaucracy or administration are served by following orders and procedures articulated by those higher in the chain of domination. These orders and procedures, and thus the bases of judgment by the higher-ups, are ideally fixed, unchanging, and routine; innovation is soft-pedaled. The best interests of the politicians, on the other hand, ideally are met by catering to the demands of those outside the formal structure of power: the constituents who put them into office. These demands tend to shift, and meeting them (so as to remain in office) often requires innovative solutions. Ultimately bureaucrats look upward in the chain of power for their support and security; politicians look downward to the voters—or to some of them, at least (Weber 1968, 3:960).

In struggles for dominance with the administration, the politicians of Congress wield the two powerful weapons of legislation and appropriation. As preludes to brandishing either of these, they can also conduct investigations of bureau activities, typically capped with command performances by administrators before congressional committees.[6]

The bureaucracy's greatest weapon in the struggle for domination is its alleged expertise. Weber insisted that there is no other possible structure ideally as rational or efficient at handling the details of running the state. Politicians' interests and expertise must shift to keep pace with changes in their constituents' concerns. Typically they do not have the time to acquire in-depth knowledge of a single area,[7] and thus must rely on the information and procedures supplied by the bureaucrats. The bureaucracy maintains The Files, the source of the accumulated information and knowledge basic to its power, and stresses the keeping of written records to augment its power base.

But knowledge is merely a prerequisite to the bureaucracy's power. Above all, knowledge must be managed effectively, which means not only retaining and retrieving it, but keeping it away from others who might be competitors in the power struggle. Hence the bureaucracy's emphasis on secrecy and its reluctance to supply information that supports positions contrary to its own (Weber 1968, 3:992). Secrecy can also be used to conceal a lack of expertise or an inability to control certain types of knowledge.

Bureaucratic structures are not only inevitable, they are essentially indestructible because of their role in the governance process. They can be prodded, investigated, publicly chastised, shifted, and renamed, but never obliterated, because of the administrative chaos that would result.

According to Weber's version of the politics-bureaucracy dialectic, the key to effective, enlightened governance lies in keeping a balance of power between the two. Without close supervision and direction the bureaucracy will come to dominate the relationship and create a system throughout government based on its own hierarchical, uninnovative worldview.[8] Weber portrayed politicians as the primary source of enlightened policy innovation juxtaposed to fundamental bureaucratic tendencies.

Still, when focusing on the dynamic of the relationship between bureaucracy and politics, a third element—the courts—is easily overlooked. Congress cannot be sued on Indian issues except for land claims; but officials in the administration can be and have been sued for alleged violations of policy or regulations. This vulnerability acts as a check on bureaucratic domination when and if the legislative branch cannot or will not act as the brake.

This brief ideal-typological prelude shapes the following discussion of relations between the tribes and the federal government over the past three decades. The basic task is to portray the nonprogressive meandering in policy articulation and implementation as a result of dynamics of power relationships within and between the various components of the policy process. The major components in this discussion include Congress, the Bureau of Indian Affairs, the federal courts, and the Indian tribes. States, non-Indian commercial interests, and an assortment of Indian-oriented constellations of interest intrude now and then as relevant components. Of course, there is a discrepancy between the reality as here described and the ideal as drawn by Weber; the point is to understand why the discrepancy exists and what it implies for the future.

CONGRESS

Characteristically, Congress waits for a crisis to erupt in Indian country before flexing its plenary muscle (cf. Taylor 1984:107). Constituents and special interest groups (i.e., constellations of interest) either favoring or opposing Indian positions in the crisis bombard members of Congress with grievances and demand redress. The legislators, as politicians, must pay attention to these demands and take action on some of them—ideally, meaningful and innovative action. In their position of power legitimized by statute they can compel executive agencies such as the Bureau of Indian Affairs to change their procedures, restructure, or even to self-destruct in keeping with demands of constituents and the results of congressional investigations. Alternatively, they can create significantly new policy directions by passing new laws.

Arguably the most significant legislative measures affecting tribal-federal relations during the last three decades were the Area Redevelopment and Economic Opportunity acts of 1961 and 1964, the Indian Self-Determination and Education Act of 1975, the creation of a *permanent* Senate Select Committee on Indian Affairs in 1984, and an explicit congressional repeal of the termination resolution in 1988. Otherwise, "policy" measures were preoccupied with services to be provided to and by Indian communities and rights or domain to be restored to specific tribes. The contradictory principles of tribal sovereignty and federal trust protection were continually invoked without being systematically articulated or integrated into legislative reform. And major investigations by Congress in 1973–75 and again in 1988–89 showed that while conditions in Indian communities have generally improved since 1960, the dismal poverty, along with flagrant mismanagement and fraud, still prevail. Congress had a hand in redirecting the Bureau of Indian Affairs toward a "technical services" role, but it has repeatedly been unable to coerce the bureau into major restructuring for the sake of efficiency. In both legislation and in oversight on Indian affairs Congress has assumed a minimalist, reactive posture, thereby abdicating much of its potential power for constructive reform. That this posture is in legislators' best political interest is the Weberian point, but it must be substantiated.

Given the need of members of Congress to appeal to the widest (or most powerful) constituency so as to be reelected, being active on issues of Indian policy is considered risky. This is the basic observation from which others related to the wielding of substantive or political power proceed. To come down strongly for or against either Indian sovereignty or federal trust protection is bound to bring on the wrath of some vociferous constituency. In an era when a single-issue mentality dominates much of the voter sensibility, what politician needs another source of polarized pressure?

Add to this risk the fact that one and a half million Indians are scattered widely over the fifty states, with only a few areas having concentrations that could affect election outcomes. The chances are that a representative or senator has a politically insignificant Indian constituency, so why take the time to become active in Indian issues? In a 1988 interview Representative Ben Nighthorse Campbell, a Northern Cheyenne representing a district in Colorado, declared: "I'd like to have a few other Indian people back here [in Congress] to spread the burden, because we get a lot of referrals. An Indian guy will go into some congressman's office from New York and they tell him, 'Oh, go talk to Ben.' Wonderful. I'll help him if I can, but some [members] are taking a hike on Indian problems and pushing them over on us. . . . [T]he thing I obviously have to be worried about is that I can't be perceived in my own district as just being an Indian congressman for Indians and for Indian problems, or I can't get re-elected" (Darcy 1988).

Then there is perhaps the major development in tribal-federal relations since 1960: the significant threat of costly court action against the government for failing to adhere to declared Indian policy; that is, to tribal sovereignty or protection of the trust. Given the prevailing obscurity of these concepts, plus the record of past court encounters, precipitous action to meddle more with either issue without intensive and comprehensive preparation would most likely spark a series of protracted court battles that would benefit only the attorneys involved. (Although Congress cannot be sued without its consent, suits can cost constituent taxpayers money and hamstring key administrators with preparations for court appearances.) Best to let sleeping dogs lie, to move only as far and as quickly as is necessary to cope with immediate problems having fairly restricted scope.

In 1978 a legislator from a Western state summarized the situation neatly to one of his staff: "Indian affairs are a no-win issue" (Bee, unpublished notes, 1978). An oft-cited manifestation of this conviction: in the mid-1970s no representative could be found to chair the Indian affairs subcommittee of the House Committee on Interior and Insular Affairs. At first the subcommittee was joined—like hens and foxes—with the subcommittee on public lands. Later, the chair of the full committee, Representative Morris Udall of Arizona, placed all Indian issues before the full committee directly, drastically curtailing the staff and committee time they received (Bee 1982:74; cf. Taylor 1984:120). The Indian affairs subcommittee on the Senate side was abolished earlier (an indication of the low priority of Indian issues but billed as a "streamlining" move). The fact that the Senate Select Committee on Indian Affairs since has become a permanent fixture to replace it is probably due more to power maneuverings among senators in the late 1970s than to a compelling concern with Indian problems (Bee 1982:153–62).[9]

The American Indian Policy Review Commission (AIPRC) of the mid-1970s was certainly an involved first step in what was supposed to become a major overhaul of federal policy. But the ensuing scenario unfolded in a familiar pattern: the report was published, the congressional lament of the prevailing conditions was dutifully delivered, the members of the executive branch covering that aspect of federal activities were hauled before congressional committees for grilling and chastisement, and little else has happened since. Again, the inference is that Indian issues do not have high priority and major reform of Indian policy is best avoided.

On the other hand, Congress cannot simply let go of the Indian tribes: the offensive termination resolution is off the books. Various bills to revive it, no matter how deceptively titled,[10] have not been able to marshal the support for passage. Then there is the memory of the termination fiasco itself. Unless they represent Wisconsin or Oregon, legislators might forget; but Indian tribal leaders will always be pleased to remind them (cf. Prucha 1984, 2:1099). Finally, the financial costs of such a move may well be intimidating, both for pretermination upgrading and for the lawsuits and shifted social program burdens that would surely follow. Accurate estimates of the cost of a termination phoenix are difficult to generate. But compared with what this would likely be, the $3 billion now annually spent on federal Indian programs seems an appropriate budgetary counterpart to the make-no-waves minimalist stance on Indian legislative reform.

So for its own best political interests Congress cannot completely ignore Indian relations, but it has not done much fundamentally to reform them. If "abdication" of policy power seems too harsh a characterization, certainly Congress has put the initiative for systematic reform up for grabs by one of the other components in the policymaking process. According to Weber's view, the administrative bureaucracy is the most likely to seize it.

THE INTRACTABLE, TERMINAL BUREAUCRACY

Perhaps Congress ought to expect major Indian policy initiatives to come from the Bureau of Indian Affairs (BIA), like those launched by Commissioner John Collier and his associates in the mid-1930s. But this expectation assumes the Weberian notion of a rational, efficient bureaucracy, which by virtually all measures the BIA is not. And surely Collier himself stood much closer to the "politician" than to the "bureaucrat" pole of Weber's spectrum.

A disgruntled ex–BIA staffer in the late 1970s declared that the BIA was like "a mindless, spastic zombie" in administering Indian affairs (Bee, unpublished notes, 1978). More recently the BIA's top official dubbed it "an intractable bureaucracy," then resigned in the midst of the 1989 Senate investigation of mismanagement in Indian affairs. For most of the past thirty years the BIA has been incapable of seizing the policy initiative— partly because it is a bureaucracy and partly because it is an ineffective one.

Back to Weber's bureaucracy-politics dialectic: the BIA's power versus Congress comes from its control of important information about Indian life and from its daily involvement in administrative detail. The BIA, or something like it, must exist if Congress is to fulfill its statutory obligations to Indian tribes. But continued dependence on the bureau's administrative effectiveness threatens Congress's ability to meet its statutory obligations.

In the 1960s at least two potentially significant policy initiatives came out of the executive. One was the so-called Indian Omnibus Bill which Secretary of the Interior Stewart Udall sent to Congress in 1967. Indians viewed it as placing too much authority in the hands of the executive, yet paving the way for eventual termination. It expired in committee. The other initiative was the creation of a presidential task force on Indian policy in 1966. To tribal leaders its report also smacked of termination, so it was buried (Prucha 1984, 2:1097–98). But for most of the rest of 1960s, and increasingly in the 1970s and 1980s, the bureau was reactive, dodging this way and that to protect its power.

The BIA's direct and largely exclusive control of Indian community development was undermined by the massive antipoverty campaign of the late 1960s. The new programs brought an enthusiastic deluge of new money, new people with new operating styles, and new channels of authority in the relationship between the tribes and Washington (see, e.g., Officer 1971:51–53; Bee 1981:122–59; cf. Castile 1974:221–22, 1976). This deluge with its self-help ideology helped to increase congressional and higher-level executive pressure on the bureau to change its administrative role: direct control of reservation programs was out; technical service for tribally run programs was in. Bureau bashing was in by the late 1960s as well.[11] As an apparent response to the criticism there was another flurry of what looked like policy initiative from the administration in President Richard Nixon's policy statement of 1970.[12]

And there was an effort by the executive to reorganize the BIA. In 1969

Louis Bruce was brought in as commissioner from outside the bureaucracy
to clean house at the uppermost BIA levels (Forbes 1981:33). This sparked a
power struggle between Bruce's reformers and a group of career administrators within the bureau who felt that their power was threatened. The battle
raged through 1971, with most of Nixon's suggested reforms being subverted by Interior and BIA people (Forbes 1981:55), giving strength to the
argument that they were never intended to be effectively implemented.

The reform proposals were further subverted by the Indians themselves:
a watershed in power manipulation came in November 1972 when the Trail
of Broken Treaties reached Washington. The ensuing occupation and sack
of the BIA building were taken as a most public signal that the bureau—
already in internal disarray—was at best an administrative and political
embarrassment (Burnette and Koster 1974; Deloria 1974; Forbes 1981).
Whatever the previous doubts about its efficiency, there was now no way the
bureau could be trusted to handle its administrative chores effectively. Now
more than ever the bureau seemed incapable of effective power manipulation as unfavorable attention from superiors and the public pushed administrators even more deeply into make-no-waves, resist-all-change behavior.

Yet no other agency had the accumulated information necessary to deal
with the daily issues of federal-Indian relations. Even though the Indians in
the takeover had taken or destroyed some of this all-important lifestuff, the
bureau's continued—if very much flawed—access to The Files allowed its
survival.

By 1977 Congress had issued explicit and strident demands for BIA
reorganization (SSCIA 1978:127–28). This was partly the legacy of the
angry confrontations with Indians in 1972–73 and the resulting AIPRC
recommendations, and partly the continuing effort to transform the bureau
into a technical service agency. The AIPRC version of reorganization was
more sweeping than that proposed in 1969–70, which is to say even more
threatening to the bureau. The new contracting process would put more
authority into the hands of the tribes and would cut both personnel and
funding for the bureau itself. In particular the control over tribes by the
twelve BIA area offices would be cut back (AIPRC 1976:8).

The bureau behaved accordingly. There was a great deal of planning with
a minimum of actual reorganization (SSCIA 1978:127, 1984). Plans called
for replacing the twelve area offices with five or six regional service centers,
two special programs offices, and three field offices.[13] By 1989—almost
fifteen years after they were proposed—these changes still had not been
implemented. The area office structure was still intact, although area directors *had* been removed from line authority in BIA education programs in

1978 (SSCIA 1984:40). The charade produced at least one classic example of dialectical symbiosis: when the BIA was finally ready to implement a plan for "realinement" (not reorganization) in 1982, the tribes reversed their earlier position and vehemently opposed elimination of the area offices. [14]

By 1978–79 the contracting system with tribes was hitting one snag after another, threatening to scuttle the process entirely. One of the major problems was the lack of BIA funding for contract support (indirect costs). There was little the bureau could do, it declared, unless it received more resources (see GAO 1978; Bee 1982:95–110, 232). Some tribes believed that the contract support controversy was partly an effort to resist the reorganization's perceived threat to bureau power (GAO 1978:16; Prucha 1984, 2:1161). Nevertheless, some of the BIA's other sources of power have been eroding. Between 1976 and 1988 the bureau lost about 3,500 personnel positions (despite strident objections by civil service lobby groups [e.g., SSCIA 1984:59–63]). In the 1980s BIA funding increased virtually every year, but these increases were wiped out by inflation, leaving a net—if relatively small—funding loss for the decade (see, e.g., FCNL 1986:7). Neither of these trends can be traced exclusively or largely to the technical services shift, however. The BIA sustained cuts along with other federal agencies in keeping with the Reagan administration's antipathy to big government.

In the wake of the 1989 Senate hearings into the poor management of Indian and federal mineral resources, members of the special investigating committee issued tough-sounding orders to the secretary of the interior: "Go in there [into the BIA and other resource management agencies] and kick butt" (McAllister 1989:A22). At least two outcomes were predictable: Interior would want more money and people to strengthen its resources administration, and there would be a call for major BIA reorganization.

The bureau for the past three decades, then: no major initiatives for policy reform, inefficiency and credibility crises, but nonetheless surviving, largely because no other agency has as much information and experience and Congress has been unwilling to risk the consequences of starting over with a new administrative structure. Weber emphasized that a bureaucracy is capable of endless adaptive adjustments necessary to sustain its existence. It is thus not only inevitable but indestructible (see, e.g., Weber 1968, 1:224).

Within the Department of the Interior itself the BIA is legendary for its lack of power (e.g., Cahn 1969, chap. 2). Certainly there is a continuing conflict of interest between the agencies that control the entire federal portion of mineral and petroleum wealth and the one that handles the social and material needs of about 600,000 Indians. Not only are the resources a higher priority, but the other agencies in the department are not about to yield any measure of their control (and thus power) to rival bureaucracies.

All administrative departments are subordinate to the Office of Management and Budget (OMB), which screens each executive department's proposals to be certain they are in keeping with the basic politics of the White House and the maintenance of the maximum amount of political power by the executive branch versus that of Congress. Ultimately, then, the major decisions by the administrative agencies, unlike Weber's ideal-typical bureaucracy, are not objective at all but must run a hierarchical gauntlet of political jockeying. To turn Karl Mannheim's comment around, administrative decisions have a way of becoming political decisions (Mannheim 1936:118).

The dialectic of politics-bureaucracy power relations is manifest not only in the BIA's relations with Congress and executive agencies but within the BIA itself. At this more specific level, too, its dynamics have helped to stifle BIA initiatives for policy reform. As in the case of Louis Bruce, the executive branch's typical reaction to the bureau's administrative lapses is to appoint new BIA leadership to shape things up. Notably, these are *political* appointees who serve only as long as they please those who appointed them; they are without the protection of civil service regulations—a way of ensuring that personal loyalty will prevail over the best interests of BIA longevity. Because these appointees also look upward in the hierarchy rather than downward, they do not fit Weber's "politician" type neatly. They are touted as the "idea people" in charge of developing long-range policy.[15] Both ideally and typically they come from outside the ranks of the BIA; that is, they are not career administrators and owe those beneath them no longstanding favors. Ideally and typically (for the past thirty years, anyway), they also know something about Indian affairs and are themselves of Indian blood. And this sets the stage for conflict between the political newcomers and the career administrators within the bureau; the running battle between Commissioner Bruce and the administrative careerists in the months prior to the BIA takeover is a well-documented example (Forbes 1981:49).

Theodore Taylor, a former BIA official, described the impacts of political appointments on bureau operations (1984:127–29). Since 1969 there have been at least eighteen appointed or acting assistant secretaries and commissioners, each with a new agenda for shaping up bureau operations. This choppy tenure means that the direction Weber found so crucial to enlightened administration has been missing within the bureau. For the rank-and-file bureaucrats, routines never become established and guidelines and procedures are temporary. For the higher-level career administrators, the frequent changes are demoralizing because there is little incentive to hone their skills and expertise; why bother? A glass wall rises between the career administrators and the top bureau officials. The political appointees move on while a few of the higher-level career bureaucrats move around from job to job in the bureau's operations, showing up at congressional hearings to whisper facts to the commissioner or assistant secretary of the moment, or occasionally filling in as an acting luminary. The two elements of bureau operations never get a chance to know one another and to work together on any long-range program. As a result, the career civil servants' best interests are served by trying to keep a low profile, to be reactive instead of innovative, and all the while to protect the span of control over people and resources.

Thus, while according to Weber's typology bureaucrats are always looking upward in the power hierarchy for direction and commands, thereby in essence linking their professional existence to that hierarchy regardless of who commands it, their obedience to politician superiors is assured only as long as it perpetuates the system. Among Washingtonians, converting administrative positions into political appointments is considered a quick fix for administrative embarrassments (Taylor 1984:129).[16] But with their high turnover, the ever-widening networks of political appointments have accomplished exactly the opposite of their anticipated effect: they have actively interfered with policy reform.

Increasing the numbers of political appointments can also lead to a subversion of all administrative objectivity for the sake of personal loyalty. This would be at least as threatening to Weber's version of democracy as the prospect of politicians being dominated by bureaucrats.

If Congress has generally failed to use a greater measure of its available power for policy initiatives, and the BIA has used most of its own power simply to exist, then conceivably Indians' power for seizing the policy initiative has become relatively greater in the past three decades.

INDIAN POWER

The federally recognized Indian tribes' leverage in the system comes ultimately from their unique sovereign status, the ramifications and limitations of which are fleetingly sketched in the Constitution and have been evolving in court findings since the 1790s. From time to time in the history of policy, public appeals to the sad plight of Indian peoples have had some influence (e.g., the late 1920s), but mostly this is an intermittent and unreliable lever. In the past three decades, mass public confrontations between Indians and state and federal authorities have generated some legislative or administrative actions, but the long-term results so far have been mixed and generally disappointing.

Because Indians occupy no formal position in the power structure of Washington, they must wage a kind of guerrilla warfare to exercise what power they have. Their strongest weapon is the threat of court action against administrative officials, states, or corporations for violating the evolved principles of tribal sovereignty, federal trust protection, or both. Several factors have combined to help them wield this threat with increasing effectiveness since 1960. The first is money. Land claims settlements and the proceeds from tribal enterprises and resources have put money into some tribal governments' hands. This allows them to hire lawyers and, in some cases, Washington-based consulting firms whose primary purpose is to influence relevant legislation. The second factor, partly related to the first, is a series of federal court decisions reaffirming the special legal status of tribes, tribal sovereignty, and the federal trust responsibility. Among the most important of these are the reaffirmation of the Boldt decision on Indian treaty fishing rights and the Passamaquoddy-Penobscots' right to sue states for the violation of the 1790 Trade and Intercourse Act. The third factor is sophistication. The antipoverty programs of the 1960s and 1970s promoted firsthand contact between tribal officials and Washington, giving them direct knowledge of how things get done in the capital city. Some tribes have been able to continue this contact despite personnel changes and heavy cuts in so-called social programs spending. And the fourth factor, also related to the other factors, is the availability of effective advocates outside the formal federal network. This includes the influence-for-hire consultants in the city, nonprofit advocacy groups such as the American Friends Service Committee and the Friends Committee on National Legislation, and, most important, the nonprofit legal advocacy groups such as the Native American Rights Fund and various state-level legal services offices.

In power struggles with the BIA, tribes are confronted by the irony that affects all bureaucracies bound to provide services for subordinate clients: the bureau cannot be responsive to Indians' wishes unless ordered to do so by its own superiors in the hierarchy of power. There is also the bureau's inevitable need to present a united front to rivals for power. So the Indians move on to Congress to try to induce it to compel the BIA or some other administrative agency to yield to the Indians' wishes.

Although the tribes and the BIA are rivals for power, they obviously depend on each other. Thus they will operate to limit or reduce each other's power vis-à-vis Congress, but will join forces against any move to eradicate the bureau or end the special legal status of the tribes. And because of the bureau's statutory administrative power, they will join forces to increase the resources of the bureau for eventual redistribution to the individual tribes. Most fundamentally, the Indians—like Congress—are forced to depend on the bureau because of its administrative apparatus and information. The linkage between many tribal governments and the bureau can be even tighter: the tribal incumbents use the administrative protection and inside information offered by the bureau to bolster their power over rival factions. The situation at Pine Ridge in 1972–73 is an example of this (see Forbes 1981:116–18; also Burnette and Koster 1974:239, 242). [17]

Mention of factionalism prompts a crucial caution. In speaking so far of "tribes" or "the Indians" there has been the implication that the Indians are united on basic issues of power relations; that is, that there is not only a constellation but a consensus of interest. This is not the case. While most tribes would agree that there should be a maximum of tribal sovereignty along with maintenance of the federal trust relationship, there are real differences both between and within tribes about the tactics and philosophy involved. There is no universal Indian voice whispering in Congress's ear.

Because tribal leaders of recognized tribes are elected, they fall into the "political" element of Weber's legal authority. This means that the concerns of their constituency (not necessarily the majority of the tribal members) must dominate their strategies. In most cases the constituents' major concerns are localized and immediate: need for money for a continuing agricultural program, more water for the crops, getting more land back for the reservation; more general issues of federal Indian policy are of less concern. It is these local issues that are most likely to bring tribal leaders to the lawyers and to Washington. And this means that localized issues dominate congressional and executive actions. This tends to deflect attention from the issues of general policy articulation and reform. The closest approach to a broader assessment may well come in the appropriations process, which, of course, ignores all important policy issues that cannot be expressed in dollars.

The major national-level Indian organizations that marshal tribal support for or against various moves by Washington reflect some of the fundamental cleavages in the Indian population across the country: the elected tribal leaders versus their opposing factions, the "progressives" versus the "traditionals" (frequently overlapping with the first-named split), urban versus reservation Indians, and federally recognized versus non–federally recognized tribes. At the national level the most persistent cleavage for the past thirty years has been between the National Tribal Chairmen's Association, the National Congress of American Indians, and the American Indian Movement (AIM). The diverse pressures leveled by these groups on Congress and the executive branch have strengthened the tendency to concentrate on localized, immediate issues at the expense of more generalized policy.

The Indians' most effective tactic for instigating broad policy initiatives by Congress or the executive since 1960 has been militant confrontation, in which the legitimacy of the federal power itself is ignored by Indians for the sake of their own bid for influence. The takeover of Alcatraz in 1969, the takeover of the BIA building in 1972, and the second Wounded Knee confrontation four months later are the primary examples. The outcomes, however, were not those intended by the Indians themselves. The crackdown on BIA operations following the takeover was decidedly not an Indian objective; and the AIPRC promised more than it delivered.

By contrast, The Longest Walk of 1978, organized as a broad-based Indian counter to a series of backlash bills introduced in both houses of Congress, was much less effective at instigating action. Once in Washington the marchers kept the peace and created only a minimal stir in the city—which by then was jaded after massive marches on the Capitol by angry farmers, schoolteachers, and antiabortion groups (Bee 1982:148).[18] Congress is more responsive when threatened than when approached.

The government's willingness in the 1960s and early 1970s to see Indian issues as primarily issues of poverty represented a threat to the tribes' power in federal relations (Deloria 1969:168–96, 1985b:251; Bee 1982:210–11). The antipoverty enthusiasm tended to ignore the special legal status of Indian tribes as distinct from all other minorities. (Ironically, for this brief period it was as powerful for tribes to be poor as to be Indian.) For this reason it has not been fruitful for Indians to join forces in a constellation of interest with the poor, or with other ethnic or racial minorities, so as to gain specific rights for Indians only. This is why Vine Deloria has made an effort to distinguish the situation of Indians from that of blacks and Hispanics in this country (Deloria 1969:168–96). Of course, broad-based social programs have helped Indians, as noted earlier. But the tribes dare not allow the impression to surface that these programs alone will meet the full measure of the government's statutory commitment to them.

The Indians have learned how to operate as effectively as possible within the legal power structure, using the same rules and the same bases of legitimation used by policymakers in Washington. AIM members have never operated according to those rules, however, and by the mid-1970s had changed their tactics to emphasize a more "traditional," more "spiritual" approach to power manipulation. This probably helped to create a broader age range among AIM supporters, but it also perpetuated the discontinuity between legal and traditional types of authority.

In some reservation communities, such as Pine Ridge or Taos, this traditional-legal discontinuity has been a long-term issue in tribal political factionalism. Tribal governments have become microcosms of the national government, with burgeoning bureaucracies and political battles over who will control them. Those favoring the traditional authority operate according to a different system, typically not hierarchical but consensual, expressing dissatisfaction by avoidance rather than by angry confrontation. To the extent that it persists as an issue in political conflict on some reservations, and to the extent that the traditional pattern spreads among tribal governments, federal authorities may once again be confronted by a power system much different from their own. The presence of this and other sources of intratribal factional conflict also threatens the constancy and intensity of tribal pressure placed on government, and the high turnover of Indian leaders caused by factionalism affects the directions the pressure favors—exactly as high turnover of political appointees has affected the BIA.

But the threat of legal action remains the most effective way for tribes to wield authority. Secretaries of the interior such as the late Rogers Morton have been named personally as defendants in tribes' suits over failed federal trust protection. Lawsuits against the Department of the Interior were filed by 17,000 Navajos and by 7,000 Oklahoma Indians for dereliction of the trust obligation in handling their mineral leasing arrangements with private corporations (*Arizona Republic,* October 4, 1987, A20). States such as Maine and Connecticut agreed to negotiate settlements of tribal land claims once they were convinced that the Indians meant business and had a case that could well hold up in court. That the negotiated settlement procedure has become so pervasive in relations between tribes, states, Congress, and executive agencies since the 1970s clearly means that a good many tribes have the potential power to be even more hurtful to their opponents' best interests should the issue go to court (cf. McGuire, *this volume*).

In a way, both the negotiated settlement process and the courtroom battles abet the fragmentary, tribe-specific tendencies of policymaking in Congress and the executive branch, and reinforce the tribes' sense that each of them is a special policy case. It is *that* tribe, after all, that goes to the expense and time and endures the anticipatory waiting as the case moves along. To be sure, other tribes or the policy process itself may be affected by any precedent set in the settlement, but the conditions of the exercise of the tribes' legal power contribute to Indians' inability to launch sweeping policy initiatives.

If for diverse reasons the initiative does not come from Congress, or from the executive, or from the tribes themselves, by default it passes to the courts. Charles Wilkinson, an expert on Indian law, wrote in 1987: "Congress has virtually unfettered power over Indian policy and . . . has adopted statutes dealing with some aspects of Indian policy. Major issues, however, have not been addressed by Congress. The result is that the task of crafting Indian law has been left in significant measure to the courts" (1987:9).

THE COURTS

On Indian issues the Supreme Court has been neither consistently liberal nor conservative over the last thirty years. Those who in 1978 were distressed at what they saw as a conservative cant in the *Oliphant* decision were cheered only sixteen days later by the Court's ruling in the *Wheeler* case (Wilkinson 1987:61–62).[19] This is to some extent traceable to a heritage of lower court findings that similarly shifted between conservative and liberal interpretations of the rights of tribes versus the other types of sovereignty (federal, state; see Wilkinson 1987:29).

Wilkinson argued that the improvement of Indians' conditions of life since 1960—and even since 1980—is predominantly due to favorable findings in the courts. Despite the apparently contradictory opinions rendered, the overall trend has been in the direction of upholding the concept of Indian sovereignty in its increasingly complex ramifications. And the persistence of those favorable findings is due to a general judicial unwillingness to cave in to realpolitik and a tendency to uphold principles and laws that were entered into in good faith in the past. Thus, he argued, the courts are not apparently or universally responsive—on this issue, at least—to the political-economic interests of the powerful majority. Congress by definition must be; administrative agencies ideally should not be but are. That is why the existing laws, the precipitate of court decisions, and the resulting threat of court action remain the most effective source of power available to the tribes. Without the law they are virtually powerless against federal, state, and private interests opposed to their own. This is one of the fundamental reasons why the status of Indian communities today cannot be sufficiently explained by their economic subordination and exploitation.

The current fuzziness of the definition and extent of the concepts of sovereignty and federal trust protection has precipitated much of the court action (Barsh and Henderson 1980:255–56). It is reasonable to expect that the clarification of these concepts will not come from some sweeping action by Congress, or bold policy initiatives from the executive branch, or a protracted, united effort by tribes, but from a step-by-step refinement based on successive court findings in cases launched by local, specific disputes (cf. Deloria 1985b:254–56). This is so partly because of the formal structure of power in policy issues and partly because of the way various components of that structure have wielded what power they enjoy—which is in turn the result of each operating according to its own best interest.

GENERAL IMPLICATIONS AND CONCLUSIONS

The past three decades of tribal-federal relations have necessarily centered on the issue of best interests and power manipulations aimed at preserving and enhancing them. It is expedient for Congress to shy away from general policy reform; it is expedient for the Bureau of Indian Affairs and other federal agencies to react passively to orders imposed on them by those above them in the power hierarchy. And it is expedient for Indian tribes to take their most strenuous actions on issues that concern them most directly rather than to band together for the extensive process of hammering out more lofty policy reform goals agreeable to all—assuming such goals could ever be found. The expediency has been traced here as an interplay of several sets of symbiotic yet contradictory factors: political and bureaucratic-administrative tendencies, tribal sovereignty and federal trust protection, the tribes and the BIA. And each set is clearly interrelated with the other two.

Weber's politics-bureaucracy dichotomy does not neatly fit the reality of the Indian policy process, of course. The reality is more typically a mixture of typologies and ideal tendencies. Members of Congress must be as concerned with hierarchies of power within their houses as with the sensibilities of their constituents, for example. In particular, political appointees as a type fit neatly into neither tendency. Like their subordinate bureaucrat-administrators, they are looking up, not down the power hierarchy. They are to this extent compromised politicians. They are also compromised as bureaucrats. Whether the bureau would be better able to seize the policy initiative were these appointees to stay in position longer is questionable; it is more probable that the short tenure is not a temporary aberration but rather a manifestation of an inherent bureaucratic nature. From this view, John Collier's decade as commissioner was an aberration.

Weber concluded that any bureaucracy has the power edge over political bodies under ideal conditions. The BIA has used most of its power merely to stay alive. Yet Weberian comparative analysis directs the analytical focus to the more fundamental issue of why the bureau has been unable to manage its power sources effectively. Although I discussed some of the important power-structural factors bearing on BIA inefficiency, I did not mention inadvertent or deliberate collusion between BIA or other agency employees and non-Indian commercial interests. The Senate investigations and *Arizona Republic* essays described such collusion (see SSCIA 1989); it can only flourish under the immortal, organizational, procedural, and personnel status quo. Like angry public confrontations, headlined acts of individual and corporate greed can be effective goads to policy overhaul, even though policy overhaul was manifestly necessary years before the press became involved.

Word of the BIA's demise is always premature. Still, the most recent grand exposé of bureaucratic inefficiency and alleged fraud may finally do it in, because it is both an active perpetrator and a convenient scapegoat (SSCIA 1989). In the Senate's overhaul plan, federally recognized tribes would be allowed to secede from the BIA and Indian Health Service bureaucracies by negotiated agreements with a proposed Office of Federal-Tribal Relations (OFTR; see SSCIA 1989:213). The OFTR would negotiate agreements and oversee their implementation. It would require money, people, offices, and regulations. An administrative department having something like the BIA's present functions is, to be Weberian about it, inevitable. And just as inevitable is the effort of any new department to enhance its own power and growth at the expense of potential rivals—including the BIA.[20] At best it would be another bureaucracy under a different name. By fall 1990 the OFTR's proposal was being ignored in favor of yet another plan for reorganizing the BIA (Joint Task Force 1991). By spring 1991 the BIA had been coerced into allowing tribes to participate in the planning.[21]

The interplay of political and bureaucratic tendencies is to a degree informed and constrained by the implications of tribal sovereignty and trust protection. Trust protection implies bureaucracy; sovereignty implies political entrepreneurship. Again the extremes overstate the reality. But if there is a search for a reasonable balance between one of the two pairs, it must necessarily involve creation of an optimal balance between the other pair.

NOTES

1. A series of investigative articles alleging fraud, waste, and incompetence in the handling of Indian resources and administration appeared in the *Arizona Re-*

public, October 4–11, 1987. The Senate appointed an investigative subcommittee of the Select Committee on Indian Affairs to look into the allegations. After staff investigations, public hearings were held in late January and February and in May and June 1989.

2. For example, President Nixon's 1970 message on executive policy toward Indians is still hailed as a sensitive and realistic statement; the American Indian Policy Review Commission's comprehensive report and recommendations in 1976–77 remain unequaled in scale. But for a variety of reasons these hopeful proclamations have not been followed by systematic policy reform (Prucha 1984, 2:1167, 1170).

3. I should emphasize a point often made about Weber: although his work is typically juxtaposed to that of Marx, he took care to stress the material basis for much of the domination he saw in social action.

4. Weber's full definition of domination through authority reads: "[T]he situation in which the manifested will (*command*) of the *ruler* or rulers is meant to influence the conduct of one or more others (the ruled) and actually does influence it in such a way that their conduct to a socially relevant degree occurs as if the ruled had made the content of the command the maxim of their conduct for its very own sake. Looked upon from the other end, this situation will be called *obedience*" (1968, 3:942).

5. Traditional authority is based on the principle that the orders and the obedience are matters of ageless truths, while charismatic authority is based on the conviction that the leader is personally and specially endowed with grace or wisdom that compels obedience.

6. In Weber's view, similar inquiry was not possible in the German parliament of 1917, a condition strengthening the control of the bureaucracy in the governance process at that time (Weber 1968, 3:1418).

7. *In-depth* here is a relative term; many members of Congress develop real (as distinct from publicly proclaimed) expertise in issues of special interest to them, and it would be inappropriate to refer to them as "dilettantes" without this qualification.

8. A case in point, he caustically observed in 1917, was the German government of his time. "Since the resignation of Prince Bismarck Germany has been governed by 'bureaucrats,' a result of his elimination of all political talent." What was needed, Weber declared, was direction by a politician, "not by a political genius, to be expected only once every few centuries, not even by a great political talent, but simply a politician" (Weber 1968, 3:1404–5).

9. It could be argued that much—if not all—of the then-hopeful movement toward Indian policy reform of the mid-1970s was due to the efforts of Senator James Abourezk of South Dakota. Significantly, he was effective because he understood how to wield power and apparently didn't give a damn about his political best interests. This political kamikaze, a vegetarian in a beef-growing state, did not run for reelection. See Stroud 1978 for a lively account.

10. One of the most sweeping of these "backlash" measures (HR 9054) was the Native Americans Equal Opportunity Act.

11. Senator Edward Kennedy told the National Congress of American Indians convention in late 1969 that the bureau was "incapable of reforming itself. It presently has the authority to contract out almost all its functions to Indian tribes" (Forbes 1981:35). See also Cahn 1969.

12. Among other things, the message called for an explicit renunciation of the termination policy, a procedure to enable tribes to take over federally funded programs when they wished to do so, tribal control of their local schools, more funding for Indian health, creation of an Indian Trust Council Authority to represent Indian resource rights without the inherent conflict of interest in the Interior and Justice departments, and creation of a new position of assistant secretary of Indian affairs to improve the clout of the BIA versus other agencies in the Department of the Interior. Bills that would accomplish some of these changes were sent to Congress by the interior secretary, but Congress waffled on passing them. Some were later revived by Congress itself and eventually passed; others were forgotten (Prucha 1984, 3:1113–15). Analysts have since wondered why an essentially conservative administration promulgated such a liberal-sounding program. A former BIA official involved in the drafting declared in 1978 that it was cynically conceived, playing up the administration's civil rights record with a small, relatively "safe" minority to offset the generally dismal executive efforts on behalf of the much larger black and Hispanic minorities. Others have suggested that the real aim was to influence white voters in an election year (Ortiz 1981:10; Forbes 1981:39).

13. The American Indian Policy Review Commission's final report included a management study of the BIA by a private firm (AIPRC 1976). The study recommended replacing the twelve BIA area offices with six regional service centers; the local BIA agencies would become local service centers. This would save about $11 million annually in 1976 dollars. Ultimately, the report went on, the regional service centers would be eliminated and the local service centers would be merged with local tribal council operations in the spirit of tribal self-determination (AIPRC 1976:52, 53). The report reiterated the special need for enforcing implementation of the recommendations, suggesting that the OMB fund and staff a special Management Improvement Implementation Review Office to see that the BIA complied. Furthermore, the report declared, "something more than problem identification and proposed resolutions is necessary" (1976:9, 55). Late in 1977 the secretary of the interior appointed a departmental task force to determine how the reorganization would proceed. At about that time a series of reports by the General Accounting Office pinpointed major BIA management problems. In April 1978 a frustrated Senator Abourezk convened a hearing of top Interior Department officials to determine why the reorganization was proceeding so slowly (SSCIA 1978:127). He was not satisfied with their testimony, including Under Secretary James A. Joseph's expressed hope that "in the next 3 to 4 years we will have a totally different

organization, one that is efficient, effective, and humane" (SSCIA 1978:129). Four years later, after more study (including another area office review in 1979), the BIA's 1982 "realinement" plan called for a consolidation of the twelve area offices into five regional service centers, two special program offices, and three field offices. In the plan there was no call for eventual withering away of this structure in favor of tribal self-determination.

14. The Senate Select Committee on Indian Affairs reported "overwhelming" tribal approval for changing the area office system in 1978 (SSCIA 1978:130). By 1982 the tribes were concerned that the BIA's plan for doing so would end up costing them more money and provide a lower level of service. They also were angered at what they considered a lack of adequate consultation between them and the BIA before the "realinement" plan was floated. The tribes and members of the civil service employees' union charged that the BIA's 1982 scheme was in no way the culmination of a long, careful planning and consultation process, but was instead prompted by OMB demands that the bureau cut its operating costs by $16 million per year (SSCIA 1984:60, 65). In fact, the tribes' reversal may not have been inconsistent; whether they would turn down a more reasoned plan for elimination of the area offices remains moot.

15. In an interview with the author and others on February 17, 1978, Assistant Secretary Forrest Gerard portrayed his ideal role in those terms but lamented the fact that he had thus far been unable to get beyond the day-to-day issues of administrative detail. Thirteen years later this problem had still not been resolved (Joint Task Force 1991:5).

16. In the midst of a crisis over the unseemly authority being assumed by some BIA area directors in 1978, Indian Affairs Assistant Secretary Forrest Gerard suggested converting all area directorships from civil service positions to political appointments (Bee, unpublished notes, February 1978).

17. As long as he remained the elected tribal chairman, the BIA steadfastly supported the incumbent, Richard Wilson, against the challenges of Russell Means and others. Excessive treatment of political rivals by Wilson's armed supporters helped spark the angry confrontation at Wounded Knee in 1973 and subsequent events on the Pine Ridge reservation.

18. The backlash bills died, but they may well have expired even if the Walk had not been organized. However, this is not to minimize the positive fallout of the Walk on communities where it paused in its way across the country, or the real—if temporary—political and strategic alliances formed among Indian groups and between them and the government.

19. *Oliphant* v. *Suquamish Indian Tribe* declared that the tribe lacked jurisdiction over crimes committed on its reservation by non-Indians. The wording of the justices' opinion was viewed as a very narrow interpretation of the concept of tribal sovereignty. *United States* v. *Wheeler* found that an Indian could be tried by both tribal and federal courts for crimes committed on an Indian reservation. The wording of the decision this time featured a strong endorsement of tribal sov-

ereignty, declaring it to be an inherent right of tribal governments (Wilkinson 1987:63). In 1991 Court watchers were dismayed by further apparent loss of tribal sovereignty in the *Duro* v. *Reina* decision.

20. The OFTR would coexist with the BIA and Indian Health Service conceivably for as long as a significant number of tribes chose to remain under the old system. The Senate recommendations did not mention non-federally recognized tribes, nor did they address programs for Indians in urban areas.

21. Tribal leaders were outraged that the bureau had drafted a plan without meaningful consultation with them, so they went to Congress to protest. As a result, the Fiscal Year 1991 Appropriations Act stipulated that the BIA could allocate none of its money for reorganization planning until the plans had been reviewed by a task force including tribal representatives (Joint Task Force 1991:7).

REFERENCES

AIPRC [American Indian Policy Review Commission]. 1976. *Bureau of Indian Affairs Management Study. Section 2 Study Provision: Report on BIA Management Practices to the American Indian Policy Review Commission.* Washington, D.C.: Government Printing Office.

BARSH, RUSSEL, and JAMES Y. HENDERSON. 1980. *The Road: Indian Tribes and Political Liberty.* Berkeley: University of California Press.

BEE, ROBERT L. Unpublished field notes, January–July 1978, in the author's possession.

———. 1981. *Crosscurrents Along the Colorado: The Impact of Government Policy on the Quechan Indians.* Tucson: University of Arizona Press.

———. 1982. *The Politics of American Indian Policy.* Cambridge, Mass.: Schenkman.

BURNETTE, ROBERT, and JOHN KOSTER. 1974. *The Road to Wounded Knee.* New York: Bantam Books.

CAHN, EDGAR S., ed. 1969. *Our Brother's Keeper: The Indian in White America.* New York: New Community Press.

CASTILE, GEORGE P. 1974. "Federal Indian Policy and the Sustained Enclave: An Anthropological Perspective." *Human Organization* 33(3):219–28.

———. 1976. "Mau Mau in the Mechanism: The Adaptations of Urban Hunters and Gatherers." *Human Organization* 35(4):394–97.

DARCY, CINDY. 1988. "Interview with Representative Ben Nighthorse Campbell, 13 October." Friends Committee on National Legislation Background Paper G-841. Washington, D.C. Mimeograph.

DELORIA, VINE, JR. 1969. *Custer Died for Your Sins: An Indian Manifesto.* New York: Macmillan.

———. 1974. *Behind the Trail of Broken Treaties.* New York: Dell.

———, ed. 1985a. *American Indian Policy in the Twentieth Century.* Norman: University of Oklahoma Press.

———. 1985b. "The Evolution of Federal Indian Policy Making." In *American*

Indian Policy in the Twentieth Century. Ed. Vine Deloria, Jr., 239–56. Norman: University of Oklahoma Press.

DELORIA, VINE, JR., and CLIFFORD M. LYTLE. 1984. *The Nations Within: The Past and Future of American Indian Sovereignty.* New York: Pantheon Books.

FCNL [Friends Committee on National Legislation]. 1986. "Here We Come Again." *FCNL Washington Newsletter* 489 (March):7. Washington, D.C.: Friends Committee on National Legislation.

FORBES, JACK D. 1981. *Native Americans and Nixon: Presidential Politics and Minority Self-Determination, 1969–1972.* Native American Politics Series, no. 2. Los Angeles: UCLA American Indian Studies Center.

GAO [General Accounting Office]. 1978. *The Indian Self-Determination Act: Many Obstacles Remain.* Report to the Congress HRD-78-59, issued March 1, 1978. Washington, D.C.: General Accounting Office.

JOINT TASK FORCE [Joint Tribal/BIA/Interior Advisory Task Force on Bureau of Indian Affairs Reorganization]. 1991. "Report to the Secretary of the Interior and the Appropriations Committees of the Congress on the Status of Activities." April 30. Unpublished typescript.

JORGENSEN, JOSEPH G. 1971. "Indians and the Metropolis." In *The American Indian in Urban Society.* Ed. Jack O. Waddell and O. Michael Watson, 66–113. Boston: Little, Brown.

MCALLISTER, BILL. 1989. "Lujan Vows to Correct Abuses in Indian Programs." *Washington Post,* June 9.

MANNHEIM, KARL. 1936. *Ideology and Utopia: An Introduction to the Sociology of Knowledge.* New York: Harcourt, Brace, and World.

NELSON, ROBERT A., and JOSEPH F. SHELEY. 1985. "Bureau of Indian Affairs Influence on Indian Self-Determination." In *American Indian Policy in the Twentieth Century.* Ed. Vine Deloria, Jr., 177–96. Norman: University of Oklahoma Press.

OFFICER, JAMES E. 1971. "The American Indian and Federal Policy." In *The American Indian in Urban Society.* Ed. Jack O. Waddell and O. Michael Watson, 8–65. Boston: Little, Brown.

OGDEN, DANIEL M., JR. 1971. "How National Policy Is Made." In *Increasing Understanding of Public Problems and Policies, 1971.* Chicago: Farm Foundation.

ORTIZ, ROXANNE DUNBAR. 1981. Foreword to *Native Americans and Nixon: Presidential Politics and Minority Self-Determination,* by Jack D. Forbes. Native American Politics Series, no. 2. Los Angeles: UCLA American Indian Studies Center.

PRUCHA, FRANCIS PAUL. 1984. *The Great Father: The United States Government and the American Indians.* 2 vols. Lincoln: University of Nebraska Press.

SSCIA [Senate Select Committee on Indian Affairs]. 1978. *Oversight on the Reorganization of the Bureau of Indian Affairs.* Hearings April 10 and 12, 1978, 95th Congr., 2d sess. Washington, D.C.: Government Printing Office.

——. 1984. *Realinement of the Bureau of Indian Affairs.* Hearings June 11, 1982, 97th Congr., 2d sess. Washington, D.C.: Government Printing Office.

——. 1989. *Report of the Special Committee on Investigations.* Report 101-216, November 20, 101st Congr., 1st sess. Washington, D.C.: Government Printing Office.

STROUD, KANDY. 1978. "James Abourezk Calls It Quits (But Won't Go Away)." *Politicks and Other Human Interests* 1(13):17–18.

TAYLOR, THEODORE W. 1984. *The Bureau of Indian Affairs.* Boulder, Colo.: Westview Press.

TYLER, S. LYMAN. 1973. *A History of Indian Policy.* U.S. Department of the Interior, Bureau of Indian Affairs. Washington, D.C.: Government Printing Office.

WEBER, MAX. 1968. *Economy and Society: An Outline of Interpretive Sociology.* 3 vols. Berkeley: University of California Press.

WILKINSON, CHARLES F. 1987. *American Indians, Time, and the Law.* New Haven: Yale University Press.

Indian Sign: Hegemony and Symbolism in Federal Indian Policy

GEORGE PIERRE CASTILE

The study of the Native American peoples has long been a major focus of American anthropology, but until recently very few anthropologists have concerned themselves with analyzing the legal-political relationship between the United States government and these enclaved peoples or the federal policy mechanisms that have defined it. With a few exceptions, study of the formation and administration of federal Indian policy, so critical to the understanding of the lives of the reservation peoples and so little in their control, has been relegated by default to political scientists and historians, who have showed little more interest (some exceptions are Bee 1982; Kelly 1983; Hoxie 1984; and Philp 1986).

While Indian policy would logically seem a subset of broader national "ethnic" policy, in fact the quasi-autonomous system of "reservations" in the United States is a unique structural arrangement between the political state and this single group of peoples. Though frequently reflecting the broader currents of federal policy, particularly the omnipresent assimilation theme, Native American policy, especially since 1930, often seems anomalous, even opposed, to the general trends in ethnic matters. Accounting for this uniqueness, a policy enigma, is the primary focus of this essay.

As with any policy, understanding the sources and direction of ethnic policy is a complex problem amounting to a sociopolitical version of vector analysis. Most models of state—ethnic group relations involve a more or less rational analysis of costs, benefits, and balances between dominant and subordinate groups and forces in the state (Despres 1975; Hechter 1975; Connor 1984). A complete chart of the course of Indian policy would require a summing of the various forces that have sought to influence it throughout its history, a task beyond the scope of a short paper. Instead I block out four broad areas that have seemed critical at a variety of turning points. I suggest that most of what has happened to the reservation peoples has had to do with (1) resource competition, (2) bureaucratic inertia, (3) reflective policy, and (4) symbolic utility.

I explore each of these in turn, but, while giving due weight to the importance of the other factors, I concentrate on the uses of Indian policy to the state primarily in terms of maintaining "hegemony"; and that is largely a question of the fourth category, symbolic utility. The integrative task of establishing cultural hegemony and ethnic solidarity is a major problem for any plural society, and Indian policy has its major benefit, at least in modern times, in that arena. Hegemonic utility, I argue, is the key to the explanation of the seeming anomaly of Indian policy in the broader range of ethnic relations.

RESOURCE COMPETITION

The almost orthodox or standard explanation of Indian policy is simple resource competition, which pictures Indian policy as based on the exploitation of Native Americans' resources for the benefit of the dominant society. Commenting on federal Indian legislation, Felix Cohen observed that "to the cynic such legislation may frequently appear as a mechanism for the orderly plundering of the Indian" (1942:xi). There have been and remain many such cynics, and resource competition–based, "neocolonial," models explain much in Indian affairs (Bee and Gingerich 1977; Jorgensen 1978; Ortiz 1984; Weiss 1984; Snipp 1986; Muga 1988). The benefits to the dominant elements in the society of the simple exploitation inherent in such a policy have a clear and obvious economic logic.

There can be no real question that the expropriation of Indians' resources—their land—is in fact the fundamental key to federal-Indian relations until approximately 1900. Where the Native Americans were once in sole possession of the entire 2.5 billion acres lying within the current U.S. boundaries, they were forced by federal policy actions onto reservations of only 155,632,312 acres by 1881. Prodigious as this confiscation was, the machinations of the General Allotment Act after 1881 reduced their resource base by a further 90 million acres, and of the approximately 60 million acres remaining to them at the end, most was not worth taking and by definition was unexploitable for economic development (Carlson 1981).

The "freeing" of land of its native inhabitants and the control of the sometimes violent resistance of the displaced created the reservation system and was unquestionably the dominant policy until 1900. A variety of other more altruistic "positive" and beneficial policy goals found frequent lip service in this era—Indians' protection, education, salvation, and civilization were frequently announced aims—but the results speak for themselves (Prucha 1976). While the land was successfully expropriated, the benevolent policies of education and civilization announced for the Native American peoples were either never pursued at all or pursued so weakly that they failed miserably.

The condition of the Indian peoples at the end of this process, as revealed by Lewis Merriam's report (1928), speaks as eloquently to the direction of federal policy as does their land loss. Their population had fallen to an all-time low of 250,000 from an estimated 10 million, and those who survived were without means of livelihood on the barren reserves. Stripped of resources, they had become the poorest of the poor with the worst life conditions of any people in America, including former slaves. Indians were ill-educated, ill-housed, in poor health, without work, and often without hope, as revealed by catastrophic alcoholism and suicide rates. Creating a dependent client population suspended in such misery can scarcely have been the intended object of the government's policy, but the reservation reality testifies to the policymakers' overwhelming interest in the Indians' land rather than in the Indians themselves.

Equally obvious is that by the 1920s the Native Americans had been picked clean of most of their usable resources. There was little left to expropriate, and by then they were no longer a military threat to anyone. The principles of control and expropriation that guided policy until that point were no longer politically compelling, and the Native Americans fell into a policy limbo. Land was no longer a national issue; indeed, after John Collier's administration as commissioner of Indian affairs, most reservation land bases stabilized, and some even grew, though these small increases were not enough to break the prevailing pattern of poverty and underdevelopment.

The end to the prevailing pattern of expropriation just short of the elimination of the reservations is part of the anomaly of Indian policy that requires us to look beyond simple economic explanations. The logic of straightforward economic neocolonialism would argue for the complete elimination of the reservations, and that remained the announced aim of policy until the 1930s, even if it was not actively pursued. Part of the answer is simply that the resources left after 1900 were not worth the candle, a question of political economy of scale. The remaining lands interested entrepreneurs in the Western states, but although such local claims continued to be supported by politicians in those states, these interests were no longer of the scale necessary to influence the policymaking interest of Congress as a whole.

Can federal Indian policy since 1900 be understood in terms of some other forms of economic exploitation of sufficient scale to justify the continued existence of the reservation system, the bureaucracy that administers it, and the sizable cost to the federal government? Many have suggested that oil, coal, and other mineral deposits belatedly discovered after the confiscatory policy period are still being expropriated, but now through the mechanism of federal control of leasing (Jorgensen 1978; Talbot 1981). There is no question that most of the remaining resources, poor as they are, are indeed in large part exploited by outsiders through a variety of such lease arrangements. On many reservations even the best farmlands are worked by outsiders through these leases, reducing the Indians to seasonal laborers on their own lands (Stern and Boggs 1971). These arrangements made by the Bureau of Indian Affairs (BIA) do often seem to have been made under terms of no great advantage to the Indian peoples. Generally they yield below-market rents and create little employment or infrastructural development.

There are limitations to the argument that this leasing pattern is the key to federal policy in sustaining the reservation system. If these resources are valuable enough to guide policy, then why not simply expropriate them as was done before 1900? The sums spent to maintain the reservation system, while not vast by federal standards, are substantial, and the yield to local Western interests who are the primary beneficiaries of these sweetheart leases is nowhere near the opportunity cost (Swimmer et al. 1984). The reservation system is a costly and inefficient Rube Goldberg device if its supposed aim is profitable exploitation of Indian resources by the larger society. The existence of these lease arrangements, on the contrary, appears to be an inadvertent function of the insignificance of Indian resources rather than a scheme based on their exploitation.

The recent hearings of the Senate Special Committee on Investigations of Indian Administration have found a clear pattern of low rates of return for reservation oil and mineral leases (FCNL 1989). But the hearings also indicate that the system is the result of bureaucratic ineptitude and mismanagement rather than any concerted scheme of intentional exploitation. The investigations suggest that *all* public domain land tends to have this characteristic low yield (FCNL 1989:2). The Native Americans suffer more than other Americans because a greater part of their economy is under inept federal management, but all Americans suffer similarly from the mismanagement of public lands. These activities so important to the reservations are more matters of oversight than intention—not policy goals at all, but mere inevitable results of their status as federally administered communities.

I do not mean to argue that there is no continued utility to resource competition–based analysis. The economic model is still clearly useful in some areas. The Alaskan Native Settlement Act and the continuing debates over its modification have a clear economic basis, as does the ongoing wrangling over *Winters* doctrine water rights in the West (Berger 1985; Miklas and Shupe 1986). But in Indian affairs in general resource competition has become something of a red herring that distracts attention from other considerations. If we assume tentatively that the exploitation of Indian resources through expropriation or lease is not the principal motive for federal policy and administration of the reservations since 1900, we are freer to explore other lines of inquiry as to the origins of policy.

Symbolic, not economic, utility is the positive policy goal I will eventually offer as the most fruitful line to explore. But first I want to introduce the two other policy considerations that frequently function to obscure understanding of what happens in Indian affairs. These operate as "uncertainty principles" that limit the rational analysis of Indian policy.

BUREAUCRATIC INERTIA

I have already suggested that Indian lands now lack "scale," and I suggest a similar lack of scale for the Native Americans themselves, which tends to induce policy indifference, which in turn leads to bureaucratic inertia. Much of what happens, or more correctly doesn't happen, on the reservations is a function of the fact that in national politics no one cares very much one way or another.

Even in the early phases of American politics, when the Indian land question had some political weight, the Indians qua Indians had virtually none. The single phrase in the commerce clause of the Constitution reflects the limited notice taken of them at a time when they were at the height of their military and economic influence. In modern times Lyndon Baines Johnson, whose administration inaugurated the vital shift to "self-determination" policy, had not one word to say about Native Americans in his retrospective account of his presidency (Johnson 1971). Once their land was secured and their resistance subdued, Indians lost what little political clout they had.

The cloutless political status of Native Americans becomes clearer when set in contrast to the scale of other ethnic groups. Among the features of an ethnic group that give it political weight and mold ethnic policy are concerns with the control of the labor of these populations and political control of their voting behavior. Persuasive arguments, for example, have been made that the various shifts in civil rights policy related to blacks have had much to do with their role as "reserve labor" in controlling wages and the shifting and increasing demographic weight of their vote (Piven and Cloward 1977; Blauner 1982).

It is difficult to make a similar argument about Indian policy. Indian labor has never been a numerically significant resource. While policy in other Latin American nations has always been guided by a concern for harnessing the large, settled native population as peasants, in the United States the prevailing policy sought land unencumbered by Indians (Spicer 1967). The critical difference is the size of the Native American populations. The ratio of Europeans to Native Americans in North America was only briefly small enough to engender the abortive attempts to harness Indian labor. But the native populations, not large to begin with, fell rapidly by depopulation through disease and the flight of the survivors to the refuge of open frontiers. European indentured servants and African chattel slaves were rapidly substituted, and the proportion of Native Americans in the labor force fell to insignificance (Nash 1974). Europeans numbered 4 million by 1790 and 31 million by 1860, and continued increasing, while the Native Americans dropped to a low point of approximately 250,000 (Merriam 1928).

Ethnic groups such as the African Americans today have considerable clout and weight in American politics because there are some 30 million of them, largely concentrated in major industrial cities. Native Americans, by the most generous estimate based on their remarkable increase by "recruitment" in the last census, number only 1,532,000—less than 1 percent of the U.S. population (Passel and Berman 1986). The reservation populations that are the primary focus of Indian policy are less than half this number (631,574) and are isolated and widely dispersed on 278 reservations (Swimmer et al. 1984). Indian labor has been insignificant since the 1700s, and, given their numbers, Indians have never been worth courting as a voting bloc. The Native Americans lack clout because they lack scale.

The result of this, as I have already suggested, is policy indifference, which results in bureaucratic inertia. In politics as in physics, "a body at rest tends to stay at rest" unless force is applied to move it; in this case political force, of which the Native Americans have virtually none. Robert Bee explores the Weberian bureaucratic implications of a similar hypothesis at greater length elsewhere in this volume. Here I want only to suggest that once the reservation system came into being, there was, after 1900, no sufficient economic or demographic interest at stake to do anything—positive or negative—further about it.

Given the lack of any directional political force, the BIA bureaucracy has by default largely been left undisturbed as a caretaker mechanism, holding the reservation peoples frozen in perpetual dependency in their administered communities. Lacking any congressional mandate for change, and charged with "trust" responsibility, the safest course of action for the BIA bureaucrat who is not interested in working himself out of a job is to do as little as posssible. The result of this is that much of what happens on reservations has no further explanation than that offered by the Tiv to Laura Bohannan: "That is the way that it is done, so that is how we do it" (1968:482). The BIA's relentless pursuit of the status quo is thus a considerable factor in understanding Native American policy.

REFLECTIVE POLICY

Things do change in Indian policy, and new mandates are periodically given to the bureaucrats. When we examine the critical turning points of such occurrences—the policies of greatest impact and significance to the reservation peoples—we tend to find that they are simply the reflections of larger events. In fact, the single greatest factor governing events on the reservations may be policies formulated entirely without direct reference to the reservations; policy applied to Indians, but not Indian policy.

Since the Indians themselves lack scale and the BIA seeks stasis, the only possible source of force to create policy action is external to the reservations themselves. Action on the reservations is the result of motivations of greater scale, of social momentum built up elsewhere and then applied as an afterthought to the reservations. This tends to lend a "deux ex machina" quality to reservation life because the often great impact of such policies is unanticipated and largely accidental. While the lack of scale explains to some extent why things don't happen, why the reservation system persists in a kind of stasis, to understand what does happen we need to look off the reservations entirely.

For example, the turning away from forced assimilation and the tentative moves toward self-government and economic development during the Indian Reorganization Act (IRA) era under the Collier administration are debatably among the most critical events in recent reservation history (W. H. Kelly 1954). Yet this was scarcely the work of the Indians themselves, as Collier tended to claim, nor was it really the result of the interest in Indian affairs of a handful of Eastern intellectual romantics such as Collier himself, inspired by the quest for the "community" of Prince Kropotkin (L. C. Kelly 1983).

The social engineering and restructuring undertaken on the reservations during Collier's administration as BIA commissioner occurred only because similar efforts on a vastly greater scale were being undertaken throughout the disrupted United States. The Native American's economic pump was primed only because the FDR administration was priming the national pump. Innovative conservation and education programs came about only because the administration was conducting a broad-spectrum social struggle against the social disruptions of the Great Depression. The Indians, long poor and powerless, got help only when "one third of a nation" found itself in similar straits and, as in the Navaho stock-reduction program, often got it in forms ill-designed for the reservations themselves (Taylor 1980).

FDR's social programs lost momentum during World War II, and the relative importance of those directed to Indian affairs was graphically illustrated when the BIA was moved from Washington, D.C., to Chicago to make room for more significant matters. The economic woes of the general society were increasingly in hand at this point, and the new deal for Indians ended with the New Deal programs for everyone else, although reservation poverty had by no means been eliminated. These programs, however, meant only as temporary and small-scale emergency measures in the general society, had unanticipated and lasting effects on the reservations. Whatever the FDR policymakers had in mind for the nation, the era, among other things, created new and stronger social structure on the reservations. The IRA tribal governments for the first time began to give the Native American peoples some potentially powerful mechanisms for self-administration.

One could argue similarly that the greatest threats to the survival of the Indian peoples have also had the quality of policy afterthought. Lawrence Kelly noted of Secretary of the Interior Albert Fall, "Foiled in his efforts to develop the public domain for private gain, Fall sought new areas of exploitation. . . . He found those in the Indian reservations" (1983:159). Similarly, when the Republicans returned to power in the 1950s they took aim at the "excesses" of the New Deal and Fair Deal social spending. The Hoover Commission, which examined federal spending, had recommended in 1949 a wide range of program cuts, and elimination of the BIA and the reservations was only a minor one of the many recommendations. Many have tended to interpret the resulting "termination" policy as a resurgence of the assimilationist philosophy, but while the policymakers did make use of that rhetoric, the policy source was clearly not this ethnic philosophy but the reflexive application of cheese paring (Felix Cohen 1953; Burt 1982; Fixico 1986).

The most recent and perhaps most hopeful policy of all, the commitment to tribal self-determination—or at least self-administration—is also arguably among these inadvertent policies. Self-administration as a policy seems to be a direct offshoot of the Office of Economic Opportunity's (OEO) "Community Action" program and its doctrine of "maximum feasible participation of the poor" (Castile 1974). The program was designed for non-Indian poverty constituencies and was applied on the reservations only as an afterthought. The OEO program quickly stalled because it was an affront to existing political balances in its efforts to "empower" the poor. But while it failed everywhere else, it succeeded on the reservations. The program provided a vehicle to revitalize Indian self-government through its system of locally administered direct federal grants and was met with enthusiasm by Indian leaders (Philp 1986).

Such successes in a morass of Great Society failures elsewhere, and the unpopularity of the Vietnam War, presumably underlay LBJ's endorsement of the trend through his announcement of the new policy of self-determination in his "Forgotten American" message (Johnson 1968). In the following administration, Richard M. Nixon, while dismantling what was left of the Great Society, also endorsed the policy of self-determination—in this case because it was consistent with the decentralizing tendencies of his own New Federalism (Strickland and Gregory 1970; Forbes 1981). Although it was a failure everywhere else, the Community Action program, like the New Deal, left a considerable if unintended legacy to the Native Americans.

It does not take such large scale swings in general social policy as the New Deal and the Great Society to affect Indian affairs. Being of small political "mass," the reservations are more easily moved than the society at large or even the larger ethnic groups. Recent Indian policy has tended to be reflexively influenced by the relatively small political forces swirling around environmental and ecological issues. Reservations find themselves in a position analogous to those of Third World countries, inasmuch as both find themselves facing developed-world demands for stringent protection of the environment amounting to a prohibition on their own development (Reno 1981). While powerful political and economic forces make such preservationist notions difficult to implement in the already developed sector, reservation resources are in large part directly administered by the federal government, so even such politically weak forces are easily heeded.

Although the rhetoric suggests otherwise, it is generally not Indian interests that are the principal motivation in efforts ostensibly aimed at preserving reservation life. The preservationists, as one group's name proclaims, are interested in "Earth First." Their energy policy focus is on wilderness, water, fish, even alligators, not the Native Americans per se. The recent federal disposal of the Phoenix Indian school involved a trade of resources once dedicated to Indian uses for resources necessary for alligators—valuable Phoenix land for Florida wetlands. To the extent that Indians themselves are a consideration, it is as a sort of human equivalent of the snail darter, with reservations as ethnographic wilderness zones. This conservationist "Indian as natural resource" view was expressed by one of Collier's stalwarts, who said of Native Americans that they were a "National Asset, having something of the value of the big trees of California, and the geysers and buffaloes of Yellowstone" (L. C. Kelly 1983:308).

ANOMALOUS POLICY?

Thus far I have suggested that much of what has happened on reservations was a function of simple exploitation, much that did not happen was the result of simple political indifference, and the rest amounted to accidents that reflected larger policy currents. But this is too facile. Even in the early resource-grabbing period there were aspects of Indian affairs that do not seem to fit such explanations. Why couldn't Secretary Albert Fall pass his Bursum bill? Why couldn't Congress complete termination? Why can't Senator Slade Gorton pass his Steelhead Trout Protection Act? Questions remain about these and other policies that seem anomalous because they are not consistent with simple economic exploitation and not only do not reflect broader trends but run directly counter to them. The recognition of Native American "sovereignty" and the related policy of self-determination are the most perplexing questions of all.

In the history of the United States one clear and unequivocal political theme is an intolerance for any form of separatism, be it regional, ethnic, or religious. The War Between the States is the most dramatic regional illustration of federal intolerance. Separatist religious movements such as the Mormon kingdom of Deseret received no greater tolerance, and all such movements have been suppressed in their territorial aspirations. More modern movements of ethnic separatism such as the various black "nationalist" groups seeking to create autonomous homelands have not been dealt with so overtly, but neither have they been granted any political legitimacy.

Yet, in Indian law, a central theme since the decisions of Justice Marshall announcing the "dependent domestic nations" doctrine is at least a limited endorsement of some degree of tribal sovereignty (Getches et al. 1979: xviii). Marshall, of course, thought this condition was "contemplated to be temporary," and policy in general has tended toward this assumption of eventual extinguishment of tribal sovereignty. Still, unique among ethnic groups or any other constituency, some degree of tribal sovereignty has been conceded even if in actual practice the extent to which federal policy actually respected it has never been great.

In the 1930s this largely theoretical political autonomy began to take on some substance with the IRA governments—puppet governments initially, but potential mechanisms for self-administration nonetheless. An even more profound turn toward actual self-government was the codification of Lyndon Johnson's self-determination theme by Richard Nixon in Public Law 638. From this point on, the condition of tribal sovereignty has appeared "contemplated to be permanent," and the threat of eventual termination has been removed.

Why would federal policymakers tolerate—and in modern times even encourage—a kind of political autonomy for this one ethnic group that they will tolerate for no other, particularly when it is a group with little or no political clout? It is disingenuous to say that the Native Americans were granted this status simply because they are the "native" or aboriginal Americans. This begs the question as to why "aboriginality" ought to grant recognition of politically unique ethnic status. Aboriginality is a matter of degree, and other groups could be arranged on a scale of aboriginality. Partial aboriginals—mestizos and Metis—could assert similar claims. Hispanic activists have in fact made such claims to aboriginal priority to "Aztlan," the Southwestern United States, but no claims but those of the Native North Americans have been heeded.

If the key, as Justice Marshall decided and the courts have maintained, is simply based in unextinguished residual sovereignty, then there is a similar problem with other competing claims. Spanish, French, Dutch, Swedish, Mexican, Russian, Mormon, and other "national" entities all had *prior* sovereign title to some part of what became the national territory of the United States. Yet all of these prior sovereignties have been completely and absolutely extinguished, leaving no residues. With all of them—except the Native Americans—we have insisted on total political integration and tolerated no forms of autonomy whatever. The search for some answer to this policy enigma moves us away from the economic and into the realm of the symbolic.

HEGEMONY

The United States is a plural society in which the Native Americans form only one very small element in the ethnic mosaic. As in all such plural states, there are inevitable political and policy problems in maintaining the cohesion of the larger state and restraining the centrifugal tendencies of the plural ethnic elements. Theorists of the plural society such as J. S. Furnivall and M. G. Smith have generally tended toward a view of such ethnically diverse states that stresses the social control of the dominant elements dependent on the coercive exercise of state power (Furnivall 1948; Smith 1965). The Marxists, perhaps because their starting point was an extreme version of the coercive model, have generated some useful theory in reaction to this view. Notable among them is Antonio Gramsci, who contrasted such coercive "domination" with "hegemony" (Adamson 1980; Gramsci 1987). The concept of hegemony suggests that the solidarity of the state is achieved primarily through securing the "consent of the governed." Hegemony is the " 'spontaneous' consent given by the great masses of the population to the general direction imposed on social life by the dominant fundamental group" (Gramsci 1987:12). In the Gramscian usage this is not simple acquiescence to democratic or other political processes. The governed are brought to *agree* with the "ruling ideas" of the state—not to grudgingly give in to these ideas but to share them. According to one interpreter of Gramsci, "The ruling ideology molds desires, values and expectations in a way that stabilizes an inegalitarian system" (Femia 1987: 45)! The hegemony model suggests that in the plural society such manipulation of ideas and symbols brings ethnic groups as well as classes and other diverse interest groups to endorse the legitimacy of the state and to reject aspirations of separatism. Gramsci thought that in the United States the "need to fuse together in a single national crucible with a unitary culture the different forms of culture imported by immigrants of differing national origins"—in short, ethnic solidarity—was the key problem in achieving hegemony (1987:20).

I have argued the economic and political insignificance of the Native Americans in federal Indian policy. I now want to suggest that in modern times, and to some extent in the past as well, the "use" of Indian policy, its rational benefit to the state, can be best understood in this context of its contribution to the securing of ethnic hegemony. Even in this symbolic task of supporting hegemony, however, the key to understanding is not the pursuit of the "consent" of the Native Americans themselves but rather the contribution of federal Indian policy to hegemony in the wider ethnic arena.

INDIAN SIGN

The symbolic "image" of the Native Americans has always been largely divorced from the reality of their lives and subject to expropriation and manipulation in political and literary form (Black and Weidmann 1976). John Collier battled on behalf of Native Americans' political rights using images of them as denizens of a "red Atlantis" and heirs to the "world's oldest democracy" while his opponents used images of savage practitioners of "obscenities and barbarisms," with neither much troubling to consult with Indian reality (L. C. Kelly 1983, chap. 9). For those who seek to make use of such dream images of Indians as savages, sages, or solons, Indian reality is irrelevant. One of the special symbolic advantages of the Indian is that few in the national audience are aware of the contrast between these images and reality. Many know what slums really look like, which limits slums' symbolic malleability; but given the general lack of knowledge, all sides are considerably freer to invent their own "Indian."

This protean unreal quality permits a unique treatment of the Native Americans among ethnic groups. There is little unusual about the exploitation of positive Indian stereotypes in naming vehicles "Comanche" and the like to imply their suitability for warriors. But while Aunt Jemima and Uncle Ben no longer shuffle about on food packages, befeathered Indian "chiefs" and "princesses" abound. While there are no ball clubs called the Boston Slaves, there are the Braves, the Redskins, the Chiefs, ad nauseum (FCNL 1988). This blatant lack of sensitivity in the treatment of Native Americans is partly because of their lack of political weight, but also because of the almost complete substitution of imagination for reality in the public mind.

These commercial and popular symbolic uses of the Indian, which constitute the ultimate expropriation—the expropriation of identity itself—deserve a good deal more exploration, but in this essay I am primarily concerned with the manipulation of Indian images as it relates to federal policy. Rather than their commercial appearances we are concerned with their casting in the theater of Congress and the federal courts, where images of Native Americans have major roles. Gramsci suggested that while all organs of the state contribute to hegemony, "lapses in the administration of justice make an especially disastrous impression on the public: the hegemonic apparatus is more sensitive in this area" (Gramsci 1987:246).

Felix Cohen observed of the symbolic role of the Indian, "Like the miner's canary the Indian marks the shifts from fresh air to poison gas in our political atmosphere; and our treatment of Indians, even more that our treatment of other minorities, reflects the rise and fall of our democratic faith" (1953:390). Less elegantly, the symbolism could be compared with Yanamamo wife beating, of which Napoleon Chagnon observed, "Apparently the important thing in wife beating is that the man has displayed his presumed potential for violence, and the intended message is that other men ought to treat him with circumspection, caution and even deference" (Chagnon 1983:16). The point in both comparisons is the same: the message sent by Indian policy finds its significance in audiences other than the Indians themselves.

Policymaking factions within the Congress who find themselves unable to carry out their aims in the larger society sometimes turn to the small-scale reservations directly under federal administrative control to "demonstrate" their policies. For example, abolitionist programs aimed at the assimilation of blacks in the South during Reconstruction were largely stalled by the 1870s. Frederick Hoxie observed that "by 1879 Republicans felt the need to affirm their 'principled' approach to politics. . . . Indian affairs raised again the possibility that the government could 'deliver' an embattled minority from tyrannical rule." "Assimilated natives would be proof positive that America was an open society where obedience and accommodation to the wishes of the majority would be rewarded with social equality." What could not be done elsewhere could at least be symbolically accomplished by a demonstration on the reservations, and the "Indian assimilation campaign promised to be popular, safe and therapeutic" (1984: 32, 34, 35).

Although in this instance there was a nice coincidence of idealistic demonstration and continuing resource expropriation, the same principle of symbolic demonstration continued after the resource base had largely vanished. Federal policy on the reservations often seems to be explicable as such a demonstration to "keep the faith," not for the Indians themselves but for larger ethnic constituencies who cannot be more directly aided. Indian policy is thus tied to "civil rights" policy, but often in oblique ways. There have been several key thematic areas in which Native Americans seem to have had such symbolic demonstration potential.

INTERPOSITION

Reconstruction ended with the Compromise of 1877, when the federal government abandoned its commitment to intervene in the South on behalf of the civil rights of blacks when these were violated by local legislative and judicial disruption. The government did not actively resume that role until after World War II—judicially when it intervened in striking down the "separate but equal doctrine" in 1954, and legislatively with the Civil Rights Act of 1957. Explaining these policy shifts is not my aim here, but persuasive arguments have been made that both the hiatus and the resumption were not a sudden recollection of somehow mislaid idealism but a reflection of the shifting importance of blacks in American political and economic life (Piven and Cloward 1977). Whatever its origin, there has, in fact, been a renewed commitment since the 1950s to interpose federal power in the protection of minority rights.

The courts have long recognized that the Native Americans themselves are threatened by such local and state forces. In *United States* v. *Kagama* (1886), the Supreme Court noted, "Because of local ill feeling, the peoples of the states where they are found are often their deadliest enemies. From their weakness and helplessness, so largely due to the course of dealing of the Federal Government. . . . there arises the duty of protection and with it the power" (Washburn 1973:2692). The extent to which such protection by federal interposition has been offered has been highly variable, but unlike the African-American situation, the variation is not explicable by shifts in the political economy of the Native Americans themselves.

The fulfillment of the dreams raised by the civil rights movement, as with those of the Reconstruction period, has often faltered. Achieving political and economic equality has turned out to be a lengthy process, in part because much of it has been left in the sometimes reluctant hands of the states. In the interim the federal government has had to maintain its hegemony and legitimacy in the eyes of the ethnic minorities even when it was unable to satisfy their aroused hopes. As the abolitionists turned to the Native Americans, so too have modern-day reformers in this latter-day quest for credibility. The modern drama over Indian affairs finds political significance and utility as a continuing affirmation of eventual federal good faith in the prolonged civil rights struggle.

One illustration of this is the struggle in the federal courts over Indian fishing rights. The state of Washington, under Attorney General Slade Gorton, carried on an astonishing assault of Indian fishing rights in the 1960s, continued into the present by now Senator Gorton (Fay Cohen 1986). The state was thwarted only by determined federal interposition. The intensity of the conflict and its analogy with the civil rights struggle were made explicit in an observation by the Ninth Circuit Court of Appeals: "Except for some desegregation cases, the district court has faced the most concerted official and private efforts to frustrate a decree of a federal court witnessed in this century" (Getches et al. 1979:649). Such protection in this and other Indian cases acts as a dramatic affirmation of federal good faith in the protection of even the most powerless minorities from powerful local majorities. The actual resources of the Native Americans in question, such as game fish in Washington, are often not nationally economically significant, but the symbolism of their protection is a reassurance to all minority groups that the faith will be kept.

INJUSTICE

Perhaps even more important than the "justice seen to be done" in interposition and other demonstrations is the avoidance of the appearance of injustice. It is often symbolically not so important that you "do right" by the Indians, but that you are not seen to do wrong. Particularly in times of ethnic upheaval, the miner's canary is watched more closely, and open or blatant violation of Native American rights is politically visible and damaging to hegemony.

The success of Collier's positive policy can to some extent be understood as a function of the inappropriateness of the continuation of open expropriation and forced assimilation in a time of almost revolutionary loss of confidence in government. The Great Depression left large numbers of Americans disadvantaged, without hope, and ready to turn to radical solutions. During such times, continuing blatant policies such as those of Secretary Fall on the reservations would only have served as a reminder to the public of governmental failure writ large. Restoring the normal state of hegemony in such troubled times required not only positive acts but the avoidance of even unimportant negative acts for symbolic reasons.

An even more compelling illustration is the halting and reversal of the termination policy of the 1950s. Beginning as an offshoot of a conservative social policy era, it ran very quickly into another time of social upheaval, the rise of the civil rights movement. Terminating the cultural existence of Indian peoples as a federal policy became visibly and embarrassingly inconsistent with the affirmative spirit of that movement. In particular, the Menominees' dramatic campaign to reverse their termination using the confrontational politics of protest served to link the struggle of the Indian peoples against termination to the larger civil rights protest in the public and federal minds (Peroff 1982). The policy of termination was not only halted by this linkage during the 1960s, it was reversed through the creation of the Federal Acknowledgment Petition process (FAP) in 1978 (Roessel 1989). The FAP process has also been more symbol than substance (only a few petitions have been approved), but it does at least constitute another symbolic commitment to the continued existence of tribal peoples.

Overall, the generally increased importance of Native Americans in federal policy since the 1960s is largely explicable by the increasing importance of ethnic and civil rights. The civil rights movement itself is readily understandable in terms of the increasing economic and political power of the larger ethnic groups in the United States. Its relation to Indian affairs can perhaps be understood in terms of political sympathetic vibration, in which a degree of sympathy clout is at the disposal of the Native Americans as proxies or surrogates for the more important minorities. "Red power," which, on the face of it, is a contradiction in terms, has had a certain reality since the 1960s (Deloria 1974). The power is not that of the Indians themselves, but the sympathetic political magic which makes an offense against Indian rights a symbolic offense against all ethnic rights.

The down side of this symbolic power is that while much rhetorical attention has been paid to Indian activism and overt offense has been avoided, there has been little practical benefit. The poverty and life conditions on the isolated reservations are not all that much improved because they are not politically visible. Although policymakers are constrained from negative actions by the sympathy clout, there is little pressure to actually do much substantial and positive. In the realm of the imaginary Indian, rhetoric and formal gestures meet the symbolic needs, and so images are manipulated, but not the underlying realities. The last thorough look at the reservations found them, as always, among the poorest of the poor (Swimmer et al. 1984).

REVERSE SPIN?

Which brings us back to the most perplexing of all messages to decode—the policy of self-determination. Since any degree of political autonomy is categorically denied to all other ethnic groups, this can scarcely be interpreted as a spin-off of larger policy, nor as an instance of a demonstration of keeping the faith—symbolically promising an eventual similar outcome to other minorities. The initial political stimulus to modern Indian self-determination policy was indeed an offshoot of the OEO Community Action efforts, but that larger movement was itself abortive. The principal political lesson of the Community Action program was yet another reaffirmation of the consistent denial of political autonomy for the other poverty-stricken constituencies it briefly attempted to empower. So what does it mean?

In fact, what we have here is reverse spin; the policy of Indian self-determination conveys a message to larger audiences which means very nearly the opposite of what it appears to mean. At one level, the granting of symbolic autonomy to Native Americans can be likened to the function of ritual acts of license such as those associated with the Roman festival of Saturnalia. The dramatic role reversals and sexual license of the festival weren't an encouragement for general debauchery but a limiting statement—"only here and now is this permitted." The fundamental message was negative, a dramatization of forbidden behavior. Similarly, the message of Indian self-determination to potentially separatist ethnic groups is that *only* Native Americans can hope to aspire to this autonomy, and "no Irish need apply."

This and other aspects of the publicly pronounced "special relationship" allowed to Native Americans and no others has yet another three-cushion effect—not on the ethnic minorities but on the dominant majority population. The federal reiteration of the special relationship inherent in Indian treaty rights (e.g., the fishing rights crisis in Washington State) inevitably touches off protests against special "privilege"; the hegemonic effect could be called "revulsion unto brotherhood." Affronted that Native Americans can catch fish when they cannot, the masses of weekend sports fishermen cry out for equality under the law and brotherhood with all minority groups (Williams and Neubrech 1976). The apparent encouragement of centrifugal tendencies functions, in fact, toward centripetal movement from both minority and majority poles.

These affirmations of self-determination are, of course, often more symbolic than real. The special access to resources is strongly federally supported for hunting and fishing, which are not economically significant, and very much hedged when it comes to matters like water rights. The autonomy implied in self-administration remains only a potential contingent on the withering away of the BIA administration and its replacement by Indian self-government, a condition now further from fruition than the demise of the dictatorship of the proletariat. Limited public and largely symbolic affirmations of self-determination suffice for the hegemonic purposes; the Ark need never actually arrive so long as it is seen to be moving toward Zion.

Their role as the miner's canary has, however, had practical benefits for the Indian peoples. It has, I think, guaranteed that threats of the complete termination of the government-to-government relationship are a thing of the past. After having elevated the relationship to an important symbol of ethnic good faith, the political costs of its betrayal would be high indeed in the great game of hegemony. In the absence of a constitutional amendment protecting the Indians' position, Congress continues to possess the power, the plenary authority, to unilaterally end the relationship, but that power has itself become more symbolic than real.

There are more benefits beyond mere political survival. Once we understand that Indian policy has little to do with the resources of the reservations or with the Indian peoples themselves, then we are in a better position to locate the actual causal vectors. For the leadership of the Native American communities, some such understanding raises the hope of being able to manipulate their symbolic position in ways that grant them a political leverage far greater than their numbers justify. By keeping a sharp eye on the political waves of ethnicity, which they cannot raise themselves, shrewd timing will allow them to ride those waves and maximize their impact in positive ways. This ability to "get something for the people" through insightful reading and understanding of federal policy trends has become the indispensable skill for tribal chairmen (Bee 1979).

REFERENCES

ADAMSON, WALTER L. 1980. *Hegemony and Revolution: A Study of Antonio Gramsci's Political and Cultural Theory*. Berkeley: University of California Press.

BEE, ROBERT L. 1979. "To Get Something for the People: The Predicament of the Modern Indian Leader." *Human Organization* 38:239–47.

——. 1982. *The Politics of American Indian Policy*. Cambridge, Mass.: Schenkman.

BEE, ROBERT, and RONALD GINGERICH. 1977. "Colonialism, Classes and Ethnic Identity: Native Americans and the National Political Economy." *Studies in Comparative International Development* 12(2):70–93.

BERGER, THOMAS R. 1985. *Village Journey: The Report of the Alaska Native Review Committee*. New York: Hill and Wang.

BLACK, NANCY B., and BETTE S. WEIDMANN. 1976. *White on Red: Images of the American Indian*. London: Kennikat Press.

BLAUNER, ROBERT. 1982. "Colonized and Immigrant Minorities." In *Majority and Minority: The Dynamics of Ethnicity in American Life*. Ed. N. R. Yetman and C. H. Steele, 302–47. Boston: Allyn and Bacon.

BOHANNAN, LAURA. 1968. "Shakespeare in the Bush." In *Everyman His Way*. Ed. Alan Dundes, 477–86. Englewood Cliffs, N.J.: Prentice-Hall.

BURT, LARRY W. 1982. *Tribalism in Crisis: Federal Indian Policy, 1953–1961*. Albuquerque: University of New Mexico Press.

CARLSON, LEONARD A. 1981. *Indian, Bureaucrats and Land*. Westport, Conn.: Greenwood Press.

CASTILE, GEORGE PIERRE. 1974. "Federal Indian Policy and the Sustained Enclave." *Human Organization* 33(3):219–28.

CHAGNON, NAPOLEON A. 1983. *Yanamamo: The Fierce People*. New York: Henry Holt.

COHEN, FAY. 1986. *Treaties on Trial: The Continuing Controversy over Northwest Indian Fishing Rights*. Seattle: University of Washington Press.

COHEN, FELIX. 1942. *Handbook of Indian Law*. Washington, D.C.: Government Printing Office.

———. 1953. "The Erosion of Indian Rights, 1950–1953: A Case Study in Bureaucracy." *Yale Law Journal* 62:348–90.

CONNOR, WALKER. 1984. *The National Question in Marxist-Leninist Theory and Strategy*. Princeton: Princeton University Press.

DELORIA, VINE, JR. 1974. *Behind the Trail of Broken Treaties*. Austin: University of Texas Press.

DESPRES, LEO A., ed. 1975. *Ethnicity and Resource Competition in Plural Societies*. The Hague: Mouton.

FCNL [Friends Committee on National Legislation]. 1988. "Racism Against Native Americans." *FCNL Washington Newsletter* (November).

———. 1989. *Indian Report* (Washington, D.C.) 1 (Summer):33.

FEMIA, JOSEPH V. 1987. *Gramsci's Political Thought: Hegemony, Consciousness and the Revolutionary Process*. Oxford: Clarendon.

FIXICO, DONALD L. 1986. *Termination and Relocation: Federal Indian Policy, 1945–1960*. Albuquerque: University of New Mexico Press.

FORBES, JACK. 1981. *Native Americans and Nixon: Presidential Politics and Minority Self Determination, 1969–72*. Los Angeles: UCLA Press.

FURNIVALL, J. S. 1948. *Colonial Policy and Practice*. London: Cambridge University Press.

GETCHES, DAVID A., DANIEL ROSENFELT, and CHARLES WILKINSON. 1979. *Cases and Materials on Federal Indian Law*. St. Paul: West Publishing.

GRAMSCI, ANTONIO. 1987. *Selections from the Prison Notebooks of Antonio Gramsci*. Edited by Quintin Hoare and G. N. Smith. New York: International Publishers.

HECHTER, MICHAEL. 1975. *Internal Colonialism: The Celtic Fringe in British National Development, 1536–1966*. Berkeley: University of California Press.

HOXIE, FREDERICK E. 1984. *A Final Promise: The Campaign to Assimilate the Indians, 1880–1920*. Lincoln: University of Nebraska Press.

JOHNSON, LYNDON BAINES. 1968. "The Forgotten American." *Indian Record*, March 1968.

———. 1971. *The Vantage Point*. New York: Henry Holt.

JORGENSEN, JOSEPH G. 1978. "A Century of Political Economic Effects on American Indian Society, 1880–1980." *Journal of Ethnic Studies* 6(3):1–82.

KELLY, LAWRENCE C. 1983. *The Assault on Assimilation: John Collier and the Origins of Indian Reform*. Albuquerque: University of New Mexico Press.

KELLY, WILLIAM H. 1954. *Indian Affairs and the Indian Reorganization Act—The Twenty Year Record.* Tucson: University of Arizona Press.

MERRIAM, LEWIS. 1928. *The Problem of Indian Administration.* Baltimore: Johns Hopkins University Press.

MIKLAS, CHRISTINE L., and STEVEN J. SHUPE, eds. 1986. *Indian Water 1985: Collected Essays.* Oakland, Calif.: AILTP/American Indian Resources Institute.

MUGA, DAVID. 1988. "Native Americans and the Nationalities Question. Premises for a Marxist Approach to Ethnicity and Self Determination." *Journal of Ethnic Studies* 16:(1):31–51.

NASH, GARY. 1974. *Red, White and Black: The Peoples of Early America.* Englewood Cliffs, N.J.: Prentice-Hall.

ORTIZ, ROXANNE DUNBAR. 1984. *Indians of the Americas: Human Rights and Self-Determination.* London: Zed Books.

PASSEL, JEFFEREY S., and PATRICIA A. BERMAN. 1986. "Quality of 1980 Census Data for American Indians." *Social Biology* 33:3–4.

PEROFF, NICHOLAS C. 1982. *Menominee Drums: Tribal Termination and Restoration, 1954–1974.* Norman: University of Oklahoma Press.

PHILP, KENNETH R. 1986. *Indian Self-Rule: First-Hand Accounts of Indian-White Relations from Roosevelt to Reagan.* Salt Lake City: Howe Brothers.

PIVEN, FRANCES F., and RICHARD A. CLOWARD. 1977. *Poor Peoples Movements: Why They Succeed, How They Fail.* New York: Pantheon Books.

PRUCHA, FRANCIS PAUL. 1976. *American Indian Policy in Crisis: Christian Reformers and the Indian, 1865–1900.* Norman: University of Oklahoma Press.

RENO, PHILIP. 1981. *Mother Earth, Father Sky and Economic Development.* Albuquerque: University of New Mexico Press.

ROESSEL, FAITH. 1989. "Federal Recognition—A Historical Twist of Fate." *NARF Legal Review* 14(3):1–9.

SMITH, M. G. 1965. *The Plural Society in the British West Indies.* Berkeley: University of California Press.

SNIPP, C. MATTHEW. 1986. "The Changing Political Economic Status of the American Indians: From Captive Nations to Internal Colonies." *American Journal of Economics and Sociology* 45(2):145–57.

SPICER, EDWARD H. 1967. *Cycles of Conquest.* Tucson: University of Arizona Press.

STERN, THEODORE, and JAMES P. BOGGS. 1971. "Whites and Indian Farmers on the Umatilla Reservation." *Northwest Anthropological Research Notes* 5(1):37–47.

STRICKLAND, BERNARD, and JACK GREGORY. 1970. "Nixon and the Indian." *Commonweal,* September 4, pp. 432–36.

SWIMMER, ROSS O., and ROBERT ROBERTSON, chairs. 1984. Report and

Recommendations of the Presidential Commission on Indian Reservation Economies. Washington, D.C.: Government Printing Office.

TALBOT, STEVE. 1981. *Roots of Oppression*. New York: International Publishers.

TAYLOR, GRAHAM D. 1980. *The New Deal and American Indian Tribalism: The Administration of the Indian Reorganization Act, 1934–45*. Lincoln: University of Nebraska Press.

WASHBURN, WILCOMB E. 1973. *The American Indian and the United States: A Documentary History*. 11 vols. New York: Random House. Vol. 4.

WEISS, LAWRENCE DAVID. 1984. *The Development of Capitalism in the Navaho Nation: A Political-Economic History*. Minneapolis: Marxist Educational Press.

WILLIAM, C. HERB, and WALT NEUBRECH. 1976. *Indian Treaties—American Nightmare*. Seattle: Outdoor Empire Publishers.

PART IV

THE RESOURCE BASE

Primitive Accumulation, Reservations, and the Alaska Native Claims Settlement Act

LAWRENCE D. WEISS AND DAVID C. MAAS

Waterdrinker, priest of the Sioux, dreamed that outlandish creatures were weaving a huge spider web around his people. He awoke knowing that was how it was going to be and said to his people, "When this happens, you shall live in square gray houses, in a barren land, and beside those square gray houses you shall starve."

—Eduardo Galeano, *Memory of Fire*

In this essay we argue that in the United States there has been a special historical relationship between the political-economic process of primitive accumulation, the determination of public policy by the state, and the history of reservation status. The Marxist conception of primitive accumulation has particular historical meaning for aboriginals because it has been the driving force by which their lands have been expropriated. The state (in the broad sense), representing principally the interests of the ruling class, has played the major role in this historical drama. The issue of reservations is tied to the larger issue of land tenure and its relationship to public policy, which, as determined and implemented by the state, typically represents the interests of capital—that is, of the ruling class. The history of native land tenure under capitalism, including the history of reservations, has been largely determined by the needs of developing capitalism at any given point in history.

The development of Indian policy in Alaska has been viewed as a sequence of events that have evolved since 1867, when there was no official distinction between native and non-native, to the most recent amendments of the Alaska Native Claims Settlement Act in 1987. These policies have also been described as an extension of American Indian law, with some local variance and lapse in time. Hence the use of sections of the Trade and Intercourse acts in 1872 to curb the sale of alcohol to Alaska natives or the passage of the Native Allotment Act in 1906 with the same premise about land, individualism, and civilization found in the original Dawes Act. We prefer a third approach, however, one that associates native policy in Alaska, including the historical question of reservations, with the growth and development of capitalism.

This essay is divided into several sections. The first section discusses selected theoretical concepts regarding the historical development of capitalism. Special emphasis is placed on the key concept of primitive accumulation. Following that section is a brief history of primitive accumulation in the United States, focusing on the relationship between capitalist expansion, public policy, and the creation and dissolution of reservations. Next is a section focusing on the Alaskan case, beginning with the early period of imperialism and the expansion of merchant capital. Subsequent sections analyze the more recent history of primitive accumulation in the nineteenth and twentieth centuries. The Alaska Native Claims Settlement Act is analyzed as the last example of massive primitive accumulation in North America.

THEORETICAL FOUNDATIONS

Internationally, the historical development of capitalism occurred largely as a result of the seizing of land, resources, and labor power of aboriginal peoples. These peoples typically lived in a socioeconomic formation (i.e., a mode of production) called a *primitive communal society* by Engels and early anthropologists (Engels 1975). In this mode of production the direct producers generally owned their own means of production and produced their own means of consumption—their subsistence. Land was not a commodity; instead, use was based on a system of traditional use rights under which the ability to use land productively gave the user de facto control over it. Commodities were traded, but only those in excess of the products needed by the producer (Weiss 1984).

In general, capitalism as a specific historical mode of production can be differentiated from various prior modes of production, including primitive communal society, on the basis of at least three main features:

1. Wealth is concentrated in the hands of a few people (the *capitalist class*) who own the means of production—that is, raw materials, factories, machines, and so on, as well as wealth in money form.

2. Large numbers of the people have no means of making a living except by selling their power to work for wages (this class of propertyless workers Marx called the *proletariat*).

3. Virtually all production is not for the personal use of the producers but for exchange, for sale on the market. Goods produced for exchange are *commodities*. Under capitalism, *commodity production* prevails (Eaton 1985: 22).

In a primitive communal society, people (the direct producers) have access to land, tools, and resources (means of production) in order to make their own food, shelter, and clothing (means of subsistence). Furthermore, most items produced by the direct producers are made for their own use. In a capitalist society the capitalist owns the means of production and the means of consumption. These commodities are manufactured not for use but for exchange in the market in order to yield a profit. The worker—the direct producer—owns no means of production and as a consequence must purchase means of subsistence from the capitalist. Having been divorced from the means of production and the means of subsistence, the worker must sell his or her labor power to the capitalist for a wage.

The development of capitalism is entirely dependent on the historical separation of the direct producer from the means of production (and consequently separation from the means of consumption) so that the means of production can be turned into commodities, and finally capital, for the capitalist. Marx referred to this initial stage in the development of capitalism as *primitive accumulation:* "So-called primitive accumulation, therefore, is nothing else than the historical process of divorcing the producer from the means of production. It appears as 'primitive' because it forms the prehistory of capital, and of the mode of production corresponding to capital" (Marx 1987:668).

Marx, for example, discussed primitive accumulation in England as the expropriation of the common lands as well as the homes and private plots of the English peasantry during the enclosure process that began in the fifteenth century. The owners of larger farms and manors forced peasants off their communal and traditionally used lands. These common lands were enclosed and became private lands for sheepherding on a capitalist, profit-making basis. The peasants were forced to flee to urban areas, where they provided cheap wage labor for early capitalist manufacture. This historic event thus terminated feudalism and gave rise to capitalism (Marx 1987: 671–93).

Marx also discussed the critical historical role that aboriginal peoples played in primitive accumulation on a worldwide basis: "The discovery of gold and silver in America, the extirpation, enslavement and entombment in mines of the indigenous population of that continent, the beginnings of the conquest and plunder of India, and the conversion of Africa into a preserve for the commercial hunting of blackskins, are all things which characterize the dawn of the era of capitalist production" (Marx 1987:703). The treasures captured in these areas by undisguised looting, enslavement, and murder flowed back to each European nation and were turned into capital there (Marx 1987:705).

The process of primitive accumulation continues to play a role in the twentieth century similar to the one it played in the earliest stages of the development of capitalism: the separation of aboriginals and other peoples from their land and resources for the benefit of capitalists. Political economist John Eaton, for example, in his discussion of primitive accumulation used the following example: "The entry of British capital into East Africa causes what is in essence the same process to be re-enacted in the twentieth century. In Kenya between 1905 and 1941, 4,400,000 acres were expropriated from the natives and given to English settlers" (Eaton 1985:51).

From the very beginning of the development of capitalism, the state has been an arm of the ruling class and has functioned principally to enhance the interests of the capitalist class as a whole. Lenin noted, for example, that "according to Marx, the state is an organ of class *domination,* an organ of *oppression* of one class by another; its aim is the creation of 'order' which legalizes and perpetuates this oppression by moderating the collisions between the classes" (Lenin 1981:9).

The role of the state in a capitalist society is critical to an understanding of the historical and contemporary relationships of expanding capitalism to primitive accumulation. Historically, during the rise of capitalism and the decline of feudalism in Europe, "the root issue was State power, that is, whether the rising capitalist class or the representatives of the old feudal order controlled legislation, administration, the armed forces, and the legal system" (Eaton 1985:49). For our purposes, the more specific historical question is: What part has the state played in primitive accumulation on behalf of the emerging capitalist class?

BRIEF HISTORY OF PRIMITIVE ACCUMULATION IN THE UNITED STATES

The history of primitive accumulation in the United States[1] is largely the history of the repeated expropriation of lands from their indigenous owners. At various periods in history Native Americans were placed on reservations or other lands, only to be removed when the lands were deemed valuable by investors and speculators. Typically as a result of state coercion, they were successively placed on smaller and smaller reservations deemed of lesser value by powerful financial-industrial interests. By the mid-twentieth century the exploitation of native lands had assumed a variety of forms, not all of which required the increasingly politically difficult removal of natives from their lands. In some cases, such as the Alaska Native Claims Settlement Act, politically acceptable ways were found to expropriate the lands in politically more sophisticated ways. This section summarizes that historical process and places the Alaska Native Claims Settlement Act in its proper historical perspective.

The British Colonial Period (pre-1776)

Commercial speculation for profit was common with Indian lands. During this time much of the land was acquired by trade with private landholders rather than by outright seizure because natives represented a formidable military threat. Frequently these lands were subdivided and sold at a profit to small farmers. The colonial governments acquired Indian lands by sale, treaty, and military might. Selective warfare resulted in expropriation of large tracts of native lands. These tracts were then offered for public sale, often to the benefit of speculators. Some of the colonies laid claim to Indian lands west of the boundaries recognized by the Crown, but after the French and Indian War of 1763, the Crown prohibited colonization west of the Appalachians. Marx discussed primitive accumulation during this period in North America in contrast with other areas:

> The treatment of the indigenous population was, of course, at its most frightful in plantation-colonies set up exclusively for the export trade, such as the West Indies, and in rich and well populated countries, such as Mexico and India, that were given over to plunder. But even in the colonies properly so called, the Christian character of primitive accumulation was not belied. In 1703 those sober exponents of Protestantism, the Puritans of New England, by decrees of their assembly set

a premium of 40 on every Indian scalp and every captured redskin; in 1720, a premium of 100 was set on every scalp; in 1744, after Massachusetts Bay had proclaimed a certain tribe as rebels, the following prices were laid down: for a male scalp of 12 years and upwards, = 100 in new currency, for a male prisoner 105, for women and children prisoners 50, for the scalps of women and children 50. (Marx 1987:705)

Trade and Treaty Reservation Agreements with Indian Peoples East of the Mississippi (1776–1810)

A principal motive for the revolutionary war against the British Crown was the Crown's insistence that there should be no colonization west of the Appalachians. Speculators and settlers wanted Indian lands, and soon after the war the Continental Congress legislated its monopoly over Indian relations. In response to these social forces public lands were acquired between the Mississippi and western boundaries of the former colonies in 1780. Vast territories were ceded by Indians to the government, but some lands were retained by native communities. These communities were often promised annuities and military protection against squatters in exchange for ceded lands. The government offered these freshly expropriated lands at public sales in huge tracts typically acquired by speculators.

Removal to Uncolonized Territory West of the Mississippi (1810–1850)

President Jefferson viewed the Louisiana Purchase as a vast uncolonized land to which Indian people could be removed from lands coveted by speculators and settlers. The Cherokees were moved to Arkansas, but armed resistance prevented other removals until the 1830s. In 1830 Congress passed the Indian Removal Act. Due to the change in the military balance of forces between 1832 and 1842, many Eastern Indians were forcibly removed to the West. The Cherokees were removed to Oklahoma and their lands were distributed through a lottery to become slave plantations. Typically, expropriated lands were offered at public sale and bought by speculators, then subdivided and offered (at tremendous profit) to settlers. Frequently treaties ceded land directly to individuals (speculators), or land was ceded to satisfy creditors.

Treaty Reservations in Colonized Territories (1850–1875)

Between 1850 and 1875, in response to intense pressure from land speculators and settlers, the federal government opened up Oklahoma, eastern Kansas, Nebraska, Iowa, and Minnesota. By 1875 most Indian peoples in these areas had signed treaties limiting them to reservations and allotments. Large tracts of expropriated native lands were added to the public domain for later distribution to the private sector.

The peak period for treaties was 1853–56, when more Indian land was alienated than at any other time. Kansas and Nebraska were flooded with settlers during this period, and additional pressure from settlers and the military forced Indians to give up additional territories in treaties. Finally, the Indians were removed to Oklahoma in 1859. Many of the treaties allowed the transfer of large tracts of land directly to the railroads, which then subdivided the land and sold it to settlers. Profits made by the railroads through speculation in expropriated Indian lands was critical to their corporate success. By 1871 the overall military conquest of natives was largely complete and Congress ruled that no more treaties could be concluded with Indians. Reservations and expropriations continued by executive order.

Allotment of Reservations (1875–1920)

During this period, as in the preceding period, pressure on Congress to accelerate Indian expropriation came from hordes of impoverished farmers, from the railroads and speculators and merchants. Mining and timber interests also wanted access to Indian lands, and therefore the speculators focused on the timber and mineral country of the Rocky Mountains and the Pacific Northwest, and the oil lands of Oklahoma as well as on the agricultural lands always sought. . . . In response to the mining and timber interest, various presidents throughout the period, especially Theodore Roosevelt, used the executive order to alienate reservation lands and allocate them to the public domain. In this way, large timber and mining companies could exploit the lands without having to deal with the more intricate Indian land-leasing procedures. (Kelley 1979:33)

While allotments had been a feature of earlier treaties, they became the dominant means of expropriation during this period, particularly on the Great Plains and in Oklahoma Territory. Beginning in 1875 Indians could homestead if they renounced all claims to Indian trust lands.

In 1887 Congress passed the Dawes Act, which parceled out small private plots of native lands to natives and dumped the rest on the market. Half of all Indian holdings were taken under the Dawes Act between 1887 and 1900. Most of the "surplus" and individual Indian holdings fell into non-Indian hands by legal and illegal methods, despite the twenty-five-year federal trusteeship established to protect native allotments.

Responding to a decade of intense pressure by the minerals industry, by the end of the 1870s the Bureau of Indian Affairs (BIA) had developed a system for leasing reservation land to private capitalists. In 1891 Congress established a system that allowed white capitalist farmers and cattle ranchers to lease allotments. By 1902, agreements were reached allowing the first oil and gas leases on trust lands. By 1908, 22,000 other leases had been concluded. Industrial oil development speeded up expropriation of Indian lands in Oklahoma.

Consolidation of Indian Reservation Lands (1920–1945)

In the 1920s, expropriation through allotments was curtailed and some native land rights were upheld in court. Lands could no longer be expropriated on the basis of executive order. The Indian Reorganization Act (IRA) was established in 1934. During the next ten years some reservation lands increased, but at the same time the BIA and Congress encouraged more leasing of native lands to profit-making corporations. Large for-profit enterprises obtained direct access to public lands through this policy. After the depression of the 1930s, "giant enterprises, mostly timber and mining companies, were the only influences on earlier federal land policy that remained significant as an economic force" (Kelley 1979:34).

Termination of Federal Trusteeship over Indian Lands (1945–1960)

After a brief respite in the 1920s and 1930s, the policy of aggressive expropriation of native lands was renewed. In 1946 Congress created the Indian Claims Commission to settle native land claims, a necessary step prior to termination. In 1953 House Concurrent Resolution 108 was passed with the intention of terminating the federal trusteeship over reservations. The assessment of the commercial value of native lands was part of the criteria for determining how quickly native lands would be terminated. Terminated lands had varied statuses: some were held by Indian corporations, some were allotted to individuals, and "surplus" native lands were sold to the government and held as public lands. In fact, however, these "public lands" were frequently handed over to timber companies, ranchers, oil and uranium corporations, and other enterprises who profited enormously from access to them. Capitalist ranchers benefited from the 1955 restriction on selling allotments that would break up timber or grazing management districts.

The New Look of Exploitation and Termination (1960–Present)

During the mid-1960s the U.S. government engineered a number of leases highly profitable to mineral, oil, and gas corporations. Manufacturing concerns acquired native land and facilities and native labor heavily subsidized by BIA and tribal funds.

The discovery of vast amounts of oil and gas on native lands in Alaska in the 1960s prompted multinational energy corporations to lobby for definitive land title settlement so they could establish the binding leases necessary for continued oil and gas exploration and development. The state of Alaska opposed the establishment of reservations because it received more revenue from state and public lands than it would receive from reservations. The Alaska Native Claims Settlement Act (ANCSA) extinguished all aboriginal land claims by Alaskan natives to 90 million acres of land, and most of the remaining native holdings were converted into land that can be taxed, bought, sold, and owned through private native corporations established by the ANCSA. This arrangement virtually ensures the eventual transfer of native lands irrevocably into the hands of speculators, multinational energy corporations, and other for-profit interests. This transfer, if it comes to pass, will mark the end of wholesale primitive accumulation in the United States.

IMPERIAL PRELUDE: THE BEGINNING OF PRIMITIVE ACCUMULATION IN ALASKA

European imperialism originated in the expansion of merchant capital in the search for increased profit, cheaper land, and more valuable goods. Marx's explanation remains the most convincing: "The circulation of commodities is the starting point of capital. The production of commodities, their circulation and that more developed form of their circulation called commerce. These form the historical groundwork from which it rises. The modern history of capital dates from the creation in the sixteenth century of a world embracing commerce and a world embracing market" (quoted in Kelley 1979:34).

Public policy concerning the indigenous peoples of Alaska is inseparable from primitive accumulation and the history of exploitation of the territory's natural resources. The Russians were the first non-native exploiters. Because of the potential profitability of sea otter and fur seal skins, the voyages of Vitus Bering and Alexei Chirikof were soon followed by hunting expeditions led by Siberian fur hunters, the *promishleniki*. Although an imperial decree was issued in 1766 claiming Russian dominion over the Aleutian Islands, there was little common authority over the traders and hunters. In response to this anarchy, and because of interference by other Europeans,[2] the Russian American Company was organized in August

1799. According to its charter the company was to "sponsor the conversion of the newly discovered people in the Christian religion and [to make] them into the subjects of His Imperial Majesty" (Chief of Foreign Law Section 1950).

The charter also expressed the hope that the islanders would be treated "amicably." The relationship between the Russians and the natives, however, was less than amicable. The Russian American Company was the brutal historical forerunner of primitive accumulation in Alaska. Though the exact numbers are not known, it has been estimated that 90 percent of the Aleut population was destroyed by murder, enslavement, and disease (Stoddard 1972:42). The survivors were in a state of servitude. The Russians exploited the Aleuts for pelagic hunting and used them in attempts to extend their empire into eastern Alaska. According to one geographer, "By 1820 there were some one thousand Aleut hunters scattered among the company's far-flung posts. In 1832 nearly one-third of all company employees were Aleuts" (Gibson 1978:52).

The conditions of employment were extremely restrictive:

> The Aleuts are forbidden to absent themselves anywhere without special permission of the authorities. [They] are forbidden to sell as well as to give away furs except to the company. They are forbidden to enter into any barter or commercial relations with anyone except the company. . . . [T]he colonial administration has the right to utilize the Aleuts to prepare the provisions of fish and fowl both during the hunting season and the rest of the year and does not have to pay them any special remuneration and . . . the company has the right or obligation to prevent the growth of luxury among the Aleuts, such as the use of bread, tea and similar items. (Okun 1951:197–98)

Despite its brutality, Russian commercial expansion into Alaska was geographically superficial. The major Russian settlements were along the coast. Although there were occasional forays into the interior, these were limited and temporary because of the inhospitable terrain, the inconsistent climate, and the "independence and hostility of the tribes" (Chief of Foreign Law Section 1950:65). By 1867, when the United States acquired control of Alaska, Russia factually ruled only a small part of the territory. Russians directly administered the Aleutian Chain, Kodiak, and the Chugach and Kenai areas; the rest remained terra incognita. The cession treaty provided that "the uncivilized tribes will be subject to such laws and regulations as the United States may, from time to time, adopt in regard to aboriginal tribes in that country" (Alaska 1867, Art. 3).

American expansion in the Northwest was propelled by the fur trade and, more important, gold. As one Russian scholar observed: "The government [Russia] not only knew of the presence of gold fields in Alaska but was actually afraid of the consequences of such a find; for in the wake of an army of prospectors armed with spades there might follow an army of soldiers armed with guns. Tsarist Russia knew very well what she was selling and the United States knew equally well what it was buying" (Okun 1951:249; Kushner 1987:295–315).

SOCIAL FORCES AND THE PROCESS OF PRIMITIVE ACCUMULATION IN EARLY TWENTIETH-CENTURY ALASKA

The Treaty of Cession between the United States and Russia contains a section that refers to future congressional action: "The Uncivilized tribes will be subject to such laws and regulations as the United States may, from time to time, adopt in regard to aboriginal tribes in that country" (Alaska 1867, Art. 3). The question of title to the land, among other matters, was left to legislative resolution. Congress recognized this obligation in 1884 when it passed the District Organic Act, which extended the civil and criminal laws of Oregon to Alaska: "Indians or other persons in said district shall not be disturbed in the possession of any lands actually in their use or occupation or now claimed by them but the terms under which such persons may acquire title to such lands is reserved for future legislation by Congress" (Alaska 1884).

Despite this disclaimer, land was always available for the economic concerns that required it. The first fish canneries were built in 1878, and within six years they were spread all along the southern coast of Alaska, cornering the mouths of the rich salmon streams. Also in 1878 the first gold-mining camp was constructed. Gold prospecting and disputes between miners resulted in the territory's first civil government and the application of mining laws and the safeguarding of mining claims and titles. Legislation in 1891, 1898, and 1900 permitted trade and manufacturing sites, town sites, homesteading, rights-of-way for railroads, and the disposal of timber.

There were no treaty reservations in Alaska, but there were four other types of reservations: statutory reservations, executive-order reserves, public purpose reserves, and IRA reserves. Legally there were important distinctions between them, but all shared a common goal: to encourage natives' economic development and therefore prevent their dependency on public welfare. Two statutory reservations were formed by Congress: Metlakatla in

1891 and Klukwan in 1957. Although these acts appear at odds with the termination mentality of the times, they were hardly an endorsement of aboriginal life. Congress was convinced that under the tutelage of William Duncan the Metlakatlans would pursue a more industrious and civilized life (Maas n.d.:7).

Missionary influence in Alaska was supported by administrative policy, judicial opinion, and economic change. William Duncan, an Anglican lay missionary who led an emigration of eight hundred Tsimpshian from British Columbia, convinced Congress to establish the first reservation (Metlakatla) in Alaska in 1891.[3] Duncan ran the community with a tight-fisted and autocratic hand, and insisted that every resident observe "the Sabbath; be loyal to the United States; vote in community elections; support the schools; abjure liquor, gambling and heathen customs; be sanitary; utilize the land; and don't give or sell land to outsiders" (Maas n.d.:7). The Klukwan reserve was established to allow U.S. Steel to explore for iron ore because the Tribal Mineral Leasing Act permitted mineral leases only on reservation lands (Case 1984:116).

Executive-order reserves were created for a variety of reasons. At the urging of Sheldon Jackson over a million acres was set aside for reindeer herding to prevent starvation and to teach the "civilizing art of animal husbandry" (Case 1984:89). In 1885 Sheldon Jackson, a well-known Presbyterian missionary and self-proclaimed publicist and lobbyist for Alaska, was named general agent for education.[4] Through his control of both mission and public schools he "provided the physical facilities and supplies . . . and permitted the missionary societies to staff the schools. Through this expediency, the missions flourished and for the first time the Native homelands were penetrated everywhere by the new cultural force" (Oswalt 1963).

Other lands were set aside for educational purposes under the supervision of the Bureau of Education until 1931, when the Bureau of Indian Affairs assumed control. By 1908 most of the major villages had designated land for schools. There were also public purpose reserves which were technically not Indian reserves but were for the educational and vocational benefit of Alaska natives.

The Indian Reorganization Act was applied to Alaska in 1936 and gave the secretary of the interior the authority to organize Indian reservations on "any area of land which has been reserved for the use and occupancy of Indians and Eskimos . . . or which has been heretofore reserved under any executive order and placed under the jurisdiction of the Department of the Interior or any Bureau thereof, together, with additional public lands

Table 1. Alaska land proscribed for native use between 1891 and 1945.

		Population	
Type of Reserve	Acres	Total	Native
Statutory reserves	87,635	1,665	1,105
Executive-order reserves	1,259,679	1,773	1,713
Public-purpose reserves	13,772	514	446
IRA reserves	1,540,270	1,248	1,111

Source: Federal Field Committee for Development Planning in Alaska, Alaska Natives and the Land (Washington, D.C.: Government Printing Office, 1968), pp. 444–45.

adjacent thereto, within the Territory of Alaska, or any other public lands which are actually occupied by Indians or Eskimos within said Territory" (U.S. Congress 1936, sec. 2). Through the extension of the IRA to Alaska, Secretary of the Interior Harold Ickes hoped to identify the different native groups and the lands they occupied and to carry out the government's moral and legal obligations to Alaska natives (Case 1984:100).

The amount of land administratively and legislatively proscribed for native use between 1891 and 1945 amounted to only 2.5 million acres, or less than 1 percent of the total land area in Alaska. The withdrawals affected only 12 percent of the native population, most of whom lived along the coast (the exact figures are in table 1). Federal reservation policy engendered much controversy and opposition in Alaska. There was first the question of leasing executive-order reserve lands, which was part of a national debate over Secretary of the Interior Albert Fall's scheme of opening reserved lands for mineral exploration. Eventually the Indian Oil Act of 1927 was passed; it authorized oil and gas leases but with the stipulation that the income derived from leasing be put into trust for those who occupied the land (Kelly 1983:349–78).

The restrictions on Alaska lands also infuriated many local leaders. White entrepreneurs wanted to seize Alaska's lands in their drive for unrestrained economic development, a recurring theme in the history of the territory and the movement for statehood.[5] One argument used to prevent native tribes from acquiring land under the IRA was typified by Anthony Dimond, the territorial delegate to Congress, who argued that Alaska natives were accustomed to small families and lacked any notion of tribe. William L. Paul, Sr., a leader of the Alaska Native Brotherhood (ANB),[6] feared rule by a distant exploitative and neocolonialist bureaucracy in Washington. Another Tlingit leader opined: "There has grown up in America by no deliberate design but by a natural though mischievous opportunism a system as inconsistent with American principles and the American spirit as could easily be devised by the ingenuity or conceived by the imagination of man[;] it has denied to the Indian those *rights* and *prerogatives* which the Declaration of Independence truly declares to belong inalienably to all men. It has made a prisoner of him instead of civilizing him."[7] Other native groups opposed the erection of boundaries around traditional hunting and fishing grounds.

There was also determined opposition to reservations from fishing and packing firms like the New England Fish Company, the P. E. Harris Company, the Pacific American Fisheries, and others who worried about losing control of the $60 million per year industry. Their lobbyists warned of the alleged negative consequences of native reservations, such as loss of revenue to the territory, discrimination, unemployment, and the limitation on future economic opportunities. These warnings from the representatives of capital find expression in current conflicts over native lands as well.

Nevertheless, many villages did incorporate under the Indian Reorganization Act and a few derived some benefit from the organization of local cooperatives and the availability of financial credit. However, because of public criticism, only six IRA reservations were approved by the secretary of the interior. Because of public criticism, judicial restriction,[8] and a shift in national Indian policy toward termination, over eighty village petitions for IRA reserves went unheeded. In 1971 the Alaska Native Claims Settlement Act revoked all the native reserves except Metlakatla. The reasons are discussed in the next section.

A good illustration of the complementary relationship between private interest and public law in Alaska's history is the passage of the Tongass Timber Act in 1947. Following World War II there was a shortage of newsprint. Industry representatives began a search for pulp and discovered the forests of southeastern Alaska. In 1946 Congress commissioned a survey of the territory's resources. The final report was favorable, and officials from three pulp companies and the U.S. Forestry Service entered into negotiations. The major snags were the question of aboriginal title and Harold Ickes's vigorous defense of Indian claims. Company executives worried about the risks of development and the possibility of litigation.

The pulp companies wanted some form of congressional protection before proceeding with their plans. The bill that eventually passed, the Tongass Timber Act, ignored aboriginal rights and allowed the secretary of agriculture to sell timber on any "vacant, unappropriated or unpatented" land. If the timbering activities touched on their land, the natives could sue in court—after the fact. In the words of one historian: "The Indians were removed from the process as active participants and were made dependent upon the Secretary of the Interior to protect their villages, on the Secretary of Agriculture to get a fair price for the timber and on the courts of the United States to determine what, if anything, they were entitled to as compensation" (Haycox 1990).

The federal government continued to overlook its obligations to recognize and protect the rights of Alaska natives through much of the twentieth century. Native lands were withdrawn for national forests, homesteads, and health and educational services. However, it was the movement for statehood that led to the expropriation of most native land.

After World War II, officials in Washington, D.C., were more aware of the strategic importance of Alaska. This realization, coupled with the influx of money and people, produced a viable statehood effort, and President Harry S Truman recommended statehood in his State of the Union Address in 1946. Owing to partisan opposition and doubts about the financial capability of the territory, statehood was delayed. Finally a compromise was reached, and Alaska and Hawaii were admitted simultaneously. On January 3, 1959, President Dwight D. Eisenhower proclaimed Alaska the forty-ninth state.

With regard to aboriginal land, the state enabling act contained a curious contradiction. On the one hand, the fourth section of the act required the state to disclaim right and title to "any lands or other property (including fishing rights) the right or title to which may be held by any Indians, Eskimos or Aleuts" (Alaska 1958, sec. 4); however, in a subsequent section Congress gave the state the right to select 103 million acres of unreserved public lands "which are vacant, unappropriated and unreserved at the time of their selection" (U.S. Congress 1958, sec. 6[b]). There were, of course, no "vacant" lands in Alaska. Inevitably the state selected land used by natives. By 1968, 12 million acres had been chosen and the Bureau of Land Management had issued patents to 5 million acres. The land was chosen primarily for its potential economic value to the state.

Native opposition arose as governmental activity increased in rural Alaska. On the Arctic Slope, the Bureau of Land Management issued a license to the Atomic Energy Commission to use 1,600 square miles around Point Hope for an experimental nuclear explosion to create a deepwater port. The Interior Department and the AEC did not bother to consult the residents of nearby villages. Another issue was the enforcement of an international migratory bird treaty between Canada and the United States. In 1961 Inupiaq Eskimos in Barrow staged a "duck in" to protest the restrictions. Many were arrested.

In March 1961 the president of the Point Hope Village Council wrote to the Association of American Indian Affairs and asked for help. The AAIA and the Indian Rights Association provided funds for intervillage meetings in which experiences were shared, rights were explained, and common solutions were proposed. Within six years, twelve regional associations and one statewide organization, the Alaska Federation of Natives (AFN), had formed to pursue the claims of Alaska natives. By 1967 all of Alaska's land—375 million acres—was under protest.

In November 1966 Secretary of the Interior Stewart Udall suspended all land transfers. The "land freeze" had three implications: all public lands were withdrawn from appropriation, the Bureau of Land Management could not process mineral leases or patent land title, and the federal courts insisted that the land rights of Alaska natives be protected until Congress acted.

The second bill to settle the claims of Alaska natives was introduced in June 1967.[9] Others authored by the AFN and the state soon followed. In December 1968 the first hearings were held by the Senate Committee on Interior and Insular Affairs. Little progress was made toward a settlement because of differences among the state, natives, and national leaders; a less than enthusiastic House of Representatives; intervening elections; and the mounting opposition of environmental groups. The key to a congressional settlement, however, was oil. Alaska's oil and gas reserves were considerable, and by 1971 the Nixon administration, powerful members of Congress like Wayne Aspinall and Henry Jackson, and the energy companies were committed to the construction of the trans-Alaska pipeline. There was only one stumbling block—aboriginal ownership. As Don Wright, president of the AFN, emphasized in a letter to Len Garment, President Nixon's special counsel, "An . . . issue of vital importance to Alaska Natives is the overriding question of aboriginal title to the land which would be traversed by the pipeline. In the recent case of *Stevens Village* versus *Hickel* in the Washington, D.C., federal District Court, Judge Hart ruled that the federal statutes prohibited the issuance of the pipeline permit without first obtaining the consent of the Natives of the village of Stevens. . . . There are many other Native groups having similar claims and protests over which the proposed pipeline would pass."

By fall 1971 each party in the claims dispute clearly saw the advantages of a settlement. The state needed the revenue that private development would generate; Nixon and the Senate wanted a domestic source of oil that would counter the increase in prices in 1970 and the shortage of fuel and heating oil; the oil industry and the House of Representatives wanted a permit to build the pipeline; conservationists wanted additional wilderness and parklands; and Alaska natives wanted their land. The Alaska Native Claims Settlement Act was signed into law on December 18, 1971.

In one sense the act was a unique legislative compromise. Unlike past federal-Indian agreements, no reservations were established, public administrative entanglements were minimized, private ownership was recognized, and an unusual amount of land and money were exchanged. Alaska natives received $962 million and 44 million acres of land. In 1978 the entire American Indian population controlled only 51 million acres, and the Indian Claims Commission, after twenty years, had awarded only $755 million in compensation for past illegal activities.

In a more general sense, however, the Alaska settlement was well within the tradition of the American political economy. Faced with the failure of past Indian policy and the need for the exploitation of Alaska's oil fields, lawmakers acted within the only frame of reference they understood—American capitalism. Legislators such as Wayne Aspinall, the powerful chair of the House Interior and Insular Affairs Committee, insisted that Alaska natives be integrated into the national economy. Some native leaders, like Alfred Ketzler, the president of the Tanana Chiefs, dutifully responded: "The major property interests must be held by Natives and not by state or federal agencies. Those who are the owners must have the greatest say. The royalty benefits must be spread widely, but with full regard to private property concepts. The legislation which we have authored and proposed through the AFN is designed to utilize modern corporate forms, so that we will be able to compete along with anybody else in a capitalistic society" (U.S. Congress 1970:369). Thus the ANCSA provided for regional and village corporations, stock ownership, fee title, and all the other appendages of Western capitalism.

While the ANCSA allotted only a modicum of land to private corporations and a small sum of money to individual natives, it was an economic and environmental bonanza for others. The settlement cleared the path for the construction of the pipeline. It permitted the Interior Department to withdraw utility and transportation corridors across public lands and to prohibit state and village selections on these lands. By 1988, oil and gas interests had gained net profits in excess of $52 billion.

For environmental groups and the federal government, the ANCSA led to the withdrawal of millions of acres of public lands for a variety of uses. Eventually 41 percent of Alaska will be designated national parks or forests, or scenic rivers, and another 19 percent of the total land area will be managed by the Bureau of Land Management for recreation, petroleum reserves, and unreserved use. Seventy percent of the wilderness lands in the United States is in Alaska. Most of the classified lands are also open to oil and gas leasing.

The ANCSA satisfied many of the demands of state representatives as well. State lands had been patented or were not subject to native selection; land grants were set aside for municipal use; and state officials were allowed to acquire the remainder of their entitlement under the Statehood Act. By 1986 the state had also collected over $26 billion in royalties and taxes from the development of the North Slope oil fields.

SUMMARY AND CONCLUSIONS

We began this essay by recounting the role of primitive accumulation in the historical development of capitalism, the expropriation of land and resources, the separation of production and consumption, and the emergence of capitalism. The new mode of production was characterized by an "industrial reserve army" increasingly separated from land and resources and commodity production. Conflicts in Alaska between natives and non-natives reveal the complexities, subtleties, and incompleteness of this process.

First was the assault on the communal societies of Alaska natives. Here familiar patterns reappear: contact, trade, pacification and Christianization, disease, demoralization, and impoverishment. The effects of conquest, colonization, and expropriation continue to find contemporary expression. While Alaska natives make up 14 percent of the population, they receive 40 percent of the benefits under food stamp and Medicare programs. Over 2,100 families collect Aid to Families with Dependent Children payments and 3,000 individuals depend on Adult Public Assistance payments. Moreover, many of those who are eligible do not bother to apply (Berman and Foster 1986). Native suicide rates have climbed from near zero in the 1950s to 4 times the national average; the suicide rate among young native males between the ages of twenty and twenty-four is 14 times the national average. Rates of crime, alcoholism, and birth defects have also risen dramatically. Unemployment in village Alaska is twice the statewide rate, and, according to one regional study, "less than half (42 percent) of the working-age Alaska Natives, in the western Alaska study group, are the active labor force, compared to nearly 86 percent of the white working-age Alaskans" (Institute of Social and Economic Research 1988).

Native lands and coastal waters have also been lost, mostly through corporate encouragement of state appropriation. By 1958 the federal government had set aside over 92 million acres, mostly for petroleum and power reserves, and a lesser amount for wildlife refuges and national parks. Between 1959 and 1980 the state of Alaska acquired rights to over 102 million acres, 2,000 miles of coastline, and navigable waterways. The federal government added another 125 million acres to the public domain after the passage of the Alaska National Lands Interest Conservation Act in 1980. State and federal properties support a wide variety of commercial interests, including fishing, a subsidized timber industry, and the extraction of oil and gas. Even protected areas are open for exploration and possible economic development; for example, the coastal plain of the Arctic National Wildlife Refuge and the U.S. Borax mine in Misty Fjords National Monument.

State policy has also sought to incorporate Alaska natives into the wider framework of U.S. capitalism. Initially, aboriginal rights to hunt and fish were eliminated. This was a legal necessity in order to clear title to lands that would be crossed by the trans-Alaska pipeline. Next was the establishment of for-profit village and regional corporations. The Alaska Native Claims Settlement Act has resulted in the loss of 375 million acres of land, over 2,000 miles of coastal waters, and indigenous rights to hunt and fish. It has also led to a major redirection of the economies, polities, and societies of Alaska natives. It is unique only because it is the most recent expropriation of native land in North America. It was fashioned in a politically sophisticated manner to make it appear that the acquisition of lands by capital was actually the fault of native mismanagement and greed. In the twentieth century primitive accumulation has assumed a variety of forms, but the intent has been the same: the actual or de facto separation of natives from their lands and resources.

Legislation passed in 1987 allowed individual tribal corporations to expand the number of shareholders, to contain the sale of stock, and to place their land in a settlement trust or land bank. Finally, land and compensation payments from the ANCSA were conveyed to these native corporations to forestall tribal ownership.

Neither the process of assimilation nor the process of primitive accumulation is complete. Over the last twenty years Alaska natives have fought to protect their local economies. In exchange for their support of the Alaska National Lands Interest Conservation Act in 1980, native rights to subsistence were partially restored. Village leaders have also demanded recognition of their tribal governments. They realize that powers not asserted are powers not realized. Consequently native councils have organized tribal courts, dissolved city governments, passed restrictive ordinances, formed regional nations, claimed jurisdiction over fish and game resources, limited entry into their communities, and declared their immunity from suit.

Despite the intense, unrelenting pressures of powerful energy corporations, and despite the heavy-handed maneuverings of their representatives in Congress, Alaska natives have generally come to understand the historical significance of the ANCSA. They have united in a variety of groups and coalitions in a struggle to retain their lands and strengthen native sovereignty. Their political awareness and the effectiveness of their struggle against some of the mightiest political and economic forces in the world have sharpened in recent years. Alaska natives' resistance to expropriation and the integrally related struggle for sovereignty have joined with comparable struggles nationally and internationally. The pervasiveness of international capital has forged an equally strong international resistance to its more destructive features.

Tribal self-determination in a capitalist economy like that of the United States is unlikely; certainly the history of capitalism offers little reason for optimism. Perhaps in the struggle to gain political independence and economic self-sufficiency, Alaska natives will become part of a larger successful movement to build a more democratic order.

NOTES

1. The brief historical review of primitive accumulation is based almost entirely on the following excellent work: Klara B. Kelley, "Federal Indian Land Policy and Economic Development in the United States," in *Economic Development in American Indian Reservations,* ed. Roxanne D. Ortiz (Albuquerque: University of New Mexico Native American Studies, 1979).

2. In the 1770s the Spanish, the English, and the French explored southern Alaska (respectively, Bodega y Quadra in 1775, James Cook in 1778, and La Peruse in 1786).

3. Duncan's efforts to obtain land for the Tsimpshians were aided by powerful individuals in business and the ministry. Individuals like Henry Solomon Wellcome and Henry Ward Beecher were helpful, as were organizations devoted to the reform of Indian legislation; for example, the Board of Indian Commissioners, the Conference of Missionary Boards, and the Indian Rights Association. The campaign to win support for Duncan's proposal was carefully planned to emphasize the problems the Tsimpshians had encountered in Canada and the avoidance of words such as *Indian* or *tribe* when talking about Duncan's followers. See Peter Murray, *The Devil and Mr. Duncan* (Victoria, B.C.: Sois Publishing, 1985), pp. 187–99.

4. Missionary work and governmental policy were intertwined in this area. Thus, as Jackson sought to support Alaska's missions and their religious and

educational endeavors, he also contributed to the passage of important legislation like the District Organic Act in 1884, which established the territory's first civil government. See Theodore C. Hinckley, "The Alaska Labors of Sheldon Jackson, 1877–1890" (Ph.D. diss., Indiana University, 1961).

5. See the territorial governor's charges of reverse discrimination and federal tyranny in *Hearings Before the Committee on Interior and Insular Affairs* (U.S. Senate, 81st Congr., 2d sess. On Orders of Secretary Julius A. Krug Creating Indian Reservations in Alaska, February 2, 1950. Washington, D.C.: Government Printing Office). Krug proposed reservations on Barrow, Shungnak, and Hydaburg.

6. The ANB was organized in 1912. It was the first native association in Alaska and it promoted citizenship, education, and the abolishment of "aboriginal customs."

7. Robert J. Peratovich, Jr., "Difficulties of the American Indian Student," *Alaska Fisherman* (September 1928). Also in 1919 the ANB sent a memorial to Territorial Governor Thomas Riggs, Jr., concluding: "Your memorial is to respectfully urge that you use your influence as Governor of Alaska to have said Indian Reservation Lands and Reservations placed on the list of taxable properties and hereby add income to the Territory Treasury, eliminate the pernicious system of reservations for Indian Americans and give political status to the qualified Indian American voter" (Memorial Records of the Office of the Governor of Alaska, R6348, National Archives file, Native Conditions 041.1919).

8. See, for example, *Hynes* v. *Grimes Packing Company*, 337 U.S. 86 (1949), which challenged the interior secretary's power to declare reserves for the exclusive use of a racial group. Confusingly, the Supreme Court upheld the secretary's right to recognize IRA reserves but ruled against the exclusion of non-native fishermen. Thus the Court agreed with the intent of the legislation—the protection of native subsistence—but disagreed with its enforcement.

9. On June 11, 1951, the first bill to settle native claims was introduced by the territorial delegate to Congress, Bob Bartlett. However, it was never referred out of committee. See Willy Templeton, "Federal Policies Toward Alaska Natives and Land in Alaska" (unpublished manuscript), p. 36.

REFERENCES

ALASKA. 1867. Treaty of Cession. *Alaska Statutes*. Charlottesville, Va.: Michie, 1983. Binder 1, pp. 49–53.

———. 1884. District Organic Act. *Alaska Statutes*. Charlottesville, Va.: Michie, 1983. Binder 1, pp. 55–60.

———. 1958. Alaska Statehood Act. *Alaska Statutes*. Charlottesville, Va.: Michie, 1983. Binder 1, pp. 77–105.

BERMAN, M., and KAREN FOSTER. 1986. *Poverty and Public Assistance Among Alaska Natives: Implications for 1991*. Anchorage: Institute of Social and Economic Research.

CASE, DAVID S. 1984. *Alaska Natives and American Laws*. Alaska: University of Alaska Press.

CHIEF OF FOREIGN LAW SECTION. 1950. First Charter of the Russian American Company. Quoted in *Russian Administration of Alaska and the Status of Alaska Natives*. Prepared by Law Library of Library of American Congress. Washington, D.C.: Government Printing Office.

EATON, JOHN. 1985. *Political Economy*. New York: International Publishers.

ENGELS, FREDERICK. 1975. *The Origin of the Family, Private Property and the State*. New York: International Publishers.

GALEANO, EDUARDO. 1985. *Memory of Fire*. Vol. 1. *Genesis*. New York: Pantheon Books.

GIBSON, JAMES R. 1978. *European Settlement and Development in America*. Toronto: University of Toronto Press.

HAYCOX, STEPHEN W. 1990. "Economic Development and Indian Land Right in Modern Alaska: The 1947 Tongass Timber Act." *Western Historical Quarterly* 21(1):21–46.

INSTITUTE OF SOCIAL AND ECONOMIC RESEARCH et al. 1988. *Alaska Natives at Risk*. Anchorage: Alaska Federation of Natives.

KELLEY, KLARA B. 1979. "Federal Indian Land Policy and Economic Development in the United States." In *Economic Development in American Indian Reservations*. Ed. Roxanne D. Ortiz. Albuquerque: University of New Mexico Native American Studies.

KELLY, LAWRENCE C. 1983. *The Assault on Assimilation: John Collier and the Origins of Indian Policy Reform*. Albuquerque: University of New Mexico Press.

KUSHNER, HOWARD I. 1987. "The Significance of the Alaska Purchase to American Expansion." In *Russia's American Colony*. Ed. S. Frederick Starr. Durham, N.C.: Duke University Press.

LENIN, V. I. 1981. *State and Revolution*. New York: International Publishers.

MAAS, JO. n.d. "William Duncan and the Tsimpshians." Unpublished manuscript.

MARX, KARL. 1987. *Capital*. Vol. 1. New York: International Publishers.

OKUN, S. B. 1951. *The Russian American Company*. Cambridge: Harvard University Press.

OSWALT, WENDELL H. 1963. *Mission of Change in Alaska: Eskimos and Moravians on the Kuskokwim*. San Marino, Calif.: The Huntington Library.

PERATOVICH, ROBERT J., JR. 1928. "Difficulties of the American Indian Student." *Alaska Fisherman* (September):2–3.

STODDARD, NATALIE B. 1972. "Some Ethnological Aspects of the Russian Fur Trade." In *People and Pelts: Selected Papers of the Second North American Fur Trade Conference*. Ed. Malvina Bolus. Winnipeg: Peguis Publishers.

U.S. CONGRESS. 1936. The Alaska Reorganization Act. Public Law 538. 74th Congr.

———. 1958. The Alaska Statehood Act. Public Law 85-508. 85th Congr.

———. 1970. Committee on Interior and Insular Affairs. *Hearings Before the Subcommittee on Indian Affairs*. H.R. 13142, H.R. 10193, and H.R. 14212. 91st Congr., 1st. sess. Washington, D.C.: Government Printing Office.

WEISS, LAWRENCE D. 1984. *The Development of Capitalism in the Navajo Nation*. Minneapolis: MEP.

Shortcomings of the Indian Self-Determination Policy

GEORGE S. ESBER, JR.

Nearly two decades ago D'Arcy McNickle cautioned that Indian peoples' "moral right to remain a separate and identifiable people is far from assured" (McNickle 1973:166). In contemporary America, the ability to make decisions and assert some modicum of control over one's own life and future is assumed to be virtually synonymous with constitutionally protected rights. People who are unable to exercise control over their own affairs feel a sense of frustration because they lack the money, power, and influential social contacts to promote their goals.

Minority peoples find themselves limited by additional factors beyond their control; namely, their own group membership. As members of social groups, they are restricted by the more powerful and controlling forces that define the dominant society. The constraints imposed on a minority group may range from a tolerance that permits varying degrees of self-expression and participation to the ultimate intolerance, merciless extermination.

Falling within that range are six different policy positions that Simpson and Yinger (1953:27–35) described in analyzing dominant group policies toward minority groups: assimilation, cultural pluralism, population transfer, legal protection, continued subjugation, and extermination. At one time or another, all of these positions were adopted by European immigrants to the New World in their contacts with Indian peoples.

Inasmuch as social scientists have not identified minority self-determination as a pattern of interaction between dominant and subordinate groups, my intention in this essay is to question the potential for self-determination as a tenable policy for Indian peoples as it is set forth in the

Indian Self Determination and Education Assistance Act (P.L. 93-638). Moreover, if self-determination is not functioning in actuality, then there is a serious need to explore the act's consequences with regard to Indian communities. I contend that the objectives of the self-determination policy are not designed to guarantee Indian self-determination, and further, that one of its effects has been the creation or intensification of divisiveness and the favoring of factions in tribal organizations that pattern their actions after an assimilationist model.

The meaning of *self-determination in Indian affairs* is not as clear as the phrase implies. By its title, the policy suggests local community control over decision making; thus, central to its implementation must be the power to make decisions. A common assumption is that Indian communities now have that power. This control, however, is not allowed by the Self Determination Act, nor is it congruent with the structure of federal-Indian relations. In actual practice the government executes its trust responsibility to serve the "best interests" of the Indian people (Gross 1989: 18–19), however those interests are defined and for whom.

The Indian Self Determination and Education Assistance Act of 1975 plainly does not address the issue of power, nor does it suggest the empowerment of Indian communities. Rather, it calls for "an orderly transition from federal domination of programs for and services to effective and meaningful participation by the Indian people" (*U.S. Statutes* 88:2203–4). One can read into this purpose the intent that the federal government will eventually grant an opportunity for Indian peoples to be included in program and service delivery. Inclusion or "meaningful participation" is not control but at best a limited exercise of power, which must be translated as "relative powerlessness" given the legal definition of the federal-Indian relationship.

The initial formation of the asymmetrical power relationship between the U.S. government and Indian tribes was rooted in the Constitution and built upon through other legislative acts such as the Trade and Intercourse acts and the Northwest Ordinance of 1787. Through these means the federal government established its position of power and authority over Indian tribes (Tyler 1973:34–43). Later, in exercising that authority, the Supreme Court in the famous Marshall decision in *Cherokee* v. *State of Georgia* defined tribes as "domestic dependent nations" and thereby confirmed them as powerless relative to the authority of the federal government. That arrangement remains the foundation of the federal domination that has prevented Indian self-determination from becoming a reality. Continued federal control, with the Bureau of Indian Affairs (BIA) acting as the government's agent, has actually become greater because of Indians' dependency on the BIA to carry out the contracting process that is supposed to more fully involve tribes in the national economy (Stull 1990:206). It is within the framework of power and control that the self-determination policy must be analyzed and critiqued.

The genesis of Public Law 93-638, like all other federal Indian policies, was a top-down decision from the legislative and executive branches of the government. Like other federal policies, the self-determination legislation provides no guarantee to Indian peoples about the shape that any future policy might take, when it might be legislated, or to what extent Indian communities might participate in its formulation. Indian peoples have never had control over the policies that affect them, nor can they expect to, given the asymmetrical relationship that has been defined by the federal government.

Federal policy continues to follow a course that shifts with the political winds, and perceptions about Indian peoples tend to follow these shifts. Under recent conservative administrations Indians have been portrayed as just another needy minority on whom federal dollars must be spent (Deloria 1985:255). From this it follows that tribes are welfare recipients whose use of government dollars must necessarily be monitored by the government.

This line of thought is erroneous because tribes do not receive welfare payments. Rather, as Richard Nixon made perfectly clear, the services and programs that are provided by the federal government are tendered as payment according to agreements made in an exchange relationship. In a 1970 message President Nixon stated:

> There can be no question that the government and the people of the United States have a responsibility to the Indians.
>
> In our efforts to meet that responsibility, we must pledge to respect fully the dignity and uniqueness of the Indian citizen.
>
> That means partnership—not paternalism.
>
> We must affirm the right of the first Americans to remain Indians while exercising their rights as Americans.
>
> We must affirm their rights to freedom of choice and self-determination.
>
> We must seek new ways to provide federal assistance to Indians—with new emphasis on Indian self-help and with respect for Indian culture.
>
> And we must assure the Indian people that it is our desire and intention that the special relationship between the Indian and his government grow and flourish. (Quoted in McNickle 1973:124)

Nixon added that the administration of these programs need not be federally controlled, but rather should be managed locally by Indians (McNickle 1973:125–26). While the spirit of Indian local control may appear to have been carried forward in the self-determination legislation and its subsequent amendments, genuine control remains impossible so long as federal domination continues.

The problem of federal interference with local control was illustrated recently when the Department of Housing and Urban Development (HUD) prepared to take over the unique Minneapolis Indian Housing Project. The enterprise was originally built as a result of Indian initiative and organization for the purpose of solving housing needs of low-income urban Indians. It has operated for roughly twenty years under Indian management, but because certain facets of the operation do not conform to HUD requirements of recordkeeping (a fascinating reason for intervention, given HUD's notorious record of unaccounted-for dollars during the Reagan years), the operation is in jeopardy and may be seized from Indian management.

The case illustrates the secondary role allocated to Indian self-determination when Indian performance does not conform to the Anglo model prescribed by the government under the authority of the secretary of the interior. The Indian Self Determination Act, in Title I, grants veto power over the issuance of Indian contracts and programs to the secretary of the interior, the secretary of health and human services, or the secretary of education—whichever is appropriate to the case. In essence, the United States is agreeing to legal compliance with the self-determination policy by granting Indian participation in Anglo activities. This is not equivalent to the governance of Indian affairs as Indian undertakings.

Actions such as those threatened by HUD are perceived as appropriate because of the underlying misconception that obligatory debts in perpetuity are temporary payments in relief. For the government to accept the idea of a perpetual debt to peoples of prior rights would be to undermine its sense of power and control—something the United States is unwilling to forfeit. In lieu of a policy that permits genuine self-determination, the current policy, as it is implemented through a variety of state and federal programs, has demanded a certain degree of assimilation from Indian communities.

Throughout the 1980s the illusion of self-determination was fostered by the Reagan administration's decision to maintain government-to-government relations with tribes (Gross 1989:71–73; Prucha 1989:96–97). Alone, the concept is consistent and supportive of the idea of Indian self-determination if tribal sovereignty is fully respected. However, tribal sovereignty and tribal self-determination are inextricably linked to communities' economies and economic development programs (McGuire 1990) and have been both directly and indirectly affected by external forces originating in the dominant society.

Tribal responses to self-determination under these terms have been mixed and exhibit a lack of unity, particularly among larger groups and those holding resources deemed valuable to the nation. Disagreements over tribal participation in the national and international market economy, as opposed to the preservation of a more locally based economy, are pronounced. Many local controversies are rooted in disagreements over approaches to stimulate recovery from fractured and insufficient economic bases. The surrender of lands and the circumscription of peoples has necessitated alternative sources of income, among which are the obligatory federal payments. But because those payments are perceived as remedial and temporary, and because of the conditional terms under which the payments are made, tribes are faced with acute pressures to produce income from sources such as business ventures, the sale of resources from tribal lands, and bingo and gambling operations. The lack of agreement among Indian peoples over the direction of tribal economies is also fueled by pressures brought to bear by national needs and interests beyond the tribal level. Seen in this light, a community's desire to exercise self-determination is hindered by pressures from national and private interests whose eyes are fixed on the resources of the reservations.

In the past, the Bureau of Indian Affairs made arrangements for the exploitation of Indian resources without ever obtaining tribal consent. Now that these economic activities have been institutionalized, they continue with Indian participation in management. When the Council of Energy Resource Tribes (CERT) sought advice from OPEC in the 1970s, it was immediately denounced by oil company executives as unpatriotic.

The role of the United States in pressing for the development of capitalistic, entrepreneurial tribal governments cannot be ignored. Not only have the economic goals and interests of the dominant society overridden those of the tribes, but social and psychological propaganda have been used against Indian peoples when tribal interests have not been subordinated to national interests. Remarks by James Watt during his tenure as secretary of the interior epitomize the unwillingness of the United States to accept tribal self-determination: "If you want an example of the failures of socialism, . . . go to the reservations. . . . every social problem is exaggerated because of socialistic government policies on the Indian reservations . . . because the people have been trained through 100 years of government oppression to look to the government as the creator, as the provider, as the supplier, and they've not been trained to use the initiative to integrate into the American system. . . . Terrible socialism" (quoted in Epstein 1983). In his statement Watt articulated a widespread opinion that self-determination is admissible only so long as tribal economies are congruent with the dominant society's economic system.

Indian self-determination was further hampered by President Ronald Reagan's policy of slashing budgets in the name of encouraging Indian self-sufficiency. These periodic threats to terminate federal indebtedness undermine the abilities of tribes to make stabilizing economic decisions that bear on their future well-being. The same economic coercion used in government-to-government relations in the international forum has been applied to reservation governments, although perhaps using more subtle tactics.

This pattern is at variance with the federal government's economic responsibility to tribes as part of the trust relationship guaranteed by executive acts and treaties (treaties that are presently threatened by anti-Indian lobby groups based in Michigan and Wisconsin). The fear of losing the trust relationship strikes at the very heart of tribal futures. If ended, it would most likely result in a final erosion of Indian landholdings. The Bureau of Indian Affairs, which for decades has supervised the trust relationship, at the same time has served as the arm of the government in managing tribal economic and resource development.

An alternative approach to economic development in the name of self-determination, the Alaska Native Claims Settlement Act (ANCSA) illustrates an extreme case of capitalist pressures on Indian peoples. Through the ANCSA, native stockholding corporations were established following the Anglo model for business enterprises. The corporations hold cash payments and land as equity and are expected to function as capitalistic stockholding companies. In a laissez-faire market, the corporations are subject to—and are experiencing—varying degrees of both success and failure. Beginning in 1992 (on the 500th anniversary of Columbus's voyage), native individuals may, by a majority agreement of stockholders, sell their shares (Anderson and Aschenbrenner 1986, 1988). In a market in which hostile takeovers and corporate competition prevail, a people with noncompetitive cultural values will be subject to pressures and inducements to sell shares, which could result in termination. The corporations that succeed will have done so because they assimilated values of competition and corporate managerial skills necessary for survival in the current world market. Corporations that fail or are sold off will leave the original native stockholders landless and without access to the resources needed for traditional subsistence patterns.

To further jeopardize the Alaskan organizations, the legislation forming the corporations is worded in a way that makes it possible to argue that corporations, and not "tribes," are the organizational entities in Alaska. If this holds up, the Department of the Interior will have no trust responsibility to Alaskan natives because they will be viewed as corporate stockholders (Anderson and Aschenbrenner 1986:1–2). A court battle won tribal acknowledgment for the Nome Eskimo community and set a precedent that the remaining 130 villages may use if they organize according to the stipulations of the Indian Reorganization Act (*NARF* 1989:17).

The Nome community and tribes in the remainder of the country presently maintain government-to-government relations with the federal government. However, this requires the formation of a tribal organizational structure whose pattern was established by the Indian Reorganization Act of 1934 (IRA) and which was implemented by majority vote on a tribe-by-tribe basis. Following the passage of the IRA, the BIA arranged elections with tribes to vote on the adoption of the IRA model. Voter turnout was poor because many traditionally oriented people chose not to participate in what was perceived as an Anglo purpose. Many tribes approved the model. Some, such as the Navajos, rejected the idea but then later approved it, while others such as the Quinaults have steadfastly refused.

The significance of these tribal organizations lies in the fact that they institutionalize an infrastructure for divisiveness within communities. Early in Indian-Anglo relations, terms like *friendlies* or *progressives* were used to identify people who were compliant with Anglo pressures, while *hostiles* or *traditionalists* were those resistant to directed change. As an implementer and enforcer of federal policy, the BIA has carried on its negotiations with progressive factions in initiating changes originating from outside rather than from within local communities.

In response to this past history of BIA domination, and recognizing the failures of paternalistic policies, the Senate Select Committee on Indian Affairs recommended that the BIA be dismantled and replaced with a system of direct grants from the federal government. The grants would be awarded to tribes with constituted governments accountable to the federal government. Among other stipulations, block grants would be issued only to "tribes willing to promise clean governments . . . and . . . the powers of tribal governments [cannot be] concentrated in one person or governmental branch" (McAllister and Lancaster 1989). Once again, the thrust of such a policy would select for a specific kind of tribal government, the purposes for which money might be spent, and, in effect, where tribal power would be recognized and by which procedures tribes must operate.

This option fails to recognize that many tribes are accustomed to decision-making procedures that use mechanisms other than a one-person, one-vote system. Tribally valid decisions might be made by less than a majority or by full consensus, or by leaders selected through a theocracy (Wilkinson 1988:7). The traditional religious leaders of Jemez Pueblo, for example, meet in December and discuss who should assume leadership responsibilities for the coming year. One does not seek office, nor does one have the privilege of declining the charge to serve. The requirements suggested by the Senate panel would find many traditional systems, such as that of Jemez, "undemocratic" and therefore unacceptable.

The path indicated by the Senate panel appears to suggest that the more a community or part of a community is held together by tradition, the more difficult it will be for its members to be involved in the politics leading to tribal self-determination. The lifeways embedded in Indian traditions and Indian religions may conflict with the kind of participation expected or even demanded by federal policy. Tradition and belief have persisted far beyond the superficial labels often used as indicators of assimilation. Though Indian communities may have Christian adherents, other values may persist within a legacy of more deeply felt meanings in daily, religious, and spiritual life. In a life history account of an Apache Christian religious leader, an elder noted that one's religion, whether Christianity or traditional Apachean, was only a vehicle for enabling one to live in harmony with others and with nature (Esber, unpublished notes).

The deep-seated meanings and cultural significance of enduring belief systems are easily lost at the interface of Anglo-Indian cultures. To the non-Indian world, Indian rituals are essentially tourist attractions and instruments for commercialization in a market economy. Indian icons have been used as trinkets and collectors' items (as when kachinas are mimicked in liquor bottles), and many of the ceremonies have been branded as deviant (e.g., the Native American church or the Hopi Snake Dance). Religious sites have been disregarded or considered obstacles to Anglo development. On the other hand, meanings in Indian religions extend into all aspects of peoples' lives and affect the degree to which and the ways in which participation may be possible.

A recent call for religious participation can be found in the Native American Grave Protection and Repatriation Act. After a considerable struggle, Indian lobby groups succeeded in having legislation passed that would enable Indians to retrieve ancestral remains and associated funerary objects from museums and institutions for proper reburial. Section 8 of the act mandates the formation of a review committee to oversee the implementation of the law. The committee membership is to consist of seven members;

three of these are to be Indians, and two of the three are to be traditional Indian religious leaders. Because the secretary of the interior is empowered to make the final selection of committee members, there remains the question of who will be chosen and from which tribes they will come. Since the Navajos have the largest tribal membership, one might expect that a Navajo representative would be appointed to fill one seat. However, in Navajo culture there are proscriptions against matters and thoughts dealing with the dead, and participation might create an impossible dilemma: either avoid involvement by following the directions of one's own culture, or turn that aside and follow the process established in Anglo culture. In this, as in many other areas of concern, traditionalists who choose in favor of self-determination with sovereignty may find that they must refuse to participate in activities that conflict with their own worldview.

Their situation is nicely summarized in a short piece by Anthony Dorame (1991:12).

The Two Worlds of the Indian

Joseph had been puzzled. He was looking for two worlds and couldn't find one of them. Ever since he was a young man, he had been admonished by his parents to prepare to live in the other world but retain his traditional world. He and his sister were carefully raised and spoke their language fluently. They danced and participated in the ceremonies, knew and practiced the rituals, and believed in the values of their people.

When they had attended school off the reservation, they were told they needed to leave the Indian world and learn the ways of the "civilized" world. Their way of dress, their language and their customs were a burden to their success in the world, they were told. The must discard these esoteric traditions and adopt new ones which would equip them for success in the competitive world out there. It all seemed logical. That is, there were two worlds, one of the Indian and one outside the reservation, and each one was basically different.

Joseph and Maria remained close to each other and often visited and reminisced about the "old days" when they were growing up. They did not forget the traditions and ceremonies and still practiced them as they had been taught.

However, they had been puzzled because of the advice about the "two worlds." They had discovered that there was only one basic world, that of their values. They took their values with them wherever they went, and problems arose if or when they abandoned these values. They could contend with their exterior world of differences in customs from culture to culture, if they kept attuned to these differences but did not discard their values.

Now if only they could share that lesson.

Through numerous challenges, Indian cultures have defied the destructive policies and efforts of Anglo society. There is no question that Native Americans are closer now to the ideal of self-determination than at any other time since Anglo domination began. They are represented by tribal councils that interface with dominant society on a government-to-government basis, by a variety of national organizations, and by spokespeople whose voices are being heard, though often ignored. Certainly in the expression of their need for and management of services, they have a much greater voice than in the past. In effect, Public Law 93-638 is doing what its policy statement says it should do; it is, however, inappropriately titled. The Indian Self Determination Act is not a self-determination policy but an invitation to participate. A more appropriate name for the policy would have been the Indian Participation Act.

The invitation to participate carries with it a divisiveness that draws some participants toward assimilation while it creates alienation among factions that choose not to participate. What has been called economic development is an ethnocentric persuasion to model tribal economies after the U.S. pattern. Tribal organization is considered valid only so far as it conforms to standards approved as "clean" government.

Indian community social and economic organizations are subject to condemnations such as those of James Watt, whose apology would be viewed as a second lie in at least one Indian writer's point of view (Martin 1989). One must question whether it was Watt's idea that was so offensive or the fact that he articulated in public an idea that is otherwise widely accepted. One must conclude that Anglo acceptance of Indian peoples is contingent on the belief that they exist only as memories of the past and that contemporary peoples are not viable communities to whom a perpetual financial debt is owed.

While I argue that a genuine self-determination policy is needed, I also contend that such a policy cannot be forthcoming unless tribal sovereignty is recognized and economic obligations are fulfilled without external control over the expenditure of funds. Recently the Quinaults and six other tribes initiated a program in which tribes prepare their own budgets, run their own programs, and negotiate directly with the federal government for funding. The BIA is not involved in this experiment and has none of the traditional responsibilities for prescribing programmatic needs (Egan 1991:9). This is the closest approximation to government-to-government relations yet achieved. The fact that tribes are able to set their own priorities and negotiate the funding for them is also much closer to genuine self-determination. Whether the experiment will be allowed to continue without the threat of federal monitoring and intervention remains to be seen.

Simpson and Yinger's omission of self-determination as a pattern of interaction between dominant and subordinate groups was not an error. Self-determination as a policy of a dominant group toward a minority people is a contradiction in terms and can never be a reality. The paradox rests on two opposing ideas: Indian self-determination and decision making, on the one hand, and federal control of policymaking and implementation, on the other. Self-determination cannot be accomplished by a policy decision of a dominant government; it can only be achieved by disempowerment of the dominant government and recognition of the genuine sovereignty of the other. Crucial to such a transition, however, must be the federal guarantee of the trust relationship in which the role of the trustee will be to protect Indian lands for Indian peoples. Along with the trust obligation, the federal government must view its own financial debt as a payment in perpetuity for the privilege that Indian peoples granted in treaties when they abdicated land crucial to the economy of their communities.

While the government-to-government relationship is a step in the direction of self-determination, a nation-to-nation relationship needs to be implemented in order for self-determination to be fully realized. Self-determination cannot be equated with participation, but rather must come to mean liberation from domination. In a nation-to-nation relationship, tribes would be able to function much as they do in the Quinaults' experiment. At worst, there might be problems such as mismanagement and corruption or errors of judgment not dissimilar to the history produced by supervision under the BIA. Of much greater importance is that Indian nations managed by their own peoples in their own ways would enfranchise Indian peoples once again.

REFERENCES

ANDERSON, BOB, and LARE ASCHENBRENNER. 1986. "Alaska Native Tribes Battle Discrimination." *NARF Legal Review* 2(3):1–7.
———. 1988. "Amendments Provide Stop-gap Protection for Native Land and Corporations." *NARF Legal Review* 13(2):1–5.
DELORIA, VINE, JR. 1985. "The Evolution of Federal Indian Policy Making."

In *American Indian Policy in the Twentieth Century.* Ed. Vine Deloria, Jr. Norman: University of Oklahoma Press.

DORAME, ANTHONY. 1991. "The Two Worlds of the Indian." *1991 Official Visitors Guide.* Eight Northern Indian Pueblos, San Juan Pueblo.

EGAN, TIMOTHY. 1991. "Sovereign Once Again, Indian Tribes Experiment with Self-Government. *Akwasasne Notes* 22(6):9, 29. Originally published in the *New York Times,* January 16, 1991.

EPSTEIN, AARON. 1983. "Watt May Raise Cain but He Also Raises Coin." *Cincinnati Enquirer,* January 21, p. B-12.

ESBER, GEORGE S., JR. n.d. Field research tapes in the possession of the author, April 28, 1990.

GROSS, EMMA R. 1989. "Contemporary Federal Policy Toward American Indians." In *Contributions in Ethnic Studies* 25. Ed. Leonard W. Doob. New York: Greenwood Press.

MCALLISTER, BILL, and JOHN LANCASTER. 1989. "Senate Panel Wants Overhaul of Federal Indian Programs." *Washington Post,* November 18, pp. 1, A-8.

MCGUIRE, THOMAS R. 1990. "Federal Indian Policy: A Framework for Evaluation." *Human Organization* 49(3):206–16.

MCNICKLE, D'ARCY. 1973. *Native American Tribalism: Indian Survivals and Renewals.* New York: Oxford University Press.

MARTIN, JOHN. 1989. "Loudmouth in the Outhouse." *Lakota Times,* December 19, p. 5.

NARF Legal Review. 1989. "Case Updates." 14(4):17.

PRUCHA, FRANCIS PAUL. 1988. *The Indians in American Society: From the Revolutionary War to the Present.* Berkeley: University of California Press.

SIMPSON, GEORGE EATON, and MILTON YINGER. 1953. *Racial and Cultural Minorities.* Rev. ed. New York: Harper and Brothers.

STULL, DONALD D. 1990. "Reservation Economic Development in the Era of Self-Determination." *American Anthropologist* 92(1):206–10.

TYLER, S. LYMAN. 1973. *A History of Indian Policy.* Washington, D.C.: Government Printing Office.

U.S. Statutes at Large. 1975. 88:2203–17. P.L. 93-638, January 4, 1975. Indian Self-Determination and Education Assistance Act.

———. 1990. 104:3048–58. P.L. 101-601, November 16, 1990. Native American Graves Protection and Repatriation Act.

WILKINSON, CHARLES F. 1988. "The Idea of Sovereignty: Native Peoples, Their Lands, and Their Dreams." *NARF Legal Review* 13(4):1–11. Originally presented at the Native Hawaiian Rights Conference in Honolulu, August 5, 1988.

Getting to Yes in the New West

THOMAS R. MCGUIRE

In 1946, the Congress of the United States mandated the Indian Claims Commission to hear "every conceivable tribal grievance" against the "fair and honorable dealings" of the nation (Barsh 1982:12). In its thirty years the commission reviewed 611 dockets, each with many specific claims—legal, equitable, and moral. Curiously, few of the alleged and documented transgressions concerned water.

That oversight provides the tribes and the government with another chance—with opportunities to establish firm entitlement to a scarce resource, to put that resource to effective use, and, critically, to reaffirm fundamental trust relationships between the government and the Indians. But that trust relationship, ambiguous as it is, is not being affirmed. Rather, in a strict sense, it is being negotiated. From the arid and semiarid West to the water-logged swamps of Seminole territory in Florida, principles of case law are yielding to processes of mediation, conflict resolution, and negotiation—the forging of consensus, formalized after the fact by congressional statute and judicial decree.[1]

Deals are cut, bargains are struck, and resources are reallocated. Past, present, and future claims against the government and the states are routinely waived by the tribes and their counsel. Indian water is being addressed with the identical finality with which the Claims Commission approached land. What will emerge from this flurry of activity—of getting to yes[2]—is likely to be a rather novel restructuring of the relationships among the federal government, the states, and the Indians. In this essay I undertake a mid-course assessment of these activities. The question I raise is this: How does the federal government's policy of negotiation affect the negotiation of policy?

My focus is on definitions of *trust, equity,* and *property,* and on who is writing these definitions. Historically, the trust responsibility of the federal government has vacillated between two poles: one the strict fiduciary duty of a private trust, the other a compromise that acknowledges the legitimate public interests of competing resource claimants (Wilkinson 1987:83–85). Equity too has been a changeable concept, defined typically by the moment at hand. Under the mandate and operation of the Indian Claims Commission, for example, equity was quantified by the value of lands at the time they were taken from their original possessors, not by the more common legal principle of restitution; that is, restoring the possessors "to the position that they would have been in had no wrong occurred" (Carlson 1985:98). Finally, property, at least in theory, admits to precise legal and economic definition. But in practice property is a "text," an enduring communicative event. Acts of possession must be both communicated and read. How they are read says as much, or more, about the reader as it does about the act itself (cf. Rose 1985).

All three concepts—trust, equity, and property—are mercurial. Moreover, they intertwine. In the context under study here, they have also been opened to negotiation. I make no claim to a final fix on the theory that will eventually emerge. First, I review judicial efforts to define Indian entitlement to water. I then look at the pressures building in the 1970s to negotiate, not adjudicate, Indian water claims. Two brief case studies in the negotiation of policy follow. Finally, tentative efforts are made to understand the discourse on equity, trust, and property.

ENTITLEMENT

The legal precedent at stake here is *Winters* v. *United States* (207 U.S. 564 [1908]), by which the U.S. Supreme Court in 1908 reserved sufficient water to fulfill the present and future purposes of Indian reservations. The Court was asked to consider a novel proposition advanced by the U.S. attorney for Montana on behalf of the Indians at Fort Belknap. The theory contradicted tenets of the emerging water law in the West, violated a Supreme Court ruling in 1907 (*Kansas* v. *Colorado,* 206 U.S. 46 [1907]) that urged strong deference to state water law, and was received with substantial ambivalence by the Indians' own trustees (the Justice Department and the Indian Service). Daniel McCool astutely observed that when "the case went to the Supreme Court, it was anybody's guess as to the outcome" (McCool 1987:46).

In its two-page opinion the Court ruled in favor of the U.S. attorney and the Gros Ventre and Assiniboin of Fort Belknap, who had been dispossessed of irrigation water from the Milk River by non-Indian farmers. The doctrine established by the decision contained the following principles: (1) the federal government reserved water for Indians when it removed reservation land from the public domain, (2) this water right was to be sufficient to fulfill the purposes of the reservation, (3) the water right would not be forfeited by nonuse, (4) the right could expand in the future if new uses required additional water, and (5) the right had a priority date corresponding to the establishment of the reservation (Folk-Williams 1988:66).

The anguish of the non-Indian settlers along the Milk—and throughout the West now—stems from the direct conflict of the reserved rights doctrine with the prior appropriations tenet of Western water law. Under this doctrine, water rights are held by order of filing, are quantified on the basis of beneficial use on defined acreage, and are lost through discontinuous use. Recently, too, there has been strong pressure throughout the water-scarce West to establish markets to permit the efficient transfer of water to "highest and best" uses. In current parlance, state water laws create a relatively well defined property right.[3] *Winters* established a right for the Indians that was patently—and purposely—ill-defined, open-ended, and attached to the very water claimed by the settlers. This troubles the West.

Subsequent to the Supreme Court ruling in 1908, the *Winters* entitlement has been ignored, assaulted, modified, quantified, applied in concept to all federal lands, extended to include groundwater, refereed in state court in contrast to virtually all other Indian questions, and now, to repeat, is being negotiated. But it has not yet been revoked. Let us assess the robustness of this incongruous doctrine.

The Indian Service and its successor in name, the Bureau of Indian Affairs (BIA), for the most part ignored the doctrine. Befuddled by the implications and given little direction by the Court as to how the doctrine should be implemented, the BIA typically relied on principles of prior appropriation and beneficial use to protect Indian water supplies. This strategy, in McCool's view, had three drawbacks: "it created even more confusion, it led to the widespread policy of leasing Indian lands, and it meant that water rights protection became a function of project funding levels" (1987:119). And, as he ably documented, those funding levels were abysmally low throughout the heyday of dam construction and irrigation development in the West (McCool 1987:122–25).

Winters was revived when the Supreme Court was finally called upon to partition the Southwest's biggest stream, the Colorado River. *Arizona* v. *California* (373 U.S. 546), decided in 1963, had profound consequences. The Court confirmed that the reserved rights principle applied to all federal lands, not just Indian reservations, and the priority of claims dated to the establishment of the reservation. Most significantly, however, the Supreme Court demanded a quantification of Indian reserved rights to end the inherent uncertainty of the original doctrine. Nonetheless, the quantification scheme—based on the water required to supply all "practically irrigable acres" (PIA) of Indian land—was liberal. It shocked non-Indian water users throughout the West. Five tribes along the lower Colorado River were awarded close to a million acre-feet (an acre-foot equals 325,851 gallons) of water from the river, accounted against the 7.5 million acre-feet partitioned among the states of California, Arizona, and Nevada. The Court announced that the water was intended to "satisfy the future as well as the present needs of the Indian Reservations" (Hundley 1975:330), agricultural or otherwise.

THE 1983 DECISIONS

The 1963 Supreme Court decision was challenged not by the non-Indians whom it jeopardized but by the Colorado River tribes themselves. The challenge centered on irrigable lands that were omitted from calculation in the 1963 decree, and the tribes asked the Supreme Court to amend their allocation.

The ambivalent ruling in 1983 (*Arizona* v. *California II*, 103 S.Ct. 1392) has been read both as a reversal of the philosophy contained in the 1963 decision and subsequent decree (McCool 1987:49) and as a narrow procedural modification of that decree (Coursen 1984:712). The second interpretation is based on a close reading of the text.

Stressing the need for finality, the 1983 Court refused to award additional water to acreage within the reservations that, upon further analysis after 1963, had been determined to be "practically irrigable." However, the Court did respond with favor to another point under contention by the Indians. Water was awarded to lands annexed to the reservations by litigation after the original decree. Thus, as Coursen observed, "the Court drew a clear line, not against granting any additional claims, but against relitigating claims that had been settled by the earlier decree . . . *Arizona v. California* is, therefore, less rigid than it appears" (1984:712).

Those who see a narrowing, even an abrogation, of *Winters* look to two additional Indian decisions handed down by the Supreme Court in 1983. In *Nevada* v. *United States* (103 S.Ct. 2906) the Pyramid Lake Paiute tribe sought to amend a forty-year-old decree—which reserved only irrigation water—to include additional supplies for preserving the lake's fishery. Drawing on the doctrine of *res judicata*,[4] the Court rejected the claim. It further concluded that the federal government, which had represented several parties in the original litigation, had intended to assert the tribe's entire *Winters* claim and could not be faulted for misrepresentation of the Indians' case. "In the Court's view," Coursen concluded, "the consequences of reopening the tribe's claims would have been an intolerable disruption of an established water allocation scheme" (1984:714).

Arizona et al. v. *San Carlos Apache Tribe of Arizona et al.* (103 S.Ct. 3201), the third of the 1983 Court's Indian decisions, validated the right of state courts to adjudicate Indian water claims. This right derives from a 1952 congressional action, the McCarran Amendment, waiving the federal government's sovereign immunity in water litigation pursued under state law. The *San Carlos* ruling, seeking to "conserve judicial resources and avoid duplicative litigation" (Coursen 1984:715), thus enabled the states to proceed with general stream adjudications involving Indian and non-Indian claims.

Indians expressed the fear that "state courts may be inhospitable to Indian rights" (Upite 1984:189), even though these courts have to abide by federal law vis-à-vis Indian claims. The Supreme Court acknowledged this concern. The decision ended with a strong warning that the Court would be prepared to review state court decisions with "a particularized and exacting scrutiny commensurate with the powerful federal interest in safeguarding those rights from state encroachment" (quoted in Coursen 1984:716).

Nevertheless, all three of the 1983 decisions stressed the need for finality and predictability in Western water rights. The open-ended flexibility of the original *Winters* theory was terminated. The federal government was absolved, in part, from accusations that it had misrepresented its Indian wards and clients in the past. And the presumed beneficence and protection of the federal judicial forum was lost.

Thus there is some substance to the "pivotal year" theory in the evolution of *Winters*. I return to it below, but a preliminary observation is necessary: the theory developed and was put to use while the massive Wind River/Big Horn Basin case in Wyoming was still pending.

"AN EQUALLY DIVIDED COURT"

On June 26, 1989, the U.S. Supreme Court reviewed the findings of the Wyoming Supreme Court in a general adjudication of the Big Horn Basin.[5] The state court, following twelve years of litigation, awarded 477,000 acre-feet of water annually to the Shoshones and Arapahoes of the Wind River Reservation. Bitterly contested by the state, with moral and legal support from nine other Western states, the award was based explicitly on "practicably irrigable acres," even though all parties suspected that there was insufficient water to supply this acreage.

The U.S. Supreme Court upheld the state court's decision and thus validated the quantification scheme for *Winters* rights put forward in the initial litigation between Arizona and California. The decision was close, and the strategy of putting the PIA standard to this highest test was a risky one (as was the original *Winters* hearing before an unpredictable Supreme Court in 1908). But the outcome again gave judicial confirmation to the doctrine of reserved rights.

Reminiscing on the Wind River case on the eve of the highest court's decision, Special Master Teno Roncalio of the Wyoming court calculated that the twelve-year suit cost $20 million in litigation fees: "Another endurance contest has evolved, and none who were or are now its key players can be proud of that. Many Wyoming lawmakers and officials regret the day the lawsuit was filed" (1989:4).

Wyoming had, in fact, taken an aggressive step when it sued Wind River in 1977. In form and process—and even to a degree in the substance of the final outcome—*Wyoming* resembled the first *Arizona* v. *California*. Both cases were long, complex, and expensive. Both resulted in the clarification of an entitlement to a valuable resource. Courts, of course, determine rights. However, the generous quantification standard established in *Arizona* and reaffirmed in *Wyoming* unsheathed "the sword of Damocles," a favorite call to arms of fearful non-Indians in the 1970s and 1980s.

THE POLICY OF NEGOTIATION

Reactions to the first *Arizona* v. *California* account only in part for the excitement over negotiated water rights settlements. The trend must also be placed in the context of parallel societal movements. The preference for "informal justice" rose strongly in the 1970s, and quasi institutions proliferated to address this trend. Such institutions—neighborhood mediation centers, consumer complaint offices, ombudsmen of all sorts—"eschew official law in favor of substantive and procedural norms that are vague, unwritten, commonsensical, flexible, ad hoc, and particularistic" (Abel 1982:2). There were complex causes for this movement toward informalism, but these are beyond the scope of the present discussion. Richard Abel is one of the critics of the movement: "Although applicants [to dispute resolution institutions] certainly want cheap, speedy justice, justice may be more important to them than speed—and they may be willing to pay for it" (1982:8).[6]

To be sure, Indian water rights settlements negotiated by lawyers, ratified by Congress, and decreed by an appropriate judiciary bear little formal resemblance to neighborhood dispute resolutions and no-fault divorces. But they share in the promise of speed, expediency, the use of imagination rather than strict case-law precedent, and, ostensibly, cost.[7]

There is ample evidence, however, that Indians met the call for conflict resolution in the 1970s with suspicion and hostility. McCool has marshaled the documentation: "An article appeared in *Akwesasne Notes,* an Indian newspaper, entitled 'Water Negotiations—A New Word for Fraud.' Writing in *Wassaja,* Rupert Costo warned that 'termination will be the ultimate result of negotiations in which Indians give up their rights piece by piece' " (1987:231).

The negotiation policy itself evolved in haphazard fashion during the Carter administration, a product of, more than an integral element in, the Western water policy reform movement. President Jimmy Carter's infamous "hit list" of water projects was compiled, in part, with an eye to unsettled Indian claims. Modifications, reductions, and deletions were threatened for projects that appeared to be economically unwise, environmentally destructive, and inequitable in the distribution of benefits to Indians (McCool 1987:229).

Yet the means to achieve water policy reform and fulfill the government's trust responsibility were still in flux. Senator Edward Kennedy attempted a legislative route in 1976 and again in 1977 to finalize allocations to five tribes in central and southern Arizona: Ak-Chin, Papago (now Tohono O'odham), Salt River, Fort McDowell, and Gila River. But the effort failed, for instructive reasons.

Unlike the bill introduced in 1976, the identical 1977 writing— S.905—received a full hearing before the Senate's Select Committee on Indian Affairs. Kennedy, not himself a member of the committee, had become deeply concerned with the federal trusteeship relationship during his tenure on the Committee of the Judiciary (U.S. Congress 1971).

The senator's defense of his 1977 bill reiterated this concern: "The federal government's treatment of the five tribes is clearly unjust and expresses itself in intense human suffering" (U.S. Senate 1977:49). Observing that the legal principles of *Winters* are well established, he invoked the full powers of Congress to settle Indian claims: "It is for these reasons that I have proposed that Congress, with its plenary power over Indian affairs, to [*sic*] enact a legislative settlement. Legislation can serve as a prompt, equitable, and socially responsive alternative to lengthy, costly, and disruptive litigation" (U.S. Senate 1977:50).

The bill, based primarily on consultation with the five tribes, called for quantification of their *Winters* rights by the standard set in *Arizona* v. *California.* The water supply—1.2 million acre-feet, equivalent to the entire flow through the Central Arizona Project—was to have been obtained through eminent domain, the enforcement of prior appropriations, and the closing of the troublesome Wellton-Mohawk Irrigation District near the Colorado River delta.

Kennedy estimated that the proposed legislation would cost the government $475 million in land purchases and aid to the tribes. But the benefits, he suggested, would outweigh the costs: tribes would become economically self-sufficient, local water users and the federal trustees would no longer be liable for damages to the Indians, and taxpayers would save $30 million a year from the reduced construction and operation costs of the Yuma desalinization plant, mandated by treaty with Mexico to cleanse Wellton-Mohawk's tailing water before it flows across the border (U.S. Senate 1977:52).

Predictably, Arizona's water users united in strong opposition to the proposed fulfillment of *Winters* claims for the tribes. And the state's congressional delegation, while supporting "in concept" the legislative settlement of Indian claims, led the fight against s.905. In 1977 Kennedy's bill failed a second time.

A handful of negotiated settlements worked out in the 1960s were on record to serve as templates for an administrative policy, although these settlements addressed specific local issues. The Navajo concluded two agreements, one to perfect a water supply for the still incomplete Navajo Indian Irrigation Project, another to provide Indian water to the non-Indian power plant at Page, Arizona (Folk-Williams 1988:75–77). And, after fifteen years of discussion, the Utes along the Duchesne River agreed in 1965 to defer development of irrigated acreage on their reservation in the interests of expediting the Central Utah Project (Folk-Williams 1988:89–91).

The U.S. Department of the Interior, it should be noted, had occasionally recommended the more conventional route of litigation during the

1970s to settle claims; for example, on behalf of the Ak-Chin community and the Papagos. But these suits—against the government and the groundwater pumpers near the Ak-Chin Reservation and against all water users in the Tucson basin, respectively—were rapidly deflected into the negotiating arena. In the process, the administration's policy of ad hoc case-by-case bargaining was forged.

On June 6, 1978, President Carter fully endorsed the negotiation-legislation strategy in his Water Policy Message to Congress (*Federal Register* 1980, 45[239]:81268). He underwrote his commitment to negotiation by signing the prototypical Ak-Chin settlement a month later.

The Ak-Chin Act—the initial one of 1978—was hailed as a landmark in conflict resolution. Introduced into the Senate by Senator Dennis DeConcini of Arizona on the same day Senator Kennedy was defending s.905 before the select committee, the legislation embodied a set of important principles. First, it explicitly acknowledged that the federal government had failed to meet its trust responsibility for protecting the 20,000-acre reservation's water sources. Second, it committed the government to the provision of 85,000 acre-feet of water annually to the reservation's farmable land. While the bill was careful not to elaborate on how this quantity was determined, it was close to the figure calculated by the PIA standard in the Kennedy legislation—89,505 acre-feet.

The critical difference from the Kennedy proposal was that the water would not come from existing users. Rather, the government agreed to study the feasibility of constructing a temporary well field on federal lands near Ak-Chin to supply the reservation until the Central Arizona Project was finished. And, again in clear distinction from Kennedy's approach, the Ak-Chin Settlement Act absolved all non-Indian water users from blame, further litigation, and any financial responsibility for past damages to the reservation's water supply. The total federal expense authorized in the 1978 package was $42 million, with provisions made for future claims should the government fail to meet construction schedules.

Juxtaposed to the Kennedy proposal, the Ak-Chin Settlement Act was a clear victory for the state's water users. Irrigators around Stanfield and Maricopa incurred neither blame nor expense for depleting the aquifer under the reservation. And the reservation, likewise at no cost, would receive a guaranteed supply of water. The act, in short, was a "win-win" solution for a local problem—at least for Arizona. The principles on which it rested, however, were questioned radically by the succeeding administration. And the Ak-Chin settlement itself—negotiated, as it turned out, too hastily—had to be rewritten entirely in 1984 (cf. McGuire 1988; Burton 1991).

Nonetheless, the 1978 settlement momentarily quieted skepticism among Indians and non-Indians alike. Rural Ak-Chin, with a long history of farming, acquiesced to having its *Winters* rights quantified and developed for agriculture. Other tribes, viewing the generosity of the federal government in developing Ak-Chin's award, began to see some wisdom in negotiated settlements of their pending claims. Western water interests likewise were generally delighted to have the Carter administration underwrite the costs of the settlement and, in Ak-Chin's proposed well field, to discover new water in the arid desert.

The Reagan administration reiterated the policy of negotiation and nudged that policy along with implicit financial threats to recalcitrant tribes (McCool 1987:237). Western water users, sensing more sympathy from the incoming Reagan administration, drafted legislative proposals in 1980 and 1981 to force tribes into inclusive negotiations and settlements. Now on the defensive, Indian leaders themselves called for case-by-case, tribe-by-tribe settlements (McCool 1987:233–34). This format has prevailed.

THE NEGOTIATION OF POLICY

Wedded to a policy of negotiation, the Reagan administration simultaneously articulated a curious position on the trust relationship. David Getches, representing the state of Colorado before a congressional hearing in 1989, suggested that the policy is still operative: "One of the few official positions announced with any clarity was that the administration considered its obligation to protect Indian water rights to be limited to engaging in litigation; thus, the trustee's perceived obligation did not include participating in the burdens of making Indian water rights useful and productive, let alone the burdens of relieving the equities of non-Indian water users" (U.S. Senate 1989:11).

There is less inconsistency here than meets the eye. By proclaiming its trust responsibility as one of litigation, the administration highlighted the ambiguities of the law. The Supreme Court decisions of 1983 yielded two interpretations—one a narrowly procedural adjustment of *Winters,* the other an abrogation of those rights. Federal negotiators and policymakers, at least those from the administrative branch, utilized this ambiguity to foster a strategy of "legal risk assessment."

Discussing the Salt River settlement of 1988 (and the appropriate level of federal financing), William Swan of the Department of the Interior offered this interpretation:

> In regard to risk assessment, this settlement process demonstrates, to Indian communities, the government and non-Indians, the need to carefully and accurately assess their respective litigation risks in order to arrive at reasonable settlement goals. Recent refinements in the law (e.g., the *res judicata* effect of early water rights decrees) along with a judicially refined understanding of the practicably irrigable acreage analysis, compels settlement participants to study and assess their litigation risks, and the risks of their opponents, in order to arrive at appropriate compromises. Without such assessments, participants may deceive themselves into believing that their relative positions are stronger than what a realistic assessment would support. (Swan 1989:92–93)

This is a significant message from the administration to litigants. It is composed most directly out of the elements of *Nevada* v. *United States.* In that case the Court invoked the *res judicata* argument over settled claims, guaranteeing, in Justice Brennan's words, that "thousands of small farmers in northwestern Nevada can rely on specific promises made to their forebears two and three generations ago" (quoted in Coursen 1984:714). The Court also absolved the federal government of trust violations for representing several conflicting interests in the original litigation.[8]

The intent of the message is clear. Local competitors must still assess the particular facts at hand. But they must do so within the context of judicial precedent. Non-Indian users face the possibility, as happened in the Wyoming litigation, that courts will indeed hold to the standard of practicably irrigable acreage. Indian supplicants, for their part, may find that claims to water have already been asserted for them, years ago, by their federal trustee, even though that trustee may have been unconcerned with (or ignorant of) the flexibility and open-endedness of the *Winters* doctrine.

Finally, in assessing its own litigation risk, the federal government may determine that it has very little "exposure"; that is, there is little possibility that a court would find it negligent in its role as trustee for Indian land and resources. This, in fact, was the position developed by analysts in the Office of Management and Budget (OMB) in the negotiations that grew out of litigation in the Salt River Valley, Arizona (Starler and Maxey 1989:104).

In intent, then, this post-1983 emphasis on legal risk assessment is designed to spur negotiations. Local litigants may lose an adjudication—

and water—and the federal government may bear little financial responsibility for developing Indian entitlements. Indeed, the purpose of the OMB's analysis of the Salt River situation was to reduce the level of federal funding in the eventual settlement and, correspondingly, to increase the cost-sharing burden on local users, Indian and non-Indian. Moreover, the OMB staff sought to develop explicit analytical guidelines for structuring and evaluating future settlements—guidelines that serve, in effect, to ratify the federal government's reading of the Supreme Court decisions of 1983.

The policy of negotiation, I suggest in the following review of two cases, has three emergent implications. First, it has allowed *equity* to be defined as a residual, as the dollars that water users and the Congress, with an eye on the Office of Management and Budget, are willing to spend to get to yes. Second, it has reduced principles of federal trusteeship to local-level bargaining. Finally, it has enabled local non-Indian bargainers to impose a restrictive definition on Indian water as a property right.

Salt River

Enacted into law late in 1988, the Salt River Pima–Maricopa Indian Community Water Rights Settlement Act (P.L. 100-512) was impelled by, and resolved, a series of suits brought by the community against the government and water users in the Phoenix area. The agreement ended the government's simultaneous role as defendant in these suits and as plaintiff, on behalf of the community, in the ongoing general stream adjudication of the Gila system in Arizona's superior court.

The government's chief local negotiator, Field Solicitor Swan from the Department of the Interior, has remarked that "the complexity of the settlement provides a new source of burden and frustration, which has caused a number of people to question whether litigation might in fact be easier" (1989:93). But he, and most others, extol the benefits: settlement of claims, fulfillment of the trust obligation, and financial aid to the community.

In the general stream adjudication, the government advanced a claim of 190,000 acre-feet yearly to water the reservation's 29,000 practicably irrigable acres. Under the terms of the negotiated agreement, the community has roughly 122,400 acre-feet at its disposal. About 30,000 acre-feet are contributed by three irrigation districts in the rapidly urbanizing Phoenix area, largely through the retirement of existing farmland. Seven cities in the region exchanged their rights to 20,000 acre-feet of water stored in the Salt River system for 22,000 acre-feet of water imported through the Central Arizona Project. This quantity is to be purchased from willing sellers in the Wellton-Mohawk Irrigation District along the Colorado River. In turn, that district will be absolved of the acreage limitations contained in the Reclamation Reform Act of 1982 and forgiven some outstanding debts to the government. In addition, the terms and intent of two earlier agreements will be fulfilled, giving the community a call on 40,000 acre-feet of stored surface water. And the community retains rights to pump a yearly average of 23,000 acre-feet of groundwater. Finally, the act allows the reservation to lease its 13,300-acre-foot allocation of Central Arizona Project water to the city of Phoenix for ninety-nine years, at a total price of $16 million (Swan 1989:91).

Money, not water, proved to be the contentious issue, the one that provoked Interior and the OMB to articulate the legal risk assessment strategy. One estimate put the cost of the 1982 Ak-Chin settlement at $160 million—borne entirely by the federal government (Simon 1989:3). The Papago settlement in 1982, vetoed initially by the administration for its paucity of local financial contributions, nonetheless has a $164 million federal price tag (Simon 1989:3). By putting a price on the government's "legal exposure" should the Salt River claims be adjudicated, the OMB determined that "$25 million represented the limit of reasonable Federal participation in the settlement" (Starler and Maxey 1989:104).

Expressing their own views, two architects of the legal exposure argument concluded that "the difference between this amount [$25 million] and the amounts suggested in various proposals during the debate on the enabling legislation represent a quantification of equity. Congress made the ultimate determination of what the U.S. should contribute in the name of 'equity'" (Starler and Maxey 1989:96).

Hidden in this spare observation is a fundamental contention about the history of water and people in the West. James Ziglar, assistant secretary for water and science in the Department of the Interior, articulated this contention at the joint congressional hearings on the Salt River bill. Threatening a presidential veto, he observed that the federal government is already subsidizing Central Arizona Project water deliveries to non-Indians, at a cost of $3 billion. Furthermore, "the federal government has invested about $60 million in the Salt River Project for the benefit of non-Indians . . . these expenditures were made early in the decades of this century, so the $60 million would be considerably greater when evaluated at today's costs. . . . I submit that these points have not been accorded sufficient weight in the judgments on the relative federal and non-federal contributions to this settlement" (U.S. Congress 1988:97).

Ziglar partially endorsed the OMB's exposure analysis and, implicitly, its definition of equity as a residual. At the same time, though, he was proposing a counterpoint—legitimate, I think—to what can be called the Australian theory of settlement in the American West. That theory has been offered up, over and over again in settlement negotiations, by local water users, state officials, and, frequently, Western delegates to Congress. The rhetoric varies in eloquence; the principle remains the same. The West was peopled by unwilling and unwitting settlers who were dragged, cajoled, and forced onto the irrigation projects being built by the Reclamation Service. And these settlers were duped into thinking it was their water, exclusively.[9]

Ziglar, referring to one of the legal claims of the Salt River community, was willing to give some credence to such a position but stopped well short of putting full blame on the government: "I think that the Federal Government has been—I don't want to use the word 'negligent'—again, less than diligent in fulfilling the mandate that Congress gave to us in 1916 to secure water supplies for some 6,310 acres of land" (U.S. Congress 1988:67).

This is a brief discourse on the trust relationship, but, for the present purpose, it is also a text on equity. The final negotiated cost to the federal government of the Salt River settlement was $60 million, not the $25 million proposed by the OMB, nor the $78 million accounted against the government in the local rounds of negotiation. Ziglar from Interior and Representative John J. Rhodes III from Arizona bantered about these figures at the hearing directly following Ziglar's acknowledgment of a failure of the trusteeship:

ZIGLAR: I think reasonable men can differ on the value that you
            place upon the United States' liability—whatever you
            want to call it—not legal liability but a certain moral lia-
            bility in this situation. I think there really is a lot of room
            to differ on that. The only way I can do things like this is
            to review it and make up my own mind about how I feel
            about it, and I am not speaking for the administration. I
            have to make that very clear. My view is that $45
            million . . . was a tad low. I also think that the $78 mil-
            lion is too much.

RHODES: I guess for those of us who were not brought up in Mis-
            sissippi, we are going to have to sit down and discuss how
            we quantify "tad." (U.S. Congress 1988:68)

Indeed, the price of equity for the Mission Bands of southern California, written into the San Luis Rey Indian Water Rights Settlement Act of 1988, was somewhat lower: $30 million. And it was higher, by an order of magnitude, for the Southern Utes and the Ute Mountain Utes in Colorado. Be that as it may, Starler and Maxey pinned settlement costs to another issue—the present state of the federal budget: "Furthermore, OMB viewed contributions related to use of water or economic development as discretionary, programmatic matters that should compete for funds with other programs in the Department of the Interior independently of settlement of monetary damages related to the deprivation of water use" (1989:104).

Whether or not Congress bought the OMB's fiscal philosophy, it quickly showed a reluctance to pay for these negotiated equities. At a hearing called in 1989 to develop—unsuccessfully—an "Indian water policy," one Arizona senator posed the question to his colleagues: "How can you have a settlement if you are not going to abide by what you agreed to?" (U.S. Senate 1989:4).

Colorado Utes

The federal government, pursuant to the McCarran Amendment, filed applications in state court for reserved rights on the Ute Mountain Ute and Southern Ute reservations in 1976. Judicial quantification of the tribes' rights was suspended, however, when the affected parties—farmers, ranchers, and rural residents of northwestern New Mexico and southwestern Colorado—began to negotiate in 1984 (*Congressional Record* 1988b: S16245).

Practically irrigable acreage on these high plateau reservations, had it been established, might not have been substantial. But the tribes did have legitimate claims, within the scope of the *Winters* doctrine, for water to process minerals. Moreover, the tribes appeared ready to seek monetary damages from the government as well as wet water from their neighbors. It was the Colorado Forum, not the Office of Management and Budget, that performed the gratuitous "legal risk assessment" for the government. The price of equity—of seventy years of forgone agricultural earnings since *Winters*—was $545 million (U.S. Senate 1987:339). The government eventually agreed to pay $360 million—not all of which goes to benefit the two tribes, however. Congressman George Miller of California argued against the Colorado Ute Water Settlement bill, H.2642 (and its Senate version, S.1415) in the House: "Let's be honest about what we are buying if this bill is enacted . . . we are buying a water project that will benefit non-Indian alfalfa farmers much more than it will ever benefit the Ute Mountain Utes and the Southern Utes" (*Congressional Record* 1988a:H9346).

There was some truth to this claim. The Animas–La Plata Project, authorized with the Central Arizona Project in 1968 as a means to develop part of the upper-basin states's share of the Colorado River, never passed the Bureau of Reclamation's cost-benefit requirements. And most observers candidly admitted that it would never have been constructed had not the Indians laid claim to the appropriated waters of the La Plata and Animas rivers and their tributaries (U.S. Senate 1987:254). The act revived the project. When completed, it will provide 200,000 acre-feet of developed supply for northern New Mexico and Colorado, of which the two tribes will receive about 25 percent. Additionally, the tribes will get a trust fund totaling $60 million and the federal government will pay 60 percent of the construction costs of the Animas–La Plata Project. Total federal costs for the Colorado Ute Water Settlement Act (P.L. 100-585) will be $360 million.

As it turned out, however, the wisdom of Animas–La Plata was not the major point of contention in the negotiations. Rather, it was the issue of water transfers—the definition of Indian property. Through the course of negotiations, several positions on the transferability of the Indians' entitlement were discussed. Ironically, the final settlement bill, designed to terminate the Utes' litigation, left the issue up to the courts. Oddly, too, this was a position the tribes endorsed—and then had to staunchly defend— throughout the discussions and debates. The discourse was about the limits of the new resource economics in the New West.

Susan Christopher Nunn, in fact, defined the New West by its emerging economic rationale, water marketing: "In the New Market coalition, city water planners are joined by fiscal conservatives, who support transfers of water from agriculture because they tend to be locally funded and appear less expensive than the traditional reservoirs; by environmentalists, who support water transfers because they do not involve building new dams; and by economists and others who feel that markets in resources will contribute to rationalizing resource use" (1987:32–33).

The economics are simple. Water, if defined as a private property right, can be transferred through market mechanisms to its highest-valued use. Municipalities will be the willing buyers, and farmers the voluntary sellers. Both will gain from the trade. There will be third-party winners as well, predominantly taxpayers relieved of the expense of underwriting new construction—such as the Animas–La Plata Project. Finally, tribes stand to gain: unused river flows can be turned into cash flows.

There are critics of the New Market Coalition, especially from dewatered rural areas. But the ranks of the skeptics seldom include policy spokespeople for the Metropolitan Water District of Southern California (MWD), which started the trend eighty-five years ago in Owens Valley.

The MWD joined forces with Arizona's Department of Water Resources, the Colorado River Board of California, and the Colorado River Commission of Nevada to curtail the transferability of Colorado Ute water rights. This powerful coalition of lower-basin water interests did not fully prevail. But it succeeded in postponing—perhaps indefinitely—a difficult policy issue facing Indians and their trustees. And this coalition was sufficiently tenacious to bring a series of colonial-era statutes, the Trade and Intercourse acts, into contemporary discourse.

Local negotiators in Colorado had already crafted a settlement agreement when the lower-basin interests spoke up. Signed by the affected parties, approved by the Departments of Interior and Justice, and ratified by the governor of Colorado, the December 1986 package formed the basis for S. 1415, the federal legislation "To Facilitate and Implement the Settlement of Colorado Ute Indian Reserved Rights Claims in Southwest Colorado." On water marketing, the 1986 local consensus was liberal. The tribes were expressly permitted to use their water entitlement outside the boundaries of the two reservations—indeed, outside the boundaries of the state of Colorado (U.S. Senate 1987:162).

The position accorded well with the formative policy of the Reagan administration. Reclamation, historically a bureau of engineers, fell under the influence of the free-marketers (and the cost-conscious OMB) in the 1980s. Finally, in 1989, Reclamation formally announced that it would "serve as a facilitator for water-marketing proposals between willing buyers and sellers" (*Arizona Daily Star,* January 1, 1989), as a means simultaneously to promote allocation efficiency and to get out of the business of constructing new public works.

Since 1983 the Department of the Interior has been advocating an equivalent position for Indian water. The position was articulated by Interior's Water Policy Advisory Group, headed up by the department's solicitor. Finding no "insuperable legal bar to marketing of Indian water rights off the reservation," the solicitor viewed the practice as consistent with the beneficial and flexible use philosophy of *Winters,* and in accord with "President Reagan's efforts to strengthen tribal economies and governments by giving the Indians more control over and benefits from their natural resources" (quoted in Storey 1988:214). The policy was consistent, in other words, with Ronald Reagan's sustained efforts to privatize reservation development (cf. McGuire 1990).

In promulgating this position, the solicitor attempted to allay the fears of non-Indian water users and water seekers. The government, as trustee, would not assert excess *Winters* claims "simply because there might exist a market for that off reservation" (quoted in Storey 1988:214). The solicitor suggested, too, that off-reservation transfers could provide a valuable tool for non-Indian bargainers in negotiating water settlements with, for example, the Colorado Utes.

The fledgling policy did not appease the MWD and its lower-basin allies. When the legislation came before the Select Committee on Indian Affairs and the Senate's Energy and Natural Resources Committee, the coalition attempted to erect the "insuperable legal bar" that the solicitor had found lacking. Its complex brief (U.S. Senate 1987:356–92) on the Law of the River—the aggregation of interstate compacts, international treaties, Supreme Court decisions, and federal and state statutes governing the allocation of the Colorado River—did not mask the transparent complaint of the lower-basin users. Under the Law of the River, water flowing downstream, unused by its upper-basin owners, is free to the lower basin. It has been appropriated by those states for decades. The prospect of having to buy that supply from the Indians in Colorado was unacceptable.

Moreover, such sales or leases of Indian property, the lower-basin coalition argued, were illegal under federal Indian law: the Trade and Intercourse acts from the 1790s to the 1830s. These acts, designed to protect Indian lands and resources from the unscrupulous activities of traders and settlers, were now invoked to prevent off-reservation transfers of water entitlement.

Earlier, the government's solicitor had easily deflected the Intercourse impediment. Congress has the power to waive this restriction, on a case-by-case basis, if it serves federal purposes toward Indians (Storey 1988:215). The Colorado Ute legislation contains such a waiver; but it is a limited waiver that stops short of a challenge to the Law of the River. The two tribes agreed in the end to allow the courts to determine their right to sell water downstream (U.S. Senate 1987:455).

Through the intervention of the lower-basin water users and their powerful congressional delegates, the final settlement has become decidedly more restrictive than the agreement negotiated by the local users in 1986. The MWD let it be known, in effect, that the tribes are not welcome in the New Market Coalition.

CONCLUSIONS

Only a handful of water claims have been negotiated to date. The sample is not large enough in time, space, and circumstance to draw firm conclusions. The financial strength of the country may improve or worsen. New administrations may bring new philosophies about federal-state-region-

Indian relationships. Tribes may define and redefine their objectives. It would be encouraging to think that these myriad uncertainties, by themselves, account for the failure of Senator Daniel Inouye's select committee to crystalize an "Indian water policy" in 1989 (cf. U.S. Senate 1989). I am less sanguine.

Predominant testimony at the committee's hearing argued against the narrow legal risk assessment strategy of the OMB. The government, it was felt, has a larger trust responsibility to develop Indian resources—even if it is unwilling or unable to actually fund such efforts. But beyond this there was little consensus. The Western Governors' Association could not come to a position on the issue of water transfers; several reasoned arguments for omnibus marketing bills met an equivocal response. Senator Inouye himself admitted that he has allowed marketing provisions to be stricken from legislation simply to get it passed. And, at the hearings, rather serious rifts appeared within the administration itself—between career bureaucrats and policy-level political appointees—over who represents the interests of the government in negotiations (U.S. Senate 1989). The senators and their witnesses did reaffirm the policy of negotiation, however. Settlements should be built around circumstance. And they should be worded cautiously to disclaim precedent—denying, almost, that these case-by-case settlements establish the will and intent of Congress.

Fundamental concepts of trust, equity, and entitlement are thus thrown open to interpretation by whatever community forms around the negotiating tables in Phoenix, Tucson, San Diego, Durango, Yakima, or Los Angeles. These communities are being given the latitude to read *Winters* in almost any fashion that works. The one consistent line that has emerged to date is this: "to execute a waiver and release" of all past and future Indian claims to water.

There is a final irony to the federal government's policy of negotiation. Parties to the disputes are being asked—told, in fact—to assess their "legal liabilities" in litigation. But the litigations that would allow them to accurately assess their risks are being voided by negotiated settlements. Combatants are indeed "getting to yes" in the West. But they are doing so through processes that guarantee, by design or by default, that no consistent policy will emerge.

NOTES

1. To date there have been nine negotiated water settlements (Simon 1989:3), most of which stemmed from, and ended, litigation. By one count (McCool

1989:127) there are currently over fifty active adjudications involving Indian water rights.

2. My title is drawn from Fisher and Ury's *Getting to Yes: How to Negotiate Without Giving In* (1981).

3. Stephen (1988:14) gives an economist's definition of well-defined property rights:

> There are three necessary conditions for the attainment of efficiency relating to property rights:
>
> (i) *Universality:* all scarce resources should be owned by someone.
>
> (ii) *Exclusivity:* property rights should be exclusive rights.
>
> (iii) *Transferability:* this is necessary to ensure that resources will be transferred from low-valued uses to high-valued uses. The three taken together ensure that some individual has the incentive to ensure that all resources are used efficiently, i.e., in their highest valued use, because that is where the individual receives the greatest reward.

4. *Res judicata* "makes a prior judgment binding in a second suit which was or could have been litigated in the initial suit. This principle is applied to ensure finality of judgment and to protect litigants from a multiplicity of suits" (Rosenthal 1985:50). Rosenthal's paper provides an excellent review of how the principle was applied—differentially—by the Indian Claims Commission and the Court of Claims.

5. The Supreme Court decision, in its entirety, reads as follows: "The judgment below [*Wyoming* v. *United States et al.*] is affirmed by an equally divided Court. Justice O'Conner took no part in the decision of this case."

6. Abel further argued that "there is considerable evidence that people want authority rather than informality. They want the leverage of state power to obtain the redress they believe is theirs by right, not a compromise that purports to restore a social peace that never existed" (1982:8).

7. The environmental dispute resolution movement offers a closer model for water rights negotiations. Again, though, it evidences many of the same contradictions as "informal justice." It was born out of the "emerging environmental consciousness" (Bacow and Wheeler 1984:1) of the 1970s and fueled by the empowerment of environmental activists contained in the National Environmental Policy Act and a host of related statutes. Significantly, it is more often than not the environmental advocates who shun mediation and negotiation in favor of litigation. Litigation, precisely because it can be protracted and definitive (Bacow and Wheeler 1984:12−16), is a useful tool against corporate wealth and power.

8. It is not clear what Swan is referring to when he speaks of "a judicially refined understanding of the practicably irrigable acreage analysis," other than the Court's insistence that such acreage be specified.

9. Editorial writers for the *Los Angeles Times* captured some of this sentiment in urging passage of the San Luis Rey settlement in the San Diego area: "It would be

fitting for the federal government to provide the final seal of approval for the complex compromise because it began the problem a century ago when the Interior Department signed away the rights of the Indians to the water that passed through their reservation" (reprinted in U.S. Senate 1986:262).

REFERENCES

ABEL, RICHARD L. 1982. Introduction to *The Politics of Informal Justice*. Vol. 1. *The American Experience*. Ed. Richard L. Abel, 1–13. New York: Academic Press.

BACOW, LAWRENCE S., and MICHAEL WHEELER. 1984. *Environmental Dispute Resolution*. New York: Plenum Press.

BARSH, RUSSELL L. 1982. "Indian Land Claims Policy in the United States." *North Dakota Law Review* 58:7–82.

BURTON, LLOYD. 1991. *American Indian Water Rights and the Limits of Law*. Lawrence: University Press of Kansas.

CARLSON, LEONARD A. 1985. "What Was It Worth? Economic and Historical Aspects of Determining Awards in Indian Land Claims Cases." In *Irredeemable America: The Indians' Estate and Land Claims*. Ed. Imre Sutton, 87–109. Albuquerque: University of New Mexico Press.

Congressional Record. 1988a. House, pp. H9344–53.

———. 1988b. Senate, pp. 16830–37.

COURSEN, DAVID F. 1984. "Reserved Rights: Water for Fish Protection and the 1983 Indian Water Rights Decisions." *Oregon Law Review* 63:699–720.

Federal Register. 1980. "Central Arizona Project: Allocations of Project Water to Indian Tribes." 45(239):81268.

FISHER, ROBERT, and WILLIAM URY. 1981. *Getting to Yes: How to Negotiate Without Giving In*. Boston: Houghton Mifflin.

FOLK-WILLIAMS, JOHN A. 1988. "The Use of Negotiated Agreements to Resolve Water Disputes Involving Indian Rights." *Natural Resources Journal* 28:63–103.

HUNDLEY, NORRIS, JR. 1975. *Water and the West: The Colorado River Compact and the Politics of Water in the American West*. Berkeley: University of California Press.

MCCOOL, DANIEL. 1987. *Command of the Waters: Iron Triangles, Federal Water Development, and Indian Water*. Berkeley: University of California Press.

———. 1989. "Indian Water Rights: Negotiation; Agreement; Legislative Settlement." In *Indian Water Rights and Water Resources Management*. Ed. William B. Lord and Mary G. Wallace, 127–34. Proceedings of the American Water Resources Association. Bethesda, Md.: American Water Resources Association.

MCGUIRE, THOMAS R. 1988. "Illusions of Choice in the Indian Irrigation Service: The Ak Chin Project and an Epilogue." *Journal of the Southwest* 30(2): 200–221.

———. 1990. "Federal Indian Policy: A Framework for Evaluation." *Human Organization* 49(3):206–21.

NUNN, SUSAN CHRISTOPHER. 1987. "Developing City Water Supplies by Drying up Farms: Contradictions Raised in Water Institutions Under Stress." *Agriculture and Human Values* 4(4):32–42.

RONCALIO, TENO. 1989. "Wyoming Adjudication of Indian Water Rights: The Big Horns of a Twelve-Year Dilemma." Paper delivered at the Indian Water Rights and Water Resources Management symposium. American Water Resources Association, Missoula, Montana, June 1989.

ROSE, CAROL M. 1985. "Possession as the Origin of Property." *University of Chicago Law Review* 52:73–88.

ROSENTHAL, HARVEY D. 1985. "Indian Claims and the American Conscience: A Brief History of the Indian Claims Commission." In *Irredeemable America: The Indians' Estate and Land Claims*. Ed. Imre Sutton, 35–70. Albuquerque: University of New Mexico Press.

SIMON, BENJAMIN. 1989. "Indian Water Claims Negotiations: Conflicting Federal Roles." In *Indian Water Rights and Water Resources Management*. Ed. William B. Lord and Mary G. Wallace, 1–10. Proceedings of the American Water Resources Association. Bethesda, Md.: American Water Resources Association.

STARLER, NORMAN H., and KENNETH G. MAXEY. 1989. "Analysis of the Salt River Pima–Maricopa Community Water Rights Settlement." In *Indian Water Rights and Water Resources Management*. Ed. William B. Lord and Mary G. Wallace, 95–113. Proceedings of the American Water Resources Association. Bethesda, Md.: American Water Resources Association.

STEPHEN, FRANK H. 1988. *The Economics of the Law.* Ames: Iowa State University Press.

STOREY, LEE H. 1988. "Leasing Indian Water off the Reservation: A Use Consistent with the Reservation's Purpose." *California Law Review* 76:179–220.

SWAN, WILLIAM H. 1989. "The Salt River Pima–Maricopa Indian Community Water Rights Settlement Act of 1988." In *Indian Water Rights and Water Resources Management*. Ed. William B. Lord and Mary G. Wallace, 87–93. Proceedings of the American Water Resources Association. Bethesda, Md.: American Water Resources Association.

UPITE, DAINA. 1984. "Resolving Indian Reserved Water Rights in the Wake of San Carlos Apache Tribe." *Environmental Law* 15:181–200.

U.S. CONGRESS. 1971. *Federal Protection of Indian Resources.* Hearings Before the Subcommittee on Administrative Practice and Procedures of the Committee on the Judiciary, October 19–21, 1971, pt. 1. Washington, D.C.: Government Printing Office.

———. 1988. *Settlement of Water Claims of the Salt River Pima–Maricopa Indian Community in Maricopa County, Arizona.* Joint Hearings of the Select Committee on Indian Affairs, Senate, and the Committee on Interior and Insular Affairs, House, March 24, 1988. Washington, D.C.: Government Printing Office.

U.S. SENATE. 1977. *Water for Five Central Arizona Indian Tribes for Farming Operations*. Hearings Before the Select Committee on Indian Affairs, May 23–24, 1977. Washington, D.C.: Government Printing Office.

——. 1986. *Indian Water Claims in San Diego County, CA*. Joint Hearings Before the Select Committee on Indian Affairs and the Committee on Energy and Natural Resources, August 11, 1986. Washington, D.C.: Government Printing Office.

——. 1987. *Colorado Ute Water Settlement Bill*. Joint Hearings Before the Select Committee on Indian Affairs and the Committee on Energy and Natural Resources, December 3, 1987. Washington, D.C.: Government Printing Office.

——. 1989. *Indian Water Policy*. Hearings Before the Select Committee on Indian Affairs, April 6, 1989. Washington, D.C.: Government Printing Office.

WILKINSON, CHARLES F. 1987. *American Indians, Time, and the Law*. New Haven: Yale University Press.

Index